# CONFLICT IN THE ARCHAEOLOGY OF LIVING TRADITIONS

# TITLES OF RELATED INTEREST

*Animals into art*
H. Morphy (ed.)

*Archaeological approaches to cultural identity*
S.J. Shennan (ed.)

*Archaeological heritage management in the modern world*
H. F. Cleere (ed.)

*Centre and periphery: comparative studies in archaeology*
T.C. Champion (ed.)

*Chalcolithic, Bronze and Iron Age cultures in South Asia*
M. Lal (ed.)

*Domination and resistance*
D. Miller *et al.* (eds)

*The excluded past: archaeology in education*
P. Stone & R. MacKenzie (eds)

*Food, metals and towns in African history: African adaptations in subsistence and technology*
T. Shaw *et al.* (eds)

*Foraging and farming: the evolution of plant exploitation*
D. Harris & G. Hillman (eds)

*From the Baltic to the Black Sea: studies in medieval archaeology*
L. Alcock & D. Austin (eds)

*Global record: semi-arid regions*
C. Gamble & O. Soffer (eds)

*Global record: temperate latitudes*
O. Soffer & C. Gamble (eds)

*Hominid evolution, behaviour and dispersal*
M.H. Day *et al.* (eds)

*Hunters of the recent past*
L. Davis & B. Reeves (eds)

*The meanings of things: material culture and symbolic expression*
I. Hodder (ed.)

*Pleistocene perspective: innovation, adaptation and human survival*
A.M. ApSimon & S. Joyce (eds)

*The politics of the past*
P. Gathercole & D. Lowenthal (eds)

*Signifying animals: human meaning in the natural world*
R. Willis (ed.)

*State and society: the emergence and development of social hierarchy and political centralization*
J. Gledhill *et al.* (eds)

*The walking larder: patterns of domestication, pastoralism, and predation*
J. Clutton-Brock (ed.)

*What is an animal?*
T. Ingold (ed.)

*What's new? A closer look at the process of innovation*
S. Van der Leeuw & R. Torrence (eds)

*Who needs the past? Indigenous values and archaeology*
R. Layton (ed.)

# CONFLICT IN THE ARCHAEOLOGY OF LIVING TRADITIONS

Edited by Robert Layton

*Department of Anthropology, University of Durham*

London
**UNWIN HYMAN**
Boston     Sydney     Wellington

Published by the Academic Division of
**Unwin Hyman Ltd**
15/17 Broadwick Street, London W1V 1FP, UK

Unwin Hyman Inc.,
8 Winchester Place, Winchester, Mass. 01890, USA

Allen & Unwin (Australia) Ltd,
8 Napier Street, North Sydney, NSW 2060, Australia

Allen & Unwin (New Zealand) Ltd in association with the
Port Nicholson Press Ltd,
60 Cambridge Terrace, Wellington, New Zealand

First published in 1989

---

**British Library Cataloguing in Publication Data**

Conflict in the archaeology of living
    traditions.—(One world archaeology;
    V.8).
    1. Cultural processes. Archaeological
    sources
    I. Layton, Robert    II. Series
    306

    ISBN 0-04-445021-4

---

**Library of Congress Cataloging in Publication Data**

Conflict in the archaeology of living traditions/edited by Robert
    Layton.
        p.   cm.—(One world archaeology)
    Bibliography: p.
    Includes index.
    ISBN 0-04-445021-4 (alk. paper)
    1. Archaeology and history. 2. Ethnoarchaeology. 3. Archaeology–
Philosophy. 4. Objectivity. I. Layton, R. (Robert), 1944–
II. Series.
CC77.H5.C66 1988
930.1—dc19          88-21617 CIP

---

Typeset in 10 on 11 point Bembo by Book Ens, Saffron Walden, Essex
and printed in Great Britain by the University Printing House, Oxford

# List of contributors

*Marjut Aikio*, The University of Lapland, Rovaniemi, Finland.

*Pekka Aikio*, The Research Institute of Northern Finland, The University of Oulu, Finland.

*Alan D. Beauregard*, Department of Anthropology, State University of New York at Binghamton, USA.

*Ellen Bielawski*, Boreal Institute for Northern Studies, The University of Alberta, Canada.

*Carlos Mamami Condori*, Institute of Historical Research, La Paz and Universidad Mayor de San Andres, Bolivia.

*Robert Cruz*, International Indian Treaty Council, San Francisco, USA.

*Angela Gilliam*, Politics, Economics, and Society Program, State University of New York, College at Old Westbury, USA.

*Jan Hammil*, American Indians Against Desecration, Indianapolis, USA.

*Jane Hubert*, Department of Psychology, University of Southampton, UK.

*Bongasu Tanla Kishani*, École Normale Supérieure, Bambili, Cameroon.

*Robert Layton*, Department of Anthropology, University of Durham, UK.

*Jo Mangi*, Department of Anthropology and Sociology, University of Papua New Guinea, Port Moresby, PNG.

*Randall H. McGuire*, Department of Anthropology, State University of New York at Binghamton, USA.

*Stephen Moore*, Native American Rights Fund, Boulder, Colorado, USA.

*Jean-Aimé Rakotoarisoa*, Museum of Art and Archaeology, University of Madagascar, Antananarivo, Madagascar.

*Lori Richardson*, National Museum of Victoria, Melbourne, Australia.

*Patricia E. Rubertone*, Department of Anthropology, Brown University, Rhode Island, USA.

*Ernest Turner*, Milam Recovery Centres, Inc., Bothell, Washington, USA.

*Pancrace Twagiramutara*, Faculté des Sciences Économiques, Sociales et de Gestion, Université Nationale de Rwanda, Butare, Rwanda.

*Larry J. Zimmerman*, Archaeology Laboratory, University of South Dakota, USA.

# Foreword

This book is one of a major series of more than 20 volumes resulting from the World Archaeological Congress held in Southampton, England, in September 1986. The series reflects the enormous academic impact of the Congress, which was attended by 850 people from more than 70 countries, and attracted many additional contributions from others who were unable to attend in person.

The *One World Archaeology* series is the result of a determined and highly successful attempt to bring together for the first time not only archaeologists and anthropologists from many different parts of the world, as well as academics from a host of contingent disciplines, but also non-academics from a wide range of cultural backgrounds, who could lend their own expertise to the discussions at the Congress. Many of the latter, accustomed to being treated as the 'subjects' of archaeological and anthropological observation, had never before been admitted as equal participants in the discussion of their own (cultural) past or present, with their own particularly vital contribution to make towards global, cross-cultural understanding.

The Congress therefore really addressed world archaeology in its widest sense. Central to a world archaeological approach is the investigation not only of how people lived in the past but also of how, and why, changes took place resulting in the forms of society and culture which exist today. Contrary to popular belief, and the archaeology of some 20 years ago, world archaeology is much more than the mere recording of specific historical events, embracing as it does the study of social and cultural change in its entirety. All the books in the *One World Archaeology* series are the result of meetings and discussions which took place within a context that encouraged a feeling of self-criticism and humility in the participants about their own interpretations and concepts of the past. Many participants experienced a new self-awareness, as well as a degree of awe about past and present human endeavours, all of which is reflected in this unique series.

The Congress was organized around major themes. Several of these themes were based on the discussion of full-length papers which had been circulated some months previously to all who had indicated a special interest in them. Other sessions, including some dealing with areas of specialization defined by period or geographical region, were based on oral addresses, or a combination of pre-circulated papers and lectures. In all cases, the entire sessions were recorded on cassette, and all contributors were presented with the recordings of the discussion of their papers. A major part of the thinking behind the Congress was that a meeting of many hundreds of participants that did not leave behind a published record of its academic discussions would be little more than an exercise in tourism.

Thus, from the very beginning of the detailed planning for the World Archaeological Congress, in 1982, the intention was to produce post-Congress books containing a selection only of the contributions, revised in the light of discussions during the sessions themselves as well as during subsequent consultations with the academic editors appointed for each book. From the outset, contributors to the Congress knew that if their papers were selected for publication, they would have only a few months to revise them according to editorial specifications, and that they would become authors in an important academic volume scheduled to appear within a reasonable period following the Southampton meeting.

The publication of the series reflects the intense planning which took place before the Congress. Not only were all contributors aware of the subsequent production schedules, but also session organizers were already planning their books before and during the Congress. The editors were entitled to commission additional chapters for their books when they felt that there were significant gaps in the coverage of a topic during the Congress, or where discussion at the Congress indicated a need for additional contributions.

One of the main themes of the Congress was devoted to 'Archaeological "Objectivity" in Interpretation', where consideration of the precirculated full-length papers on this theme extended over four and a half days of academic discussion. The particular sessions on 'Archaeological "Objectivity" in Interpretation' were under my overall control, the main aim being to focus attention on the way that evidence of the past – including archaeological evidence – has been used and viewed by particular groups (whether local, regional or national) at different times. Essential to this aim was the exploration of the reasons why particular interpretations might have been chosen, or favoured, by individual societies and traditions at specific points in their development, or at certain stages in their activities. The whole theme attempted, therefore, a unique mix of critical assessment of the basis of archaeological methodology with critical awareness of the social contexts of the use (and possible manipulation) of the evidence of the past.

Central to this re-evaluation of the strengths and weaknesses of archaeological approaches to the interpretation, and indeed 'display', of the past – whether through academic articles or by means of formal or informal curricula, or through museums or site presentation – is an assessment of the methodologies and approaches to the significance of material culture. This has long been a core issue in archaeological discussion, but it badly needed re-examination. Throughout the history of archaeology as a discipline material culture, or at least the repetitive association of distinctive material culture objects, has been taken to reflect activities of specific social groups or 'societies' whose physical movements across a geographic stage have often been postulated on the basis of the distribution patterns of such objects, and whose supposed physical or ethnic identity (see also *State and society* , edited by J. Gledhill, B. Bender & M.T. Larsen) has often been assumed to correlate with such artefactual groupings. More recently archaeologists have been forced to recognize, often through lessons gained from ethnography, that a distinctive material culture complex may represent the activities of a vast variety of social groupings and subgroups, and that archaeological classification may often serve to camouflage the more subtle messages of style and technique (see also *Animals into art*, edited by H. Morphy, and *Domination and resistance*, edited by D. Miller, M. J. Rowlands

& C. Tilley) which probably symbolize complex patterns of behaviour, as well as individual aspirations – within any society.

If the very basis of the equation between a material culture complex and a social grouping is ambiguous, then much of archaeological interpretation must remain subjective, even at this fundamental level of its operations. Whenever the archaeological data of material culture is presented in museums, on sites, in literature, in schools or in textbooks, as the evidence for the activities of 'races', 'peoples', 'tribes', 'linguistic groups' or other socially derived ethnic amalgamations, there should be at least scepticism if not downright suspicion. In a large number of such cases, what we are witnessing is the non-too-subtle ascription of racial/cultural stereotypes to static material culture items. ·

The overall theme therefore took as its starting point the proposition that archaeological interpretation is a subjective matter. It also assumed that to regard archaeology as somehow constituting the only legitimate 'scientific' approach to the past needed re-examination and possibly even rejection. A narrow parochial approach to the past which simply assumes that a linear chronology based on a 'verifiable' set of 'meaningful' 'absolute' dates is the only way to tackle the recording of, and the only way to comprehend, the past completely ignores the complexity of many literate and of many non-literate 'civilizations' and cultures. However, a world archaeological approach to a concept such as 'the past' focuses attention on precisely those features of archaeological enquiry and method which archaeologists all too often take for granted, without questioning the related assumptions.

Discussions on this theme during the Congress were grouped around seven headings, and have led to the publication of five books. The first subtheme, organized by Stephen Shennan, Department of Archaeology, University of Southampton, which lasted for almost a day, was concerned with 'Multiculturalism and Ethnicity in Archaeological Interpretation' and the second, under the control of Ian Hodder, Department of Archaeology, University of Cambridge, which occupied more than a day, was on 'Material Culture and Symbolic Expression'. The fourth subtheme, 'The Politics of the Past: Museums, Media, and other Presentations of Archaeology', was organized by Peter Gathercole of Darwin College, Cambridge, and also lasted for more than a day. Each of these subthemes has led to a separate book: *Archaeological approaches to cultural identity* (edited by S. J. Shennan), *The meanings of things* (edited by I. Hodder), and *The politics of the past* (edited by P. Gathercole & D. Lowenthal, of the Department of Geography, University College London). The fifth subtheme, on 'The Past in Education' was organized by Robert MacKenzie, of the Central Training Department, National Association of Citizens Advice Bureaux, and discussion of this topic (which lasted formally for half a day at the Congress and informally throughout the week by means of displays and educational events) has been expanded into the book *The excluded past*, under the editorship of Peter Stone (of English Heritage) and R. MacKenzie. David Bellos of the Department of French, University of Manchester, was responsible for a short discussion session on the sixth subtheme 'Mediations of the Past in Modern Europe', and contributions from this subtheme have been combined either with those from the third on 'Contemporary Claims about Stonehenge' (a short discussion session organized by Christopher Chippindale, of the Department of Archaeology, University of Cambridge), or with those from the seventh subtheme on 'Indigenous Perceptions of the Past' which lasted for almost a day. Robert Layton of the Department of Anthropology, University of Durham, was in charge of this seventh topic and has also edited the two resulting books, the present volume and *Who needs the past?* The former also incorporates several contributions from a one-day discussion on 'Material Culture and the Making of the Modern United States: Views from Native America', which had been organized by Russell Handsman of the American Indian Archaeological Institute, Washington, and Randall McGuire of the Department of Anthropology of the State University of New York at Binghamton.

The whole of the 'Archaeological "Objectivity" in Interpretation' theme had been planned as the progressive development of an idea and the division of it into subthemes was undertaken in the full knowledge that there would be considerable overlap between them. It was accepted that it would, in many ways, be impossible, and even counter-productive, to split for example, education from site presentation, or literary presentations of the past from indigenous history. In the event, each of the books resulting from this overall theme has its own coherence; they also share a concern to make explicit the responsibility of recognizing the various ways of interpreting humanly-created artefacts. In addition they recognize the social responsibility of archaeological interpretation, and the way that this may be used, consciously or unconsciously, by others for their own ends. The contributions in these books, directly or indirectly, explicitly or implicitly, epitomize the view that modern archaeology must recognize and confront its new role, which is to address the wider community. It must do this with a sophisticated awareness of the strengths and the weaknesses of its own methodologies and practices.

A world archaeological approach to archaeology as a 'discipline' reveals how subjective archaeological interpretation has always been. It also demonstrates the importance that all rulers and leaders (politicians) have placed on the legitimization of their positions through the 'evidence' of the past. Objectivity is strikingly absent from most archaeological exercises in interpretation. In some cases there has been conscious manipulation of the past for national political ends (as in the case of Ian Smith's Rhodesian regime over Great Zimbabwe, or that of the Nazis with their racist use of archaeology). But, apart from this, archaeologists themselves have been influenced in their interpretation by the received wisdom of their times, both in the sort of classificatory schemes which they consider appropriate to their subject, and in the way that their dating of materials is affected by their assumptions about the capabilities of the humans concerned. Nowhere is archaeological explanation immune to changes in interpretative fashion. This is as true of Britain as of anywhere else – Stonehenge especially has been subjected to the most bizarre collection of interpretations over the years, including all sorts of references to it having been constructed by Mycenaeans and Phoenicians. Although, at first sight, it is tempting to assume that such contentions are different from attempts by politicians to claim that the extraordinary site of Great Zimbabwe was constructed by Phoenicians using black slaves, the difference is not very easy to sustain.

Realization of the flexibility and variety of past human endeavour all over the world directs attention back to those questions that are at the very basis of archaeological interpretation. How can static material culture objects be equated with dynamic human cultures? How can we define and recognize the 'styles' of human activity, as well as their possible implications? In some contexts these questions assume immense political importance. For example, the archaeological 'evidence' of cultural continuity, as opposed to discontinuity, may make all the difference to an indigenous land claim, the right of access to a site/region, or the disposal of a human skeleton to a museum, as against its reburial.

All these factors lead in turn to a new consideration of how different societies choose to display their museum collections and conserve their sites. As the debates about who should be allowed to use Stonehenge, and how it should be displayed, make clear, objects or places may be considered important at one time and 'not worth bothering about' at others. Who makes these decisions and in what contexts? Who is responsible, and why, for what is taught about the past in schools or in adult education? Is such education based on a narrow local/regional/national framework of archaeology and history, or is it oriented towards multiculturalism and the variety of human cultural experiences in a world-wide context? What should the implications be for the future of archaeology?

The main themes in *Conflict in the archaeology of living traditions* have been discussed in detail in its editorial introduction. My aim in what follows is to examine a few of the points which have struck me personally as being of particular note or fascination.

In this book Robert Layton and his contributors are inevitably drawn into that area of intense interest about which there is currently so much debate: is there, in any sense, a 'real' past somewhere 'out there' which can be 'discovered' and 'objectively' analysed, if only we can 'get at it'? (a topic also discussed in *Archaeological approaches to cultural identity*, edited by S. J. Shennan and *The politics of the past*, edited by P. Gathercole & D. Lowenthal). If the answer to this question were 'yes', it would be easy to move on to the assumption that if the views of members of non-Western cultures about the past are opposed to those of archaeologists, then they are, at best, erroneous, and those people who are not interested in the works of archaeologists and historians are at worst obstructive and politically motivated. However, it is possible, as suggested by the editor himself, that there is no inherent conflict in the situation, as may appear at first sight, and that no single explanatory theory can account for all the aspects of any specific data set. Different approaches and views about the past would, in this view, be able to coexist without any one approach necessarily obviating any other.

*Conflict in the archaeology of living traditions* is a unique statement about the complexities of the interpretation of the past, bringing out – in chapter after chapter – a fascinating set of case studies which demonstrate, in a very wide

variety of contexts, the way that particular interactions between 'Natives' and
'Europeans' (in the very recent past as well as in the 16th and 17th centuries)
have had diverse consequences. Even more significantly, this book shows how
these complex results can be reinterpreted by those alive today in strikingly different ways, according to the different perspectives of those carrying out the
interpretative exercises (see also *Domination and resistance*, edited by D. Miller,
M. J. Rowlands & C. Tilley, and *State and society*, edited by J. Gledhill, B.
Bender, & M. T. Larsen).

As if these problems were not already daunting enough there is little doubt
that other factors – also examined in this book – compound the complexities of
the situation. Legislation, deriving in all cases from government of some sort
(whether of indigenous, local or external origin), may suddenly (and often
totally without consultation with the peoples who are to be profoundly
affected) reclassify the legal status of indigenous peoples and their most important sites and objects. Such legislation (and see *Archaeological heritage management
in the modern world*, edited by H. F. Cleere) may place movable or static evidence of the past such as manufactured objects, bones or sites under
governmental bureaucratic systems of protection or even exploitation (for tourism, etc.), or may even class the peoples themselves as part of a 'Parks' system
or as mute participants in some 'Wilderness' scheme. In many of these examples
such action disenfranchizes the people concerned by removing from their own
control both the actual evidence and, often, the possibility of continuing ritual
expression of their own cultural, ethnic or group identities. Such actions appear
to be closely linked to loss of civil liberties within the larger society.

In a strikingly powerful chapter – almost poetic in its language and its
strength – Carlos Mamami Condori makes it clear what it *feels like* for him, a
Bolivian Indian, to be condemned to being part of prehistory, to having to pay
for admission to his own sites, and to having the past taken away from him and
his people – thus placing the present and the future beyond their control. This
chapter exemplifies many of the points made elsewhere in this book (and in
several other books in the *One World Archaeology* series) including, for example,
the insensitivity of archaeology's unquestioning assumption that lands are only
really 'discovered' when Europeans have arrived; its apparent message that
literacy is the only way to 'have history' (and see *State and society*, edited by
J. Gledhill, B. Bender & M. T. Larsen), and so on. Such assertions amount to
the conscious or unconscious denial of other cultures.

These are not, unfortunately, exceptional situations limited to rare events
and to countries in some sort of crisis. Such deprivation is commonplace in
countries such as the USA, Australia and New Zealand, where effective political
control of a living peoples' past is assumed, and guaranteed by statutes and legislation, to belong to others than the peoples themselves; in fact, to belong to
archaeologists and other professional academics.

Such conflicts can have even more damaging consequences. Not only do
archaeologists and anthropologists often have a vested interest in minimizing
the role and significance of living traditions – and often even questioning their
bona fide nature – but there is a pressure to assume, before adequate research

has been carried out, that sites and objects are 'prehistoric'. In Australia, for example, I have shown (Ucko 1983a) that a whole rock art complex in Cape York may have been rendered dead by academic research at the same time that at least some of the practitioners may have been very much alive, yet forcibly displaced by government and mission to far away locations in the State of Queensland. In many parts of the world whole communities of living peoples have been forcibly moved to new locations in the cause of 'development', or to ensure political control of them (and see *Centre and periphery*, edited by T. Champion). Such peoples are often literally cut off from their roots, with inevitable social consequences. But, by such means, the archaeology of such regions becomes easier of access, and easier to control and subject to legislation. Frequently, also, in countries such as Finland, Canada, and Australia, there has been a totally unfounded, but very convenient, assumption that such indigenous peoples and cultures were on the verge of dying out.

Recently, however (e.g., Diaz-Polenco 1987; and see *Archaeological approaches to cultural identity*, edited by S. J. Shennan), a powerful argument has arisen which claims not only that the very concepts of ethnic identity and ethnic groups are part of imperialism's way to divide and rule, as in South Africa and Ian Smith's Rhodesia, but that even 'liberals' who wish to recognize the prior and powerful rights of indigenous peoples to their own lands, rituals and objects are thereby effectively joining strategy organized by certain dominant nations. The nations, such as the USA, classify such people apart from non-indigenes in similar situations of abuse and disadvantage. To recognize a special quality about indigenous ethnicity, the argument runs, is to weaken the power base both of these people and that of other, non-indigenous immigrant groups. Whether these claims are valid or not, they are at least thought provoking, especially since (as *Conflict in the archaeology of living traditions* makes clear) the concept of ethnicity has now become accepted as a biological reality by countries who may first have received the concept from imperialist sources.

The strength and depth of genuine feeling of those who are affected by some of the practices of archaeology have convinced some archaeologists of their social and ethical responsibilities in the modern world. In discussing these openly in this book, rare glimpses are afforded both of the nature of archaeology as a pro-fession, and of archaeologists themselves. These are not confined to the conflict-ridden situations of site recording at 'sacred sites' or the appropriation of skeletal material, but are found, as in the case of Madagascar for example, in the choice of research undertaken by archaeologists in the expatriate control of both the research area and period in which work is undertaken, and today, in the pressure for the Malagasy interpretation of archaeological evidence to conform to the needs of modern politics.

Many of the concerns of this book are also pursued in related volumes in the series, but are no less poignant in the context of this examination of conflict in archaeological practice. It is salutory for archaeologists to be made aware that according to several of those affected by this academic discipline of archaeology, it is archaeology itself which has led to: (1) switches in peoples' ways of think-ing about time, such as the invention in Bolivia of a cyclical time system in order to be able to place European invasion into a manageable social context, (and see *Who needs the past?*, edited by R. Layton), (2) new modes of disposal of the dead such as cremation, in order to prevent the possibility of archaeologists disturbing their ancestors at some time in the future, and (3) changing attitudes to language and culture itself, as when English is used for the study of history.

This book also asks why do archaeologists do what they do? From many of the indigenous peoples' points of view, the nature of archaeological enquiry is intrinsically irrelevant, since the past is already known to them through countless myths and traditions. Even when such people accept that – for whatever reason – archaeologists do indeed want to investigate the evidence of the past in their own particular way, they insist on their own prior rights over some of this potential evidence.

Many contributors to *Conflict in the archaeology of living traditions* make it clear that it is human remains which create the most contentious and sensitive area of conflict and concern. Even those few Australian Aborigines, Sámi and American Indians who have become archaeologists nowadays refuse to have anything to do with the disturbance of the dead. The complexities of this situation world-wide are reviewed in this book, including the fact that, in both past and present cultures, graves have apparently often been disturbed and plundered not only by outsiders but also by members of the same culture.

However aware one may be of these complexities it is nevertheless staggering to discover that, for one American Indian author in this book, antipathy towards, and lack of understanding of, archaeologists and their practices led him as a child to conclude that archaeologists should not be classified as human beings (and see *What is an animal?*, edited by T. Ingold). Against strength of feeling such as this it is difficult to be sanguine about the future of archaeology when it currently depends, in many Third and Fourth World contexts, either on a chance development whereby archaeology can be seen to be of assistance to indigenous causes (such as judicial Land Rights cases – see Ucko 1983b), or recognition that archaeology may have an important role in building national identity (such as in the present situation of Papua New Guinea – see Mangi, ch. 17, this volume).

This book is about the future of archaeology in the world, and about its social role in that context (and see *The politics of the past*, edited by P. Gathercole & D. Lowenthal). Jane Hubert's review of the conflict over skeletal and other human remains stresses that, if there is to be any future at all at least in this area of archaeology, effective control over decision making must be, and must be seen to be, in the hands of the social and cultural groups whose ancestors may be disturbed if archaeological investigations are allowed to proceed. This is by far the most important point at issue. Only when such effective political control is acknowledged by all concerned will consultations between archaeologists and others have a real chance of long-term resolution and movement. At the moment not even the consultation and explanation are adequate.

Cecil Antone, an American Indian who has himself been involved in excavations, and who is personally known to most archaeologists in the southwest of the USA, holds strong views about the desecration of human remains. Yet, on a recent visit to Arizona, I was told by one of these same archaeologists that she had had no idea of Antone's views on this subject until she had listened to tapes of the World Archaeological Congress meetings. It is such lack of awareness of other peoples' cares and concerns which is the real threat to the future development of archaeology.

The nature of the evidence presented in this book is such that it is even possible to actually believe a recent newspaper report which stated that the Ashes, for which English and Australian cricketers have contended since 1883, might indeed be the cremated remains of the skull of Australian Aborigine 'King Cole'.

P. J. Ucko
*Southampton*

## References

Diaz-Polenco, H. 1987. *Neoindigenismo* and the ethnic question in Central America. *Latin American Perspectives* **14**(1), 87–100.

Ucko, P. J. 1983a. The politics of the indigenous minority. *J. Biosoc. Sci., Suppl.* **8**, 25–40.

Ucko, P. J. 1983b. Australian academic archaeology: Aboriginal transformation of its aims and practices. *Australian Archaeology* **16**, 11–26.

# Contents

# *Preface*

All but four of the chapters in this book are based on precirculated papers presented at the World Archaeological Congress in Southampton. The chapter by Hubert and my own were written specially for this book and aim to provide critical reviews of the issues addressed by contributors. The Aikios' chapter is based on their verbal presentation at the Congress. The contribution by Turner is based on the transcript of his various contributions to the session on 'The Making of the Modern United States', and includes here the full text of Chief Seattle's speech (of which only a part was read to the Congress). Most chapters have been revised by their authors in the light of discussion at the Congress. Only Gilliam and Bielawski were unable to attend the Congress.

Many people were involved in the initial organization of these sessions and in contacting potential participants. The volume is therefore the result of collective effort by its contributors and the Congress organizers, including Peter Ucko and Jane Hubert, Randall McGuire and Russell Handsman (who organized the session on 'The Making of the Modern United States'), Olivia Harris and Steve Shennan.

I would particularly like to thank Randall McGuire, Daniel Ndagala and Olivia Harris for chairing sessions at the Congress from which this book derives.

Robert Layton
*Durham*

# Introduction: conflict in the archaeology of living traditions

ROBERT LAYTON

Recent controversy surrounding the exhumation and reburial of indigenous human skeletons in the United States and Australia has called into question the relationship between archaeologists and contemporary native peoples. This in turn has led some archaeologists to deny the existence of a continuous native cultural tradition linking living people with the remains of the past, upon which indigenous claims for control of those remains frequently rest. The debate has raised a number of issues concerning the connections between archaeological theory, research methods and politics.

The US archaeologist B. D. Smith, for instance, challenges contemporary Native American demands for the reburial of indigenous skeletons held in museum and other collections, on the grounds that Native American beliefs varied over time and place, and that no cultural or genetic continuity is demonstrable between modern Indian groups and many pre-colonial skeletons. He characterizes the linked contentions that there exists a cultural unity among all Native Americans, which permits living people to demand the reburial of skeletons, as ' "articles of faith" which are not open to logical debate . . . the defense of their initial assumptions rests on the inherent rejection of the western concept of logical reasoning' (Smith n.d., p. 15).

In a recent public lecture the Australian archaeologist John Mulvaney takes a more cautious line with regard to Australian Aboriginal participation in archaeology. He accepts that Aboriginal people are the guardians and custodians of Aboriginal history and culture (Mulvaney 1986, p. 56), but argues that custodianship should not be equated with an exclusive right to interpret that material. In particular, Mulvaney challenges the view of some Aboriginal Australians that their race originated in Australia, a contention which 'could produce unforeseen political consequences. Obviously', he continues, 'if scientific evolutionary theory is rejected by Aboriginal creationists, who also ignore the archaeological evidence for human antiquity in South-East Asia, the claim is lodged for a separate human origin within Australia' (Mulvaney 1986). Like Smith, Mulvaney also takes exception to the claim that there exists a unitary Aboriginal culture which privileges contemporary Aboriginal interpretation of the remains of past indigenous culture (Mulvaney 1986, p. 54).

Both archaeologists quoted appeal to scientific method, and its ability to examine data objectively, to validate their stance. Smith dismisses the native position as one which lies wholly beyond the limits of scientific method. Although Mulvaney sees scope for dialogue over the proper interpretation of data derived from the past's remains (Mulvaney 1986, p. 55), not surprisingly he dismisses the theory of a separate origin for Australian Aborigines as unscientific. Smith considers that the value of skeletal evidence justifies control of indigenous skeletons by archaeologists, but Mulvaney distinguishes between ownership and study. Neither archaeologist addresses a set of issues which, to indigenous peoples, appear crucial: to what extent does archaeological theory itself embody subjective assumptions about cultural process? Have archae-ologists' presuppositions prevented them from correctly interpreting the response of indigenous peoples to colonial domination? Have they similarly neglected the dynamics of non-Western society prior to colonial contact? Can indigenous peoples contribute to a reassessment of their own past, or does Western culture have a monopoly on scientific method?

The reburial issue has confronted American and Australian archaeologists with the kind of moral dilemma that faced British anthropology at the end of the colonial era (Asad 1973), and American anthropology during the Vietnam War (Berreman 1968, Hymes 1974). Research supposed by its practitioners to be disinterested was found to have contributed to the furtherance of partisan political goals at odds with the aspirations of indigenous peoples. Some academics respond to such challenges by retreating from the real world. It is my view that the popularity of structuralism in British anthropology during the late 1960s had something to do with the manifest irrelevance of structural imagery in myth, or dietary restrictions, to contemporary political issues, and was motivated in part by the fear that politics compromised scholarly activity. The rise of structuralism coincided with claims that anthropology had up until then furthered the aims of colonialism, (e.g. Asad 1973). Opponents of reburial such as Smith and ACPAC (1986), on the other hand, respond to the challenge in a different way, by evoking the image of science as a kind of intellectual Gatling Gun: whatever happens, we have got science and they have not. A more meas-ured response to either of these is to ask whether archaeological theories or methods themselves need to be revised if they are clearly at variance with other peoples' perceptions of the data. This was the response advocated by Asad, Berreman, and Hymes, and is the theme of contributors to this book.

## Can we be objective about objectivity?

Objectivity is often something one seems to possess in greater measure than one's opponents. Before considering the issues addressed by contributors it is necessary to establish some common grounds for assessing competing theoretical stances. Otherwise the debate is vulnerable to the accusation that it is merely a matter of competing subjectivities.

What, then, is objectivity? The word objective refers to an object of perception or thought, as distinct from the perceiving or thinking subject; it is, in other words, something that is, or is held to be, external to the mind. Sometimes it is used in a medical sense, to refer to symptoms observed by the practitioner, in distinction to those which are only felt by the patient (*Shorter Oxford English Dictionary*). In the social sciences, the view that the objective consequences of a person's behaviour do not correspond to their subjective intentions is comparable to the SOED's medical sense of the word. The view, often adopted in the history of science, that the presuppositions of earlier generations of scientists prevented them from objectively noticing some aspect of variability in the data under study, corresponds to the SOED's more general sense.

The former usage is exemplified by the Functionalist theory of religion, proposed by Durkheim (1938) and relied upon in many ethnographies from the 1920s to the 1950s. According to this interpretation the objective consequence of practising religious rituals, apparent to the detached observer, is to promote social harmony. The participants (subjectively) believe they are worshipping spirits, the observer finds the (objective) consequence to be increased solidarity in the congregation.

The second usage is illustrated by Ardener's discussion of Newton's belief in 1669 (Westfall 1980) that the spectrum should display seven discrete colour bands, even though cross-cultural comparison shows that other cultures classify colour variation in other ways. Newton reversed the received view that white is a pure colour, and showed it rather to be a composite of other colours. Unable to identify discrete bands in the spectrum by his own observation, Newton attributed this to his poor eyesight, and requested a friend to trace the boundaries between the colours for him. Newton felt there should be seven bands of colour in the spectrum, a presupposition apparently based on the existence of a seven-note scale in music. The name indigo was adopted for a seventh, supposedly discrete band (Ardener 1971, pp. xx, lxxxiv). His subjective expectations prevented Newton from objectively recognizing that the spectrum exhibited continuous variation.[1] The Linnean classification of species is a similar case. The 18th-century naturalist Linnaeus did not (except in limited instances) believe in evolutionary change. His classificatory system treated natural species as discrete and immutable (Davis & Heywood 1963). For that reason, he regarded variation within a species as nothing more than the effect of soil and climate. Our understanding of genetics allows us, with hindsight, to recognize such an approach as subjective, and a consequence of his presuppositions about natural order.[2]

How do these two definitions of objectivity relate to the issues addressed in this book?

In the context of the reburial debate, the first usage identified above resembles Smith's indictment of the Native American position on reburial. Contemporary Native Americans conceive of burial as a means of caring for the spirit of the deceased, but really the objective consequence of burial was to store archaeological data for the future scientist. The second usage is adopted by a number of contributors to this book in their critical assessment of archaeological theories. Static models of culture areas, the equation of material culture complexes with genetically distinct populations, concentration on certain eras of history, all betray an insensitivity to the full character of variability in archaeological data, and result from prior suppositions on the part of the analyst which do a disservice to the people whose history is under investigation.

What is not contended here is that political expediency justifies selection of a particular theoretical orientation. To this extent contributors are in agreement with the position taken by Binford in a recent paper. Although strict empiricism, that is, observation of data without the guidance of a theory is impossible (Binford 1987, p. 394), nonetheless we cannot adhere to a theory merely because it seems politically expedient or morally right (Binford 1987, pp. 401–2). We must test our theories against observation. Trigger reaches a similar conclusion, namely that, although a 'value-free' archaeology is probably impossible to achieve, 'the findings of archaeology can only have lasting social value if they approximate as closely as possible to an objective understanding of social behaviour' (Trigger 1984, p. 368). On the other hand, any theory that has a bearing on the real world may have political implications, if it is used to formulate or justify policy, even though this consequence may be unintended by the analyst.

There are cases when it is hard to believe that a particular interpretation of archaeological data is not advanced for political reasons, since it seems palpably contrary to the empirical evidence. For some years an institution in Canberra publicly displayed a case containing the skulls of a gorilla, an Aboriginal and a White Australian, arranged in ascending order. The caption asserted that the three skulls displayed the principal trends in human evolution. In other cases, the political implications of a scientific interpretation may be less apparent. The view that Tasmanian Aborigines were extinct disregarded the descendants of Tasmanian women and White Whalers (Ryan 1981). From their point of view, the assertion could underpin the denial of land rights or the right to dispose of indigenous skeletons in a culturally appropriate manner (Bickford 1979, Ucko 1983). In such cases of conflict, the use of theory to underpin policies imposed on indigenous minorities by power inevitably politicizes archaeology. Mere protestations of objectivity cannot free the archaeologist from the political implications of research. Ucko has documented the way in which Australian archaeology was transformed by Aboriginal participation, bringing to archaeologists a new awareness of the implications inherent in their theoretical positions (Ucko 1983). I have elsewhere reviewed the use of alternative anthropological theories in interpreting the evidence for Australian Aboriginal land claims, and the practical consequences which ensued in the success or failure of the claim (Layton 1985). Mulvaney points out that although the Australian Institute of Aboriginal Studies was never expected to formulate policy for the government, its research findings on such matters as education and health were bound to have policy implications (Mulvaney 1986, p. 51).

Where Binford's (1987) argument is misleading is its apparent rejection of Hodder's insight that much archaeological material is the product of conventional cultural codes that had meaning for the participants (e.g. Hodder 1982). The discovery that cultural codes are relatively arbitrary or conventional does indeed deny the archaeologist access, in the absence of informants, to specifc meanings (Binford 1987, pp. 396–9). Objectivity here consists rather of attempting to construe the intersubjective meaning of material for members of the culture that produced it. An archaeologist examining the jaw of an ancient skeleton, for instance, might discover toothware patterns that allowed him to deduce aspects of diet by comparison with toothware on unrelated living populations. But if certain teeth had been artifically removed before death, only ethnographic information about that cultural tradition would allow the archaeologist to deduce the significance of the missing teeth (Mulvaney 1986, p. 54, cf. Geertz 1973). Another good example is provided by Rubertone in Chapter 2 where she argues that historical ethnographic sources throw a different light upon 17th-century New England culture to that previously inferred by archaeologists from inspection of the material. Rubertone finds evidence of resistance to domination rather that passive assimilation.

## Objectivity and intersubjectivity in the study of culture

In the physical and natural sciences it is assumed that the data under investigation exist independently of any theory about them. In the social sciences there is a limit on the extent to which an observer, inspecting the material elements of a cultural tradition, can 'objectively' determine their significance. This is because the meaning of artefacts, their place in a system of signification, is largely determined by cultural convention. Even representational art is less open to naive interpretation by members of other cultures than is sometimes supposed, since different artistic traditions select different aspects of the perceived world to represent, and organize their representations according to different styles (Layton 1977). The meaning of artefacts is culturally constituted, and to discover what it is the analyst must go to the negotiated, intersubjective and sometimes changing elements of cultural interaction. This imposes a limit on the use of ethnographic analogy, as Binford recognizes (1987, p. 399). But Binford has himself employed such analogies (e.g. Binford 1980), and inferences having some degree of probability are not precluded. The sciences of information theory and linguistics have demonstrated that the patterning of messages into 'bits' of information can be objectively studied both in human and animal communication. Although we will probably never know what the mental construct 'bison' symbolized in Palaeolithic European culture(s) we can document the relative frequency with which bison, horse, etc. were depicted, and the non-random selection of caves to decorate (Layton 1987). We do not need to attempt to intuit the precise symbolism of prehistoric burials to appreciate that deliberate burial signified, beyond reasonable doubt, something different to the casual abandonment of the body (cf. Binford 1971, but see Ucko 1969). The failure to attend to cultural patterning in the archaeological record would be to disregard important aspects of variability in the data, even if the uninformed outsider cannot fully explain it.

It was a weakness of the Functionalist theory mentioned above that it paid relatively little attention to the intellectual content of religion. The same accusation can be directed at the opponents of reburial, who oppose the 'objective' explanations of science to the 'subjective' explanations of religion. The Functionalist stance seemed permissible as long as Durkheim's explanation was accepted. Durkheim, as is well known, believed that religious experience was generated by the congregation's coming together, creating a social current such as may grip people in a crowd. Once this interpretation was rejected (see Needham 1963), the question which Durkheim had hoped to answer, why do beliefs persist which appear to the outsider to be contradicted by experience, is posed once again. The answers which anthropologists have offered throw light on the general issue of the limits of objectivity. Horton, in a series of papers (e.g. 1960, 1964), argued that religion offers a type of explanatory model which conceives of non-human forces as socialized entities. He argued that such models appeal to communities who experience social life as ordered and predictable, but do not seem useful to members of cultures undergoing rapid social change.

Much anthropological and philosophical attention has been devoted to the case of the Azande, described by Evans-Pritchard (1976 [1937]). Although not a naive Functionalist, Evans-Pritchard explained the persistence of Azande witchcraft beliefs and practices in terms of their functional consequences rather than their intellectual content. Fear of being thought a witch discouraged anti-social behaviour, and the procedures for identifying witches gave Azande the confidence to act, in the belief they could limit misfortune. When an accused witch promised to desist, this helped to resolve quarrels. But how could the beliefs persist if experience refuted them? Evans-Pritchard had less success in explaining the intellectual content of the beliefs. He was particularly puzzled by the technique for identifying a witch that involved feeding 'poison' to chickens and posing the questions to the 'poison': 'if x is the witch kill (or spare) the chicken' (Evans-Pritchard 1976, pp. 131–40). Evans-Pritchard admitted that he found conformity with Azande practice as reasonable a way as any of conducting his affairs during fieldwork with them (1976, p. 126). He even admitted once seeing a witch (1976, p. 11). Yet he believed there were inconsistencies in Azande thought which they were unable to address because they were trapped inside their (more limiting) system of logic (1976, pp. 155–9). Consequently, he held, they could not recognize empirical disproof of their belief even though they recognized empirical evidence within the system of thought (1976, p. 25).

Philosophers and later anthropologists have attempted to better Evans-Pritchard's analysis. Three of their proposals are particularly relevant to the kinds of problem concerning objectivity posed in this book. Gellner (1970, p. 241) points out that it is in the political interests of Azande princes to maintain the system even if they recognize its logical shortcomings (cf. Evans-Pritchard 1976, p. 7). Both parties in the reburial debate might interpret their opponents' position in these terms. Winch (1970, p. 82) alternatively argued that Azande want to explain events which we dismiss as accidental. Their valuation of human life demands that unexpected death be attributed a cause (cf. Evans-Pritchard 1976, pp. 18, 23). The explanations offered by witchcraft and science are therefore directed to different ends. Ahern (1982) argues a more fundamental point, that every explanatory theory rests on certain constitutive rules, which are not open to question within the theory. The exercise of objectivity is directed by these rules. Ahern draws an analogy with the rules of a game. Tennis is constituted by certain rules; it would be silly or meaningless to ask a player why he didn't knock two balls over the net to be sure of beating his opponent with one – it wouldn't be tennis. In a parallel fashion, Azande oracles are constituted on the principle that the 'poison' is not a chemical but a sentient force. When Evans-Pritchard asked what would happen if you went on feeding more and more poison to a chicken (Evans-Pritchard 1976, p. 147), he intended the Azande to realize the chicken would inevitably die. But Evans-Pritchard's frame of reference was constituted on the supposition that the poison acted chemically. The Azande, on the other hand, replied that they supposed the chicken would eventually burst! They found such questions silly, and told Evans-Pritchard 'you do not understand such matters'. Contrary to his expectation, they did not seem distressed, nor did they feel their position to be insecure; the fault lay with Evans-Pritchard's failure to understand (Ahern 1982, pp. 308–9). Ahern's concept of constitutive rules is derived from linguistic theory (Ahern 1982, p. 305), but it may be compared with Kuhn's concept of the unquestioned rules that constitute a scientific paradigm (Kuhn 1970, pp. 4–5, 44–8) and Geertz's contention that cultures must be understood in their own terms (Geertz 1973). Trigger's paper 'Alternative archaeologies' (1984) examines some of the assumptions underlying three basic types of archaeology (Nationalist, Colonialist and Imperialist), and his conclusions match closely those of some contributors to this book. No theoretical orientation is exempt from constitutive propositions.

## Does Functionalism itself have constitutive rules?

Suppose Functionalist explanation is subjected to this type of critique. Functionalists modelled their approach on the natural sciences, and prided themselves on having devised an objective approach to studying other cultures.

The School of Functionalism arose in reaction to the earlier theories of Evolutionism and Diffusionism, the former tending to explain customs as survivals from earlier 'stages in social evolution', the latter explaining customs as elements that had spread more or less randomly from 'centres of civilization'. The rise of Functionalism was closely connected with the development of lengthy field research in a single community as a method of investigation. It offered a much more detailed explanation of human social behaviour, viewed at first hand from a synchronic perspective. Nonetheless Functionalism rested on certain constitutive propositions: that the history of a custom was irrelevant to its current function, or contribution to social solidarity (Radcliffe-Brown 1952, p. 185), that societies tend naturally to remain in equilibrium (1952, p. 183), that communities are governed by consensus (1952, p. 180, but see p. 181 note 1). Although Radcliffe-Brown emphasized that the notion of functional unity among the customs of a community was an hypothesis (1952, pp. 181, 184), these propositions were not normally tested in functional analysis, partly because the relevant historical data often seemed unobtainable, partly because the analysis often sought implicitly to reconstruct the society as it was imagined it would be in the absence of colonial domination.

Yet the Functionalists' research also depended, to a significant extent, upon the colonial order for prolonged access to the field. This, in Asad's view, played an important part in determining how research findings were presented: 'anthropology does not merely apprehend the world in which it is located, but the world also determines how anthropology will apprehend it' (Asad 1973, p. 12). 'It is because the powerful who support research expect the kind of understanding which will ultimately confirm them in their world that anthropology has not very easily turned to the production of radically subversive forms of understanding' (Asad 1973, p. 17).

The realization that a theory does not wholly explain variability in the data under investigation does not necessarily negate its usefulness in circumscribed areas. Functionalism provided a useful guide to the fieldworker which helped him or her to examine the structure of social life in the community under study. The same is true of archaeological theories (cf. Trigger's appraisal of Soviet archaeology, 1984, pp. 365–6), and more generally. Although the theory that the stars revolve around a sphere with the Earth at its centre has long since been discredited, charts which predict the location of stars in the sky through successive nights are still constructed on this principle. Although Linnaeus' creationist theory is no longer accepted in the biological sciences, his principles of classification are adequate to describe natural species, even though contemporary theory regards genetic variation within more or less transient breeding populations as of equal importance to barriers inhibiting cross-fertilization between populations. It is when such theories are applied inappropriately that they become dangerous. No space programme could be predicted on the pre-Copernican theory of the universe. The view of species as fixed and 'pure' has led by extension to the obscenities of Nazi policy toward 'Jews' and 'Slavs', and recent South African policy on so-called mixed marriages.

Whether Functionalists intended their research to provide an ideological justification for colonialism is a moot point. It is true that some argued, without much success, for the practical value of social anthropology to colonial regimes (Kuper 1983, Ch. 4, Grillo 1985, pp. 9–16). Others contend that their intention was to improve the lot of colonized peoples (e.g. Gulliver 1985). One could, however, turn the Functionalist approach to religion (see above) upon the Functionalists themselves and argue that the objective consequences of their practice were quite different to their stated goals. Wherever archaeological theories become used to justify policy, it is equally essential to look again at the assumptions that underpin them and ask whether they are used to promote injustice.

# Theories of stability, change and adaptation

## Static models

The chapters in this book examine two related topics. The first is the ability of archaeological theories to account for change in non-Western societies, both those wrought by colonialism and those which took place earlier. The second topic concerns the disjunction that sometimes arises between the research aims of non-Western people, whether archaeologists or not, and the archaeologists of Western society. The two issues are related, for we must understand how Third and Fourth World communities responded to the colonial impact to appreciate why, today, they may hold different analytical objectives and evaluate the use of information about the past in different ways. Chapters 1–9 discuss the first topic and chapters 10–16 deal with the issues related to the disposition of the dead. Chapters 17 and 18 pick up some of the threads of the previous chapters, and concentrate on the ways forward for co-operation between archaeologists and indigenous communities.

The relationship of Functionalism to colonial policy is raised in Gilliam's chapter (5), where anthropology is held particularly responsible for the view of Third World cultures as discrete and inherently static. The critique of Olderogge, whom Gilliam cites, resembles that of Eric Wolf in his survey of interaction between *Europe and the people without history* (Wolf 1982), which emphasizes the dynamism of human cultures and their continual interaction.

Beauregard and Rubertone (Chs. 1 & 2) similarly contend that the 'culture area' principle does little justice to the dynamics of interaction between native Americans and early colonial settlers, endowing the principle with misleading political implications. Beauregard demonstrates the ·diversity of economic strategies adopted in response to new modes of production imposed on the area during the colonial period. Both contributors conclude that Indians were not passively becoming assimilated to colonial society, an argument which puts the modern Indian struggle in a different light.

## Evolutionary models

For many contributors, the application of evolutionary theories has been responsible for even greater misrepresentation of the evidence of social process. Any theory that ranks human societies in successive stages rests on the constitutive principle that evolution has a single goal. It is extraordinary how little acknowledgement exists in the social sciences that the concept of unilinear progress has no part in the neo-Darwinian theory of evolution. Since genetically determined traits can only be defined as 'useful' (i.e. contributing to the individual's reproductive success) by reference to a given environment, the concept of natural selection provides no objective basis for speaking in general terms of 'higher' or 'lower' forms of life. This applies just as much to the evolution of social behaviour as it does to physiological evolution (Trivers 1985, pp. 31–2).

In Darwinian terms the evolutionary value of agriculture over hunting and gathering, for instance, is to be measured in the contribution of the new behavioural strategies to reproductive success. In some environments a hundred-fold increase in population resulted, but in environments to which agriculture is maladapted, hunting and gathering continued to provide the most effective set of behavioural strategies (Irons 1983, pp. 172–3, 198).

To the extent that Native American and Aboriginal Australian peoples have succeeded in surviving the colonial onslaught this is due in part to their ability to adapt indigenous cultural strategies. Once the persistence of distinctive cultures is acknowledged (Castile 1974) it becomes of immediate interest to investigate how it was achieved. Rubertone and Beauregard examine this issue. The origin of such flexible strategies in pre-colonial tradition further challenges the assumption that non-Western societies are characteristically static, as Rakotoarisoa shows in his contribution to this book (Ch. 6, and cf. Trigger 1984, pp. 361–2).

Twagiramutara (Ch. 7) interprets the origin of agriculture in sub-Saharan Africa as an adaptation to climatic change. He argues that historically related communities adopted different modes of production, according to the diversity of ecological niches they occupied. This, as he shows, is not incompatible with the view that innovations in technology, crops, and methods of production could enhance specific adaptations, and the latter may legitimately be described as 'progress', in a specified context. Such judgement, however, would not deny the adaptive quality of a hunting and gathering way of life in other settings, due either to the drought-prone character of the natural environment or to displacement by more powerful social groups.

Kishani (Ch. 8) argues that linguistic diversity in Africa is not the sign of barbarism (conceived as a stage in social evolution) that some Europeans have contended, but has specific historical causes: partly the failure of any single indigenous empire to establish lasting dominance, but also the continual disruption and fragmentation brought about by centuries of slave raiding. The Aikios (Ch. 9) document the response of Sámi (Lapp) reindeer herders to the encroachment of farmers upon their land, and to the closing of national borders across which Sámi had previously moved without constraint. Attention is drawn to the irony that outsiders asserted the Sámi to be politically weak and immature, even though their life-style was well adapted to the subarctic environment. In order to sustain their way of life, moreover, the Sámi had to master many languages and become expert at the interpretation of legal agreements; the idea of nomads living outside civilization is, the Aikios conclude, a politically convenient myth created by outsiders.

Rubertone (Ch. 2) argues that US colonial archaeology's view of the past confirms popular beliefs about the past without calling them into question. It disregards evidence that indigenous peoples contributed actively to the construction of colonial society, and remains constituted upon the ideology that colonization represents the successful challenge of civilization to savagery. Rubertone shows how an alternative model can account more fully for the ethnographic and archaeological data.

Condori (Ch. 3) cites the predilection among descendants of Spanish settlers in Bolivia to describe the pre-colonial past as 'prehistoric'; a contention that fits Western evolutionist thought, but is refuted by ethnohistorical research which shows that techniques existed in the pre-colonial state for keeping records pictorially. He further contrasts the Western tendency to regard the future as lying 'before us' – something we strive to attain – with the Aymara concept that it is the past which lies, visible, before our eyes, and the future, unknown, behind our backs.

Gilliam (Ch. 5) points out that it is the politically dominant who assign 'backwardness' to others, thereby not only denying the validity of alternative contemporary cultures and alternative directions for economic development, but justifying the continued expropriation of other people's land, labour and resources in the name of progress. Assertions that Western technology offers the only means to bettering a community's condition denies the value of localized traditional knowledge for self-reliant development.

### Race and culture

Historically, the assumption that evolution constituted progress has been rather closely linked in Western thought with the view that the 'level' of cultural attainment of non-Western populations (so-called 'races') is linked to their biological constitution. Although this provided archaeologists in the past with a convenient shorthand – 'the Beaker People', 'the Battle-Axe people' – the premise has no part in neo-Darwinian theory. On the contrary, socioecologists generally accept that humans as a species have evolved a substantial capacity for learned behaviour, the content of culture. The capacity is genetically determined, but not the content (Alexander 1979, pp. 65–7, Irons 1983, p. 199). Culturally acquired traits may in turn influence our genetic constitution, as is shown by the evolution of sickling and the maintenance of lactose in adulthood in response to agriculture (Irons 1983, pp. 172–3). Genetic variation in humans, however, occurs predominantly within rather than between populations (Lewontin 1972). There are a number of ethnographic studies which demonstrate that individuals may rapidly shift from one cultural configuration to another if it appears a profitable strategy: from hunter-gatherer to pastoralist or vice versa (Schrire 1980, Hodder 1982, p. 98); from farmer to pastoralist (Barth 1967); from shifting cultivator to member of a centralized state (Leach 1954, Ch. 3).

Twagiramutara argues in his contribution to this book (Ch. 7) that the Rwanda categories *Twa*, *Hutu*, and *Tutsi* are cultural constructs, the names aiding recognition between heterogeneous social units, so that anyone integrated into a neighbourhood practising a predominantly agricultural mode of production was considered a Hutu, and so forth. He regards the concept of them as genetically distinct populations on different levels of cultural evolution as a colonial imposition. Twagiramutara further questions the likelihood that people attributed the widespread clan name Abasinga (and its variants) constitute a biologically discrete unit. Rakotoarisoa (Ch. 6) criticizes Malagasy researchers for their willingness to identify with their Arab or Austronesian antecedents, but not with their Africanness. He plausibly argues that this attitude derives from the supposition that certain ethnic groups are intrinsically superior to others, and points out that the absurdity of such a contention in the light of evidence that later Austronesian settlers possessed a different mode of production to earlier groups from the same region, which allowed them to impose their political and economic system upon the earlier arrivals. Mangi (Ch. 17) questions the need to explain the diversity of contemporary cultures in Papua New Guinea in terms of waves of immigration from Asia, arguing that local diversification offers a more likely explanation.

Richardson (Ch. 12) describes how Tasmanian Aborigines were formerly thought to be related to the Neanderthals, and gives instances of the barbaric treatment of Aborigines brought about by the consequent rush to acquire specimens. Similar evidence regarding the treatment of Native Americans is cited by McGuire (Ch. 11). Just as Australian Aborigines were at first regarded as a dying race, incapable of adjusting to the colonial onslaught, so the excavation of Indian graves was misled by the assumption that either as a race or cultural group the Indians would inevitably disappear, either because they were already 'the veriest ruines of mankind' or because contact with civilization had reduced them to 'savagery'. Indians were said to be incapable of progress along the supposed unilineal evolutionary ladder, and doubt was cast on their ability to have constructed complex monuments (cf. Trigger's assessment of 'Colonialist archaeology', 1984, pp. 360–3). Westerners frequently have difficulty accepting the scale of non-Western cultural achievements. Mangi draws attention to the achievements of New Guinea peoples, having developed the technology to cross to offshore islands by 10,000 years ago, and constructing irrigation channels in the Highlands 9000 years ago (cf. Trigger's 'Nationalist archaeology', 1984). Gilliam's opening quotation is apposite (Ch. 5).

## Appropriation of the past's remains

Perhaps the most pervasive theme of this book is the extent to which outsiders' research interests fail to match the concerns of indigenous communities. A number of contributors conclude that this problem cannot be rectified unless indigenous peoples take control over access to their own past. Rakotoarisoa (Ch. 6) graphically documents the obsession of archaeologists working in Madagascar with the colonial period. The Aikios (Ch. 9) note a similar imbalance between the paucity of archaeological research into the nomadic Sámi's past as against research into the incursion of peoples practising agriculture. Beauregard (Ch. 1) finds a tendency among New England archaeologists to assume that changes in indigenous culture arose from continuous European contact, and that 'events prior to the establishment of the colonies there were relatively unimportant'. Kishani (Ch. 8) looks at the way in which Africans have been encouraged to believe that only European languages provide an adequate vehicle for the analysis of African culture. The Inuit, according to

Bielawski (Ch. 18), class archaeologists with other whites, as people who will never stay for long, will barely begin to understand Inuit culture, and will at worst take something away with them for profit: income, minerals or artefacts.

More contentious even than these instances are those in which indigenous material remains are appropriated as symbols of national identity, and human skeletons exhumed for purposes of biological research. The former is documented by McGuire (Ch. 11) and Condori (Ch. 3). The latter problem constitutes another major theme in this book. Hubert (Ch. 10) has provided an overview of this issue, bringing together for the first time the evidence of variability in Judeo-Christian practices, as well as the current demands and problems of indigenous peoples. Her information derives both from interviews of participants at the World Archaeological Congress and from first-hand experience in American Indian and Australian Aboriginal communities.

McGuire notes that the notion of the Indian as the first 'American' was part of the effort to construct a distinctive national identity in 19th-century United States, in much the same way that Australians and New Zealanders have appropriated indigenous art styles as emblems of their country's uniqueness on tea towels, tourist advertisements, and commercial logos. But McGuire argues that Native American cultures were more specifically appropriated by archaeologists and natural historians as the base on which to establish themselves as academic disciplines. When efforts to conserve the natural wonders of the United States landscape were initiated, the surviving features of indigenous culture were regarded as national monuments and archaeological resources, not as elements of a continuing and distinct Indian way of life.

It is not surprising that American Indians construe such activities as an attack on their religious practices, customs and traditions, as Hammil & Cruz (Ch. 14) make plain. The same is true in Australia where, Richardson (Ch. 12) argues, indigenous groups are entitled to be involved in handling material that is both spiritually and morally theirs. Condori (Ch. 3) describes a similar situation in Bolivia.

## Who owns indigenous burials?

A careful examination of the arguments against indigenous control of Native American skeletons shows that there is more to them than empirically orientated propositions. No doubt, as Reeder has put the anti-reburial position, 'human skeletal remains are particularly useful in studying prehistoric social structure and status systems, health and diet, and demography' (Reeder 1985, p. 8). The validity of such a position is not called into question by pointing out that its proponents also voice constitutive propositions that are not open to empirical test. The assertion that 'ancient skeletons are the remnants of unduplicable evolutionary events . . . ' is empirically testable. To continue ' . . . which all living and future peoples have the right to know about and understand. In other words ancient human skeletons belong to everyone' (ACPAC 1986, p. 2) is to move to another level. There is no obvious way in which the value of an object determines who owns it. It will determine how anxious people are to keep or acquire ownership. The analogous claim 'all peoples value good art, therefore no valuable paintings should remain in private collections' may make its political implications clearer.

Smith puts a similar view, contending that although it is not ethical to accede to requests for reburial unless they come from living members of the dead person's tribe (Smith n.d., pp. 12, 14), it is ethical for archaeologists to 'protect the data base of their discipline' by opposing reburial (p. 13); in other words, the value of the exhumed skeletons for archaeology is deemed sufficient to determine who owns them. A second constitutive proposition which emerges from the ACPAC Newsletter cited is that living Native Americans are 'Indians', not Indians. By some unspecified criterion, the continuous transformation of Indian culture in response to colonial domination has been represented, rather in the manner adopted by Newton and Linnaeus, as an absolute dichotomy. Smith adopts a similar, but not identical, position by choosing the 'tribe' as an arbitrary cut-off point. If the dead person did not demonstrably belong to the tribe of those who demand reburial, 'the biological/genetic or cultural tie to the skeletal remains is so weak, so tenuous, that any reburial request should be denied' (Smith n.d., p. 12). Statistics are notoriously open to several interpretations but Smith cites a survey which showed not only that 39 per cent of Indian tribal leaders felt non-Indian burials should be avoided in construction work, but that 54 per cent felt 'non-tribal prehistoric' burials should be avoided, in support of his position (Smith n.d., p. 11).

The opponents of reburial have no difficulty in detecting beliefs in the fate of the soul as constitutive propositions. They are less ready to accept that the pro-reburial lobby also has empirical evidence to support its position. Buried skeletons are not purely biological material. The act of burial demonstrably renders them artefacts of culture, and their value is therefore in part constituted on cultural premises. American Indians Against Desecration contend that native burials contain the remains of their ancestors, and physical anthropologists are generally prepared on empirical evidence, to identify a skeleton as indigenous or European. Christy Turner's assumption 'that the present state of knowledge about worldwide genetic prehistory is so inadequate that very few if any living populations can scientifically validate claims for exclusive *genetic* ancestry with prehistoric skeletal populations' glosses over this general congruence of Indian and White opinion (cited ACPAC 1986, p. 2).

The link between the advocacy of archaeological theory and the enactment of policy emerges clearly from the differential treatment accorded White and Indian bones in the United States. The handling of White people's bones is premised on the contention that they are meaningfully located in a continuing cultural tradition, albeit one in which, as McGuire (Ch. 11) shows, burial practices have changed markedly over time. Indian bones, however, are consigned to a lapsed cultural tradition or, worse, are considered not to constitute cultural artefacts at all but mere biological data. McGuire deals frankly with the different constraints that guided his research into colonial and native burials. He concludes that relations of power govern such differences, and that the political dimension is obscured, both to the public and to the archaeological community, by historically constructed ideologies. Zimmerman (Ch. 4) describes his similar experience, and the poignant effect upon him of discovering personal goods in an Indian burial. He argues that archaeologists make political use of their theories in defence of access to Indian skeletal material. Moore (Ch. 15) documents the way in which US federal law continues, with the support of archaeologists, to define Indian grave sites as 'archaeological resources', sanctioning the storage of Indian skeletal material and grave goods in museums. Why, he asks, should the bodies of Custer's soldiers who died at Little Big Horn be reburied, but not those of the Sioux? Moore shows that from the outset, Indian burials were deemed in federal legislation to be 'scientific resources'. It is fair to ask whether 'science' should rest content with thus becoming an agent of government policy. In other words, does such policy do justice to the nature of the data constituted in burials? The premise that indigenous human bones constitute biological, not cultural artefacts is discussed by a number of contributors. Richardson describes how Australian Aboriginal skeletons were studied to answer questions supposedly raised by Darwin's theory of evolution. McGuire argues that Native Americans were similarly regarded, in the 19th century, 'as objects of natural history, their remains to be collected like fossils and botanical specimens'. Zimmerman contends that such an approach continues among some modern archaeologists.

It is noteworthy that the Louisiana Court of Appeals, cited by Moore, recognized in 1986 that the burying of goods in a grave did not constitute their abandonment. Chief Seattle, whose speech is quoted by Turner (Ch. 13), expressly stated that in ceding land to the Whites, his people did not relinquish an interest in the graves of their ancestors. Hammil & Cruz present ample evidence that other Indian communities continue to hold such concerns.

Respect for Indian graves does not demand a denial of empirical evidence, but rather an acceptance that within the data lies part of the evidence that indigenous burials belong to an alternative cultural tradition. The issue, as Hammil & Cruz, Moore, and Zimmerman argue, is one of the right to cultural self-determination, to religious freedom, not the suppression of objectivity.

## The situational relevance of cultural unity

Although some archaeologists are willing to accept that changes in indigenous material culture over time refute Indians' contention that the sanctity of burials has a basis in cultural tradition, much of the material of value to colonial archaeology was once household refuse or abandoned house sites. Does this prove the argument a developer might advance, that the value archaeologists attribute to broken or discarded artefacts had no basis in colonial cultural tradition? Of course it does not. The contemporary value of surviving artefacts for archaeologists lies precisely in the transformation of White American culture through time. The concern of living Indians for indigenous burials regardless of arguments about tribal affiliation derives in part from the opposition *brought about by the colonial impact*, between indigenous and European cultures. Smith, I consider, misrepresents King's arguments on this score (Smith n.d., pp. 13, 14, 16). Mulvaney, similarly, neglects to note that although Australian Aboriginal cultures vary in time and space, when contrasted to other hunter-gatherer traditions, let alone European Australian culture, they do have a distinctive unity (cf. Layton 1986).

The narrowness with which a continuing interest in the remains of the dead is defined in US law is arguably a consequence of the fact that disputes over exhumation will normally arise within the community. The parties are situationally defined as those uniquely connected to the deceased versus the proponents of other interests within the community, such as road widening or building construction. Where the opposed parties belong to different cultural traditions, the situational relevance broadens.

As McGuire notes (Ch. 11), the ability to demonstrate genealogical connectedness is conditioned by cultural factors. Evans-Pritchard argued that among the Nuer of East Africa, socially recognized common descent was situationally relevant. He exemplified his point through an analogy with British culture: if asked where he belonged his answer would depend on who posed the question. To another resident of Oxford he would give the name of his street; elsewhere in Britain he would reply 'Oxford'; if abroad, and asked by a foreigner, the appropriate reply would be Britain. In the same way Nuer identify themselves as members of a hamlet, lineage or tribe according to context (Evans-Pritchard 1940). The Louisiana Court of Appeal finding cited by Moore captures this phenomenon without abandoning the notion of genealogical connectedness, reasoning that at least some members of the Tunica-Biloxi tribe are descendants of the buried Indians, and therefore the tribe is the owner of their remains. In some cases the situationally defined opposition is even wider. It may seem an irony that a sense of national identity among native Americans or Australians has been brought about by external domination, but it is this which explains why, for instance, a modern Sioux is concerned about the exhumation of the skeleton of an Indian from another group (Zimmerman, Ch. 4), and why pan-Indian groups such as American Indians Against Desecration (Hammil & Cruz, Ch. 14) form collectively to oppose the actions of European Americans.

It is not only in the definition of legally valid objections to reburial that the law may favour certain sectors of society. The Aikios refer to the recurrent legal convention that nomadic peoples possess no ownership rights over the land they exploit. This doctrine contributed to the failure of the first attempt to gain legal recognition of Aboriginal land ownership in the Northern Territory of Australia. Nancy Williams has published a detailed study of the origin of the concept that nomadic people lack land ownership in the period of the colonial expansion (Williams 1985). She demonstrates that it was not based on empirical evidence of land tenure among nomads, but on speculative theoretical constructs which presented the opposition between European and exotic societies in terms favourable to European expansion.

# The way forward

It is not the intention of contributors to argue that the interests of archaeologists must always be opposed to those of indigenous communities.

Mangi (Ch. 17), putting the view of an indigenous researcher from Papua New Guinea, looks at ways in which the findings of archaeology might be communicated to ordinary citizens. Bielawski (Ch. 18) reports on the success with which young Inuit have been involved in an archaeological field school. Richardson (Ch. 12) urges that research results be communicated more freely to Aboriginal communities in Australia (a view also promoted by the Australian Institute of Aboriginal Studies), and notes that information about past diet, medical, and cultural practices may be of benefit to such communities. For this reason, she argues, indigenous control over archaeological material will not necessarily prevent further research. Research funded by the AIAS must have the approval of the Aboriginal community involved. Hammil & Cruz (Ch. 14) report the benefits gained from collaboration between American Indians and archaeologists, as do Zimmerman (Ch. 4) and Reeder (1985). Bielawski (Ch. 18) notes that indigenous Inuit organizations are hiring their own archaeologists. The Avataq Cultural Institute of Northern Quebec encourages outside agencies to consult with Inuit prior to undertaking research which directly involves Inuit cultural and environmental concerns. Kishani (Ch. 8) laments the failure of Western linguists to involve Africans as equal partners in their research, with the consequence that informants may not benefit from the research to which they have contributed. The Avataq Institute has sought to establish an Inuit language commission.

Several contributors question the academic assumption that indigenous communities lack an interest in their own past, a fallacy which is examined in detail in the related volume in this Series, *Who needs the past?*

While contributors to the present book urge their fellow archaeologists in various ways to take account of the values, aspirations, and knowledge of indigenous peoples, they consider that the result will in the long run benefit both archaeological theory and practice. Zimmerman takes archaeologists to task for their arrogant assumption that they alone are interested in Native American peoples' past. He links the inference with the propensity to regard Indian culture as extinct. In his second chapter (16), however, Zimmerman notes that Native Americans do not regard their history as a series of discrete episodes; there is, rather, continuity between past and present. Bielawski similarly observes that traditional Inuit views of the past were structured in a very different way to the archaeologist's chronology. Gilliam and Kishani see such different modes of interpretation in a positive light, although Rakotoarisoa and Twagiramutara anticipate that archaeology may undermine indigenous cultural constructs. Rakotoarisoa concludes that it would be politically imprudent to propagate archaeological evidence which undermines political ideology. Mangi and the Aikios, however, demonstrate that the results of archaeological research may have an effect on policy of benefit to indigenous communities, in the first instance by providing evidence of a common origin for the diverse groups of Papua New Guinea, in the second by substantiating long-term occupation by Sámi.

Co-operation with archaeologists from the Third World and minority groups will frequently mean that Western archaeologists must modify their goals, or rethink their ideas. It is no longer possible to make the comfortable assumption that non-Western peoples live in a timeless present, that their cultures are inherently unchanging or that such people have willingly assimilated to Western ideas and practices. Appropriating the material remains of other peoples' past can no longer be justified by the arrogant assumption that 'we know best', that the advance of knowledge is a Western prerogative. All explanatory models rest on certain assumptions and are capable of political application. When archaeological theories are used to justify policy decisions it is not enough to disclaim an interest in politics and retreat into an ideal world of pure 'science'. Rather, the archaeologist must ask whether the theoretical premisses on which he or she relied remain justifiable, or demand revision. The intimate connection between the politics of colonial domination and the collection of exotic material must be acknowledged (Gidri 1974). Much of the evidence archaeologists use to reconstruct the past is the product of cultures whose values differ from those of the West, but it is through these values that the significance of much archaeological evidence is constituted. If people from other cultural traditions question the archaeologist's models of stability, change, and discontinuity, or the association of cultures and genetic populations, their criticisms should not too hastily be dismissed as unscientific. Instead, the evidence should be looked at afresh. This book sets out to show how archaeology can benefit from such a reappraisal.

## Acknowledgements

I am grateful to David Knight and Malcolm Smith for their help in examining the two case studies in the notes. A special note of thanks is owed to Rob Foley. Our discussions about the problems of recognizing objectivity formed the germ of this introduction. Peter Ucko made helpful comments on a draft version.

## Notes

1    The quotation which Ardener provides from Newton's published correspondence for the year 1675 (Ardener 1971, p. lxxxiv) seems unequivocal; Newton sought a friend's help 'to draw with a pencil lines cross the image . . . where every one of the seven aforenamed colours was most full and brisk, and also where he judged the fullest confines of them to be'. However, the story is more complex. Westfall points out that Newton's theory of colour reversed the basic assumption of 2 000 years of optical research in positing that white was not the pure and simple colour it seemed, but a heterogeneous mixture of individual, pure and simple colours

(Westfall 1980, p.170). Newton at first thought in terms of a two-colour system comprising blue and red (Westfall 1980, p. 161); by 1666 he had identified five – red, yellow, green, blue, purple; from 1669 he frequently spoke of seven colours (Westfall 1980, pp. 171, 213). In Westfall's assessment, however, although Newton compared the positions of the seven colours 'in the spectrum to the divisions of the musical octave, he understood that such divisions were wholly arbitrary' (Westfall 1980, p. 213).

2   In later life, Linnaeus modified his position and contended that God had created a smaller number of species than exist at present, many extant species and genera having arisen through hybridization between members of the original set. Linnaeus had experimental evidence for hybridization (Davis & Heywood 1963, pp. 19–20).

# References

ACPAC 1986 *ACPAC Newsletter*, November 1986. Garden Grove, Calif.: The American committee for the preservation of archaeological collections.

Ahern, E. M. 1982. Rules in oracles and games. *Man* (n.s.), **17**, 302–12.

Alexander, R. 1979. Evolution and culture. In *Evolutionary biology and human social behaviour*, N. Chagnon & W. Irons (eds), 59–78. North Scituate, Mass: Duxbury.

Ardener, E. 1971. Introductory essay: social anthropology and language. In *Social Anthropology and Language*, E. Ardener (ed.), ix–cii. London: Tavistock.

Asad, T. (ed.) 1973. *Anthropology and the colonial encounter*. London: Ithica Press.

Barth, F. 1967. On the study of social change. *American Anthropologist* **69**, 661–9.

Berreman, G. 1968. Is anthropology alive? Social responsibility in anthropology. *Current Anthropology*, **9**, 391–6.

Bickford, A. 1979. The last Tasmanian: superb documentary or racist fantasy? *Filmnews* (Sydney), January, 11–14.

Binford, L. R. 1971. Mortuary practices: their study and their potential. In *Social dimensions of mortuary practices*, Memoir No. 25, Society for American Archaeology. *American Antiquity*, **36**, 6–29.

Binford, L. R. 1980. Willow smoke and dogs' tails. *American Antiquity*, **45**, 4–20.

Binford, L. R. 1987. Data, relativism and archaeological science. *Man* (n.s.), **22**, 391–404.

Castile, G. 1974. Federal Indian policy and the sustained enclave: an anthropological perspective. *Human Organization*, **33**, 219–28.

Davis, P. H. & V. H. Heywood 1963. *Principles of angiosperm taxonomy*. Edinburgh: Oliver & Boyd.

Durkheim, E. 1938. *The rules of sociological method*. (Trans. S. A. Solovay & J. H. Mueller.) New York: Free Press.

Evans-Pritchard, E. E. 1940. *The Nuer*. Oxford: Oxford University Press.

Evans-Pritchard, E. E. 1976. *Witchcraft, oracles and magic among the Azande*. Oxford: Oxford University Press. First edition 1937.

Geertz, C. 1973. Thick description: toward an interpretive theory of culture. In *The interpretation of cultures*, C. Geertz, 3–30. London: Hutchinson.

Gellner, E. 1970. Concepts and society. In *Rationality*, B. Wilson (ed.), 18–49. Oxford: Blackwell.

Gidri, A. 1974. Imperialism and archaeology. *Race*, **15**, 431–59.

Grillo, R. 1985. Applied anthropology in the 1980s: retrospect and prospect. In *Social anthropology and development policy*, R. Grillo & A. Rew (eds), 1–36. London: Tavistock.

Gulliver, P. H. 1985. An applied anthropologist in East Africa during the colonial period. In *Social anthropology and development policy*, R. Grillo & A. Rew (eds), 37–57. London: Tavistock.

Hodder, I. 1982. *Symbols in action*. Cambridge: Cambridge University Press.

Horton, R. 1960. A definition of religion and its uses. *Journal of the Royal Anthropological Institute* **90**, 201–26.

Horton, R. 1964. Ritual man in Africa. *Africa* **34**, 85–104.

Hymes, D. (ed.) 1974. *Reinventing anthropology*. New York: Random House.

Irons, W. 1983. Human female reproductive strategies. In *Social behaviour of female vertebrates*, S. K. Wasser (ed.), 169–213. New York: Academic Press.

Kuhn, T. S. 1970. *The structure of scientific revolutions*. Chicago: University of Chicago Press.

Kuper, A. 1983. *Anthropology and anthropologists: the modern British school*. London: Routledge.

Layton, R. 1977. Naturalism and cultural relativity in art. In *Form in indigenous art*, P. J. Ucko (ed.), 33–43. Canberra: Australian Institute of Aboriginal Studies.

Layton, R. 1985. Anthropology and the Aboriginal land rights act in northern Australia. In *Social anthropology and development policy*, R. Grillo & A. Rew (eds), 148–67. London: Tavistock.

Layton, R. 1986. Political and territorial structures among hunter-gatherers. *Man* (n.s.) **21**, 18–33.

Layton, R. 1987. The use of ethnographic parallels in interpreting Upper Palaeolithic rock art. In *Comparative anthropology*, L. Holy (ed.), 210–39. Oxford: Blackwell.

Leach, E. R. 1954. *Political systems of highland Burma*. London: Bell.

Lewontin, R. C. 1972. The apportionment of human diversity. *Evolutionary Biology*, **6** 381–98.

Mulvaney, J. 1986. 'A sense of making history': Australian Aboriginal Studies 1961–1986. *Australian Aboriginal Studies* **2**, 48–56.

Needham, R. 1963. Introduction. In *Primitive classification*, E. Durkheim & M. Mauss. xii–xviii. London: Cohen and West.

Radcliffe-Brown, A. R. 1952. On the concept of function in social science. In *Structure and function in primitive society*, A. R. Radcliffe-Brown, 178–87. London: Cohen and West.

Reeder, R. L. 1985. Reburial: science versus religion? *Missouri Archaeological Society Quarterly* **2**(4), 7–16.

Ryan, L. 1981. *The Aboriginal Tasmanians*. Brisbane: University of Queensland Press.

Schrire, C., 1980. An enquiry into the evolutionary status of San hunter-gatherers. *Human Ecology* **8**, 9–32.

Smith, B. D., n.d. URPIE logic: an analysis of the structure of the supporting arguments of universal reburial proponents. Washington D.C.: Department of Anthropology, National Museum of Natural History, Smithsonian Institution.

Trigger, Bruce G. 1984. Alternative archaeologies: nationalist, colonialist, imperialist. *Man* **19**, 355–70.

Trivers, R. 1985. *Social evolution*. Menlo Park, California: Cummins.

Ucko, P. J. 1969. Ethnography and archaeological interpretation of funerary remains. *World Archaeology* **1**, 262–80.

Ucko, P. J. 1983. Australian academic archaeology: Aboriginal transformation of its aims and practices. *Australian Archaeology* **16**, 11–26.

Westfall, R. S. 1980. *Never at rest: a biography of Isaac Newton*. Cambridge: Cambridge University Press.

Williams, N. 1985. *The Yolngu and their land*. Canberra: Australian Institute of Aboriginal Studies.

Winch, P. 1970. Understanding a primitive society. In *Rationality*, B. Wilson (ed.), 78–111. Oxford: Blackwell.

Wolf, E. 1982. *Europe and the people without history*. Berkeley: University of California Press.

# 1 Relations of production and exchange in 17th-century New England: interpretive contexts for the archaeology of culture contact

ALAN D. BEAUREGARD

This chapter develops a form of enquiry into the archaeology of culture contact by examining the utility of the concepts of mode of production and the articulation of modes of production as a means of identifying and coming to terms with the variability and discontinuity engendered by culture-contact relationships. For illustrative purposes, the presentation examines relationships between English settlers and Native American groups in southern New England during the years of early contact between AD 1620 and AD 1676.

## Present issues and past paradigms

The kind of enquiry proposed here is appropriate in the light of challenges to paradigms which have traditionally sought to organize empirical social science research within broad, generalizing frameworks. Such challenges, collectively characterized by Marcus & Fischer (1986) as a 'crisis of representation in the human sciences', have included critiques of logical positivism in both the social sciences and economics, and have called for an epistemological shift of attention away from grand theorizing and towards more particularistic explanations of social change at more circumscribed levels of analysis.

Archaeologists who have participated in the crisis of representation have expressed similar uncertainty about the appropriateness of those bodies of theory which have guided research over the past generation. Trigger (1984) has related this criticism to what he perceives as the changing relationship between archaeology and sociocultural anthropology, specifically calling attention to approaches derived from sociocultural anthropology which have treated archaeological cultures and culture areas as closed systems. Trigger's critique of the New Archaeology called for the abandonment of such an approach in favour of the study of how relationships between social groups serve as mechanisms for social change. Explanations of social change advanced from this kind of perspective, argues Trigger, will benefit by moving away from abstract general models towards more realistic modelling of specific social forms, constructed in the context of religion or area intergroup relations.

Archaeological and ethnohistorical studies focused on southern New England Native cultures have until recently been influenced both implicitly and overtly by the concept of the culture area, and scholars working there have historically worked from a cultural landscape which represents the distribution of its indigenous populations as a mosaic of bounded spatial units, each internally homogeneous but at the same time qualitatively distinct from other units. Trigger (1980) has discussed the development of the culture area concept and its conflation with the concept of the tribe during the early history of American anthropological research. Specifically, he has demonstrated how Boas' late 19th-century critiques of cultural evolutionary sequences promoted the association of the concept of the tribe with the concept of the culture area.

This tradition of research in southern New England archaeology and ethnology was firmly established with Speck's 1928 monograph, *Territorial Subdivisions and Boundaries of the Wampanoag, Massachusett, and Nauset Indians*, produced for the Heye Foundation's Museum of the American Indian. The intent of Speck's monograph, as can be gleaned from its title, was to establish unambiguously both the nature of tribal identity in the region and to delineate clearly the extent of tribal boundaries; these issues were viewed as a necessary and crucial prerequisite for resolving a number of then-important research questions, including the distribution of culture traits, the compilation of trait lists for culture areas, and the use of such lists in addressing hypotheses about the timing and impact of migration into the area.

Studies of historic contact in southern New England since then have represented social change in Native cultures as homogeneous transformations of the social systems conceptually located within culture-area boundaries. Scholars currently working on the archaeology and ethnohistory of southern New England's period of historic contact now recognize the need for a new research agenda (Rubertone 1986), and have begun to address such issues as variability of social forms within traditionally recognized culture areas (LaFantasie 1986); social relations between distinct indigenous groups (Salisbury 1986, Starna 1986); relations between various segments of the Native and European populations (Bourque 1986, Malone 1986, Salisbury 1986, Snow 1986); and the necessity of pursuing all of these research goals in historical contexts (McBride 1986, Rubertone 1986).

Although the reassessment of culture-area formulations has invited debate on the nature of cultural diversity in native southern New England, few have challenged assumptions about temporal continuity which have traditionally influenced the interpretation of archaeological data in the region (Juli & Lavin 1986, Salwen 1986). Syntheses of prehistoric and protohistoric culture history have recognized the impact of 16th- and 17th-century contact on native groups throughout New England, but have not always confronted the ramifications of such contact. Rather it has been conventional to model the results of direct European contact on Native society as an orderly transformation of Late

Woodland Native social forms. In so doing, however, southern New England scholars have assumed that changes in Native social forms and cultural institutions can be attributed to continuous contact with English colonies, and that events prior to the establishment of the colonies there were relatively unimportant. These assumptions must now be re-evaluated as archaeological and ethnohistorical research continues to investigate the nature, extent, and consequences of contact prior to colonization.

The period of early contact in southern New England began with Verrazzano's initial exploration of the eastern seaboard in 1524 (Wroth 1970, Brasser 1978). The years following Verrazzano's 1524 encounter were marked by sporadic exploration, trade, and offshore fishing, with contacts increasing in frequency from approximately 1580 onwards, when the English and French crowns began a spirited competition for the resources of this region (Brasser 1978, p. 80). Following the death of Philip II of Spain in 1603 and coincident with the decline of Spain's sea power, the number of colonies placed in the New World increased markedly as European powers sought to take advantage of new opportunities to exploit the periphery of their expanding world-system (Bergesen 1979). Southern New England was visited less frequently by Dutch explorers and Spanish slave traders, and the presence of Basque fishing fleets in waters to the north was no doubt felt indirectly. During this phase of early contact, coastal aboriginal groups had steady access to a broad range of European material culture, including metal tools and cauldrons, items of clothing, foods and manufactured goods, and in one instance, even a small English shallop [a light boat] (Brasser 1978). Some native groups were regularly employed as fishermen by French fishing fleets (Cartier 1924), and numerous individuals had learned to speak European languages with varying degrees of fluency (Brasser 1978).

On the basis of these documented events, it is clear that the establishment of trading relationships with European merchants and fishermen, even in the absence of permanent European settlements, initiated demonstrable changes in aboriginal material culture and, to some degree, linguistic conventions and world view. Recent research has begun to demonstrate that Native groups were by no means passive recipients of European trade goods, and that the movement of such goods need not have been directly mediated by European traders. Knight (1985), working from an archaeological and ethnohistorical data base in the American South-east, has demonstrated how Native groups were able to control and exploit trade relationships for their own benefit, and has discussed the implications of such action for the transformation of the social structures of individual Native groups. Bourque & Whitehead (1986), working on data from northern New England and the Great Lakes region, have considered similar issues in the Native exploitation of early contact trade relations, with implications for the study of transformations of relationships between Native groups on a regional scale. Leacock (1954) and Snow (1968) have discussed the implications of these transformed relationships on local Native economic strategies and land tenure.

In addition to Native manipulation of the influx of trade goods, warfare and disease vectors represent additional forces which altered the distribution and character of Native groups prior to permanent European settlement. Evidence for the institution of warfare has been associated with the introduction of maize horticulture in the Late Woodland period; Snow cites the occurrence of palisaded villages, particularly near the frost line in northern Massachusetts and southern New Hampshire, as one line of evidence in support of this inference, along with the occurrence of projectile points lodged in articulated skeletons there (Snow 1980, pp. 88, 134). The ethnohistorical record (see especially Mourt 1963) is replete with evidence for the continuance of such internecine conflicts into the period of early contact, and a comprehensive study of the ramifications of European presence on these conflicts, both prior to and after the onset of permanent settlement, has yet to be conducted.

Disease vectors which have disrupted the lives of southern New England groups have been most recently described and summarized by Dobyns (1983, Ch. 1, but cf. Kelley 1986). Besides listing the well-documented outbreak of bubonic plague which affected the area from 1617 to 1619, Dobyns has also compiled evidence to suggest that the area was subjected to a far-ranging pandemic of smallpox introduced by the Spanish in 1519. In addition to this possible initial pandemic, Dobyns presents evidence for an outbreak of smallpox in New England during 1592 and 1593, and an unidentified but severe epidemic from 1564 to 1570.

It therefore seems appropriate to regard the history of contact between Europeans and Natives in the New World as a time of disorder and discontinuity marked by increasing variability in native social organization. European presence profoundly disrupted aboriginal lifeways even before the establishment of permanent colonies, and native settlement and subsistence patterns were radically different and diverse by the close of early contact. Such changes cannot be satisfactorily explained within a paradigm which models diachronic change as a continuum.

## The need for new analytical tools

The concepts of mode of production and the articulation of modes of production present us with necessary analytical tools for further understanding the diversity of relationships among the various European and Indian groups in southern New England, and should enable us to use archaeological data from the contact period to contribute to that understanding.

Wolf's definition of a mode of production as 'a specific, historically occurring set of social relations' (Wolf 1982, p. 75) allows us to move farther away from the culture area concept by focusing enquiry on variation in the social relations of production within any study area. Wolpe's definition of the articulation of modes of production presents the idea of social formations as a satisfying alternative to the culture area: 'The social formation is not given a necessary structure. It is conceived of as a complex . . . object of investigation which may be structured by a single mode, or by a combination of modes none of which is dominant, or by a combination of modes one of which is dominant' (Wolpe 1980, p. 34).

This characterization of social transformation seems well suited to a region and time period in which social change was sudden, intense, and widespread. The flexibility afforded by this formulation is useful in analysing culture change in this region because it seems that modes of production articulated there in a number of different ways, even within circumscribed areas. A reading of ethnohistorical primary sources on colonial southern New England suggests some dimensions of variation in the articulation of modes of production there.

## Plymouth as a case study: transformations in relations of production and exchange

The relationship between English colonists and Native groups can be represented as a dialectic which was transformed at least twice during the period between the initial settlement of the region in 1620 and the beginning of King Philip's War in 1675. In overview, this period can be conceptualized as a three-stage process consisting of early dependency on Native horticulture from 1620 to about 1625; trade partnerships between colonial and Native groups, lasting from 1625 to about mid-century; and a final period of English dominance which culminated in 1675 with the onset of war. My dating of these periods is based on a reading of ethnohistorical sources pertinent to the early history of the Plymouth colony (Bradford 1970, Mourt 1963), and the actual timing of the stages can differ in other areas of southern New England; as we will in fact see, the timing is quite different in the Connecticut River Valley.

The period of dependency began with the arrival of the first English colonists on the southern New England mainland. Had the Plymouth Company's ship *Mayflower* reached its intended destination in Virginia, the Plymouth colonists would have debarked into a considerably milder environment which would have become part of a larger settlement system of Middle Atlantic English colonies (Ver Steeg 1979, p. 27). Their actual landfall at Cape Cod, however, placed the *Mayflower* party in a setting where their prospects for survival were considerably diminished. Their arrival in December of 1620 precluded planting crops for the duration of the winter, forcing them to rely on the ship's stores and on the largess of the Natives. The grains which the settlers had hoped to plant were unsuited to the acid soils of New England, forcing them to examine other options for subsistence and survival. Maize quickly became the staple food, and the Native settlements in the vicinity of the colony became an essential source of supply. Maize was appropriated from storage caches at villages abandoned either because of inland seasonal migration or because of the plague which ravaged the area from 1617 to 1619. As contact between the colonists and local Native groups became regular and cordial, maize was obtained in trade (Bradford 1970, pp. 111–15, 122).

For the next few years, the Plymouth settlers depended on the Natives' surplus maize and on the sporadic arrival of goods shipped from London, and became involved in dialectical relationships with both the neighbouring Native groups and with the London merchants. The Plymouth colony bartered manufactured goods and imported foods for maize, in the process becoming indebted to the London merchants whom they could not immediately repay. The nearby Wampanoags recognized the potential of Puritan armaments in altering the balance of power in their conflicts with other Native groups, and had struck an alliance with Plymouth almost immediately after the *Mayflower*'s landfall (Mourt 1963, pp. 56–7). In return for their military assistance, the Plymouth colonists benefited by gaining a working knowledge of the Wampanoags' horticultural techniques and of their specialized knowledge of the environment.

The colony was simultaneously involved in a contradictory relationship with the London merchants who had financed their settlement. In order for the Company to realize a return on the Puritans' labour, it was necessary for them to provide their colonists with material support in the form of needed supplies and manufactured goods for themselves, and with the important trade goods which drove the entire set of relationships. The Plymouth colonists could not at that time have maintained their tenuous hold in the New World without maintaining both sets of relationships, and the production and shipment of trade goods from London to the New World was crucial.

These contradictions were resolved with the establishment of a self-sufficient agrarian economy in Plymouth before the close of the first decade of settlement. Once this necessary condition was achieved, the directors of the colony were free to initiate an extensive fur trading network, initially with the Wampanoags and later with Native groups farther north. When the problem of dependence on Native surplus was solved, the colonists were able to trade more extensively for beaver pelts. The labour of the Puritan colonists, invested in agricultural self-sufficiency, supported the fur trade by making available trade goods which had heretofore been exchanged for Native crops. Thus, the Plymouth Company profited indirectly from the agricultural labour of its shareholders insofar as it permitted a steady and substantial supply of beaver pelts which could be sold at a profit in Europe. At the same time, the Company continued to keep its colony in debt by charging its colonists for supplies and trade goods.

During this period the Native economy was transformed as Natives became alienated from the products of their labour. To obtain English trade goods and wampum [strings of shell beads (see Rubertone, ch. 2, this volume)], which entered the trade network after 1628 (Bradford 1970, pp. 203–4), fur trapping became the dominant activity of Native hunters, and the Native economy was reoriented from production for use to production for exchange (Leacock 1954, Snow 1968).

Thus, the London merchants, the colonists and the Natives engaged in an interlocking set of exchange relationships. For the colonists, particularly those who tilled the colony's fields, the fur trade was a means of paying debts and fulfilling obligations to the Plymouth Company; for the Natives, it was a means of obtaining preciosities which could be used to enhance prestige and social standing; and for the trading company, it was a source of commodities which could be sold at a profit in Europe.

The most telling contradiction of this system lay in the intensity with which the beaver population was exploited to drive these relationships. By mid-century, the system no longer generated the volume of beaver hides produced in earlier years (Moloney 1931). As the beaver trade began to wind down, the relationships of the English colonies to their sponsoring trading companies were redefined or terminated altogether. The colonies reoriented their economies by instituting an agrarian market system and by directing their mercantile economy to the triangular trade with Africa and the West Indies. The institution of an agrarian market economy transformed the relations of production between colonists and Natives, and further alienated Natives from the products of their labour, and from the land itself. As the colonies expanded their agricultural activities, they consequently interfered with the remaining Native subsistence activities (Thomas 1976). Competition for agricultural land became problematic. The clearing of new agricultural fields altered the productivity of hunting territories, cattle grazing diminished the supply of grasses used for the manufacture of straw matting and thatch, and also frequently damaged Native agricultural fields which were generally not fenced. The creation of mill dams adversely affected the distribution of fish in the rivers and streams of the hinterlands. Hence, economic systems which had interlocked at the peak of the fur trade now became at odds when the fur trade was no longer feasible.

In response to these alienating forces, Native populations were faced with a number of unsatisfactory alternatives, including participation in the agricultural market economy, craft production for the market, and wage labour. In some outlying locations, Native groups developed an eclectic strategy which combined some of these options with planting, hunting, and fishing. Some individuals opted for relocation in the missionary 'praying towns' of central Massachusetts. The diversity of strategies pursued by individual members of corporate Native groups in the region is evidence that at this point notions of 'tribal' affiliation virtually lost their meaning altogether.

## Interdigitated modes: the northern Connecticut River Valley

Although the articulation of modes of production in southern New England can be viewed as a developmental sequence, it is also possible to observe all three stages in simultaneous operation. Thomas (1981) has presented data from the northern Connecticut River Valley which can be used to illustrate the simultaneous operation of relations of dependence, mutually profitable trade, and the alienation of Natives in the face of a developing agrarian economy.

Thomas has observed that throughout the period of early contact, new towns established in the northern valley depended on Native-grown agricultural surplus until they became self-sufficient. Simultaneously, the more well-established towns were involved in fur trading relationships similar in character to those described for Massachusetts. Thomas's synthesis of data on the production of beaver pelts in the Connecticut Valley shows that the beaver population there did not decline as sharply as in Massachusetts, but nevertheless began to fluctuate during the late 1650s and 1660s. As a temporary solution to the occasional shortages of beaver fur, Native leaders traded use rights to their agricultural fields in order to continue the supply of preciosities, under condition that the leased land would revert to Native control once the beaver population replenished itself. Hence, though the conditions and relations of production in the northern Connecticut Valley resemble those characteristic of the Massachusetts colonies, Native and colonial modes of production articulated differently in these two areas with different implications in each case for the recovery and analysis of archaeological materials.

## Towards an archaeology of early contact

It is evident that an archaeology of early contact in southern New England must remain sensitive to the identification and evaluation of diversity and variability in the archaeological record. Sites and assemblages dating to early contact are best interpreted in terms of their relations to regional and local economies rather than in terms of culture area affiliations. Since the articulation of Native and colonial modes of production is not uniform over the region, background research designed to make inferences about the articulation of modes of production should be conducted for specific study areas and the archaeological record of early culture contact must be interpreted in light of such evidence.

Since artefact assemblages will reflect the differential distribution of goods through regional and local economic systems, both the classification of artefact assemblages and the analysis of settlement patterns must be informed by a knowledge of the constraints posed by contradictions engendered by the articulation of modes of production and by the range of economic strategies made possible within those constraints.

## References

Bergesen, A. 1980. Cycles of formal colonial rule. In *Processes of the world-system*, T. K. Hopkins & I. Wallerstein (eds). Beverly Hills: Sage.

Bourque, B. J. 1986. Ethnicity on the maritime peninsula, 1600–1750. Paper presented at Peoples in Contact: Indians and Europeans in the 17th Century. Symposium held at the Haffenreffer Museum of Anthropology, Brown University, Bristol, Rhode Island, 26–27 September.

Bourque, B. J. & R. H. Whitehead 1986. Tarrentines and the introduction of European trade goods in the Gulf of Maine. *Ethnohistory* **32**, 327–41.

Bradford, W. 1970, orig. 1630–1650. *Of Plimoth plantation* (edited by S. E. Morison). New York: Alfred A. Knopf.

Brasser, T. J. 1978. Early Indian–European contacts. In *Handbook of American Indians*, B. G. Trigger (ed.), vol. 15, 48–88. Washington: Smithsonian Institution.

Cartier, J. 1924. *The Voyages of Jacques Cartier* (edited by H. P. Biggar). Publications of the Public Archives of Canada no. 11.

Dobyns, H. F. 1983. *Their number become thinned: native American population dynamics in eastern North America*, Chapter 1. University of Tennessee Press.

Juli, H. & L. Lavin 1986. Archaeology at the Hillhouse Site: late prehistoric settlement on the southern New England coast. Paper presented at the annual meeting of the American Anthropological Association.

Kelley, M. 1986. Disease, warfare and population decline among seventeenth century New England Indians. Paper presented at Peoples in Contact: Indians and Europeans in the 17th Century. Symposium held at the Haffenreffer Museum of Anthropology, Brown University, Bristol, Rhode Island, 26–27 September.

Knight, V. J. 1985. Tukabatchee Consumers. In *Tukabatchee: archaeological investigations at an historic Creek town, Elmore County, Alabama, 1984*, 169–83. Report of investigations no. 45, Office of Archaeological Research, Alabama State Museum of Natural History, University of Alabama.

LaFantasie, G. 1986. The elusive Indians of early New England. Paper presented at Peoples in Contact: Indians and Europeans in the 17th Century. Symposium held at the Haffenreffer Museum of Anthropology, Brown University, Bristol, Rhode Island, 26–27 September.

Leacock, E. 1954. The Montagnais 'hunting territory' and the fur trade. *Memoirs of the American Anthropological Association* **78**.

Malone, P. 1986. Muskets in the forest: the arming of the New England Indians. Paper presented at Peoples in Contact: Indians and Europeans in the 17th Century. Symposium held at the Haffenreffer Museum of Anthropology, Brown University, Bristol, Rhode Island, 26–27 September.

Marcus, G. E. & M. M. J. Fischer 1986. *Anthropology as cultural critique*. Chicago and London: Chicago University Press.

McBride, K. 1986. Native American cultures in transition: the eastern Long Island Sound culture area during the sixteenth and seventeenth centuries. Paper presented at Peoples in Contact: Indians and Europeans in the 17th Century. Symposium held at the Haffenreffer Museum of Anthropology, Brown University, Bristol, Rhode Island, 26–27 September.

Moloney, F. X. 1931.*The fur trade in New England 1620–1676*. Cambridge, Mass.: Harvard University Press.

Mourt, G. 1963, orig. 1622. *Mourt's relation* (edited by D. B. Heath). New York: Corinth Books.

Rubertone, P. 1986. Introductory remarks. Peoples in Contact: Indians and Europeans in the 17th Century. Symposium held at the Haffenreffer Museum of Anthropology, Brown University, Bristol, Rhode Island, 26–27 September.

Rubertone, P. 1989. Archaeology, colonialism and 17th-century Native America: towards an alternative interpretation. In *Conflict in the archaeology of living traditions*, R. Layton (ed.), ch. 2. London: Unwin Hyman.

Salisbury, N. 1986. Southern New England Algonquians and native North America in the seventeenth century. Paper presented at Peoples in Contact: Indians and Europeans in the 17th Century. Symposium held at the Haffenreffer Museum of Anthropology, Brown University, Bristol, Rhode Island, 26–27 September.

Salwen, B. 1978. Indians of southern New England and Long Island: early period. In *Handbook of American Indians*, B. G. Trigger (ed.), vol. 15, 160–76. Washington, D.C.: Smithsonian Institution.

Snow, D. R. 1968. Wabanaki 'family hunting territories'. *American Anthropologist* **70**, 1143–51.

Snow, D. R. 1980. *The archaeology of New England*. New York: Academic Press.

Snow, D. R. 1986. The impact of contact on Mohawk settlement and demography. Paper presented at Peoples in Contact: Indians and Europeans in the 17th Century. Symposium held at the Haffenreffer Museum of Anthropology, Brown University, Bristol, Rhode Island, 26–27 September.

Speck, F. G. 1928. *Territorial subdivisions and boundaries of the Wampanoag, Massachusett, and Nauset Indians*. Indian notes and monographs, no. 44. New York: Heye Foundation.

Starna, W. 1986. Culture contact and change: the view from Iroquoia. Paper presented at Peoples in Contact: Indians and Europeans in the 17th Century. Symposium held at the Haffenreffer Museum of Anthropology, Brown University, Bristol, Rhode Island, 26–27 September.

Thomas, P. A. 1976. Contrastive subsistence strategies and land use as factors for understanding Indian–White relationships in New England. *Ethnohistory* **23**, 1–18.

Thomas, P. A. 1981. The fur trade, Indian land, and the need to define adequate 'environmental' parameters. *Ethnohistory* **28**, 359–79.

Trigger, B. G. 1980. Archaeology and the image of the American Indian. *American Antiquity* **45**, 662–76.

Trigger, B. G. 1984. Archaeology at the crossroads: what's new? *Annual Review of Anthropology* **13**, 275–300.

Ver Steeg, C. L. 1979. *The formative years: 1607–1763*, 18th printing. New York: Hill and Wang.

Wolf, E. R. 1982. *Europe and the people without history*. Berkeley: University of California Press.

Wolpe, H. 1980. Introduction to *The articulation of modes of production*. London: Routledge & Kegan Paul.

Wroth, L. C. (ed.) 1970. *The Voyages of Giovanni da Verrazzano, 1524–1528*. New Haven: Yale University Press.

# 2 Archaeology, colonialism and 17th-century Native America: towards an alternative interpretation

PATRICIA E. RUBERTONE

## Introduction

There is a growing concern in archaeology and related disciplines about the interpretation of Native America in the 17th century. What is being questioned is the manner in which the history of Indian people has been rendered and how their relations with Europeans have been portrayed (Axtell 1978, Cronon 1983, Fitzhugh 1985, Jennings 1975, Kehoe 1981, Martin 1987, Trigger 1980, Wolf 1982). In spite of these concerns, archaeological enquiry and interpretation have been slow in offering viable alternatives, i.e. which do not mirror the dominant society's convenient justification for colonial expansion and settlement. By casting Indians and their actions according to images defined by popular stereotypes and those dictated by the paradigms operative in archaeological science, archaeology has contributed to the support and verification of versions of the 17th-century history that fail to recognize the identity of native Indian groups, their autonomy or their ability 'to counter the cultural offenses of Europeans' (Axtell 1985, p. 4).

While the opinion presented in this chapter is critical of the conceptual frameworks that have guided archaeological studies of 17th-century Native America and their role in legitimizing the inhumanity of the 'civilizing process', my aim is not simply to trace the manner in which ideological colonization is promoted through archaeology. Rather, this critical awareness is used as a basis for suggesting that different, if not more accurate, interpretations of Native America are attainable through archaeology (see Leone 1982). According to this position, the archaeology of 17th-century Native America serves as a source of information on Indian history that exists independent of written accounts produced by European observers (Trigger 1980). It contains information about how Indians thought, carried out their everyday lives, and conducted their relations with others. By deciphering this unwritten record, it is possible to determine what was absorbed, converted into advantage, and even challenged by Indians given the conditions created by European global expansion and colonial settlement. It is this latter response to colonialism, resistance, which remains virtually unknown, or at best unnoticed, in written sources.

Yet, the failure to account for these political actions on the part of native

Indian societies, groups or individuals impedes our understanding of historical processes in the 17th century. Without political histories, we are denying the politics of the past (Jennings 1986), but also we are dismissing issues about the past that concern Indian people today, including their struggles to preserve their traditional religious beliefs and the graves of their ancestors. A recent attempt to explore the archaeology of 17th-century native resistance is presented to illustrate how archaeology may help in writing the history of these struggles and challenges to colonial domination.

## The archaeology of colonialism

Studies of the archaeology of 17th-century Native America are dominated by two principal research themes. The first of these, which may be termed colonial archaeology, has as its subject of study early American life – not of all Americans, but of those of European, predominantly Anglo-Saxon descent. Whereas this research gives little attention to, or at best downplays, the social, economic, and cultural relations that emerged between Indian people and Euroamerican settlers, or among the native societies themselves, the other category of studies extols them. Orientated around the theme of acculturation, this research emphasizes the transformations in native societies brought about by European influence and domination. In spite of the differences in subject matter, both colonial archaeology and acculturation studies are linked by common premises about Native America and about the nature of Indian responses to European colonialism.

In colonial archaeology, we have been presented with an enormous amount of detail on everyday life in colonial America that has resulted from excavations of domestic sites, villages, trading posts, forts, and other European enterprises in eastern North America. A considerable portion of this research has been centred around places such as Plimoth Plantation in Massachusetts, Jamestown and Williamsburg in Virginia, and St Mary's City in Maryland that have been developed into outdoor folklife museums, which re-create the internal workings of small-scale societies (Fitzhugh 1985, p. 3). Although the colonists who settled at each of these places often had close relations with Indian people, these interactions are given relatively little attention. I will draw on the research carried out in association with the re-creation of Plimoth Plantation to illustrate how colonial archaeology has depicted Native America, and its relations with European settlers.

Although Plimoth Plantation is envisioned as 'a museum that seeks to create an understanding of the seventeenth century, the Pilgrims, and the Wampanoag tribe who lived in New England when the Pilgrims first arrived' (Yentsch et al. 1980), we get a very different impression from the principal monograph (Deetz 1977) that has resulted from years of archaeological research in and around Plymouth Colony. In it, we are provided with information on how the colonists thought, lived and behaved in a way that is interesting and entirely plausible to both a professional audience and the public alike (Handsman 1983, p. 67). Its emphasis on the lives of ordinary people caught up in the routine of doing ordinary, everyday things has given us a very strong impression of the colonial past. It is one that depicts European colonial expansion as a matter of establishing enclaves of settlement in 'a virgin land, or wilderness, inhabited by non-people called savages' (Jennings 1975, p. 15), and of transplanting the seeds of modern American society in the form of European medieval culture onto North American soil. No mention is made of these emigrants' role in securing new sources of raw material and new markets for Europe's merchant classes. No reasons are given for the success of their colonial experiment in firmly embedding itself in eastern North America, nor is there any discussion of how they managed to surround, contain and supplant the existing native societies with a new system of order.

Colonial archaeology's view of the past supplements an ideology that permeates much of contemporary historiography, and confirms popular beliefs about our past without at all questioning them. It is an ideology that ignores the participation of non-Europeans and their contributions to the past, and separates our history from their history (Jennings 1975, Wolf 1982). According to Wolf (1982, p. 5), this ideology implies 'that there exists an entity called the West, and that one can think of this West as a society and civilization *independent* [emphasis added] of and in opposition to other societies and civilizations'. This is an ideology of exclusion that denies, or at best ignores, the rights and claims of native inhabitants, but at the same time challenges them. Created to morally and politically justify European colonial expansion into North America after AD 1500 and the appropriation of Indian land in subsequent centuries, this ideology contends that American society was formed by Europeans in their struggle to bring Western civilization, albeit in a medieval cloak, to this new world frontier. In this struggle, civilization was pitted against savagery, as was Christian against heathen, and European against Indian.

The oppositional dualism which permeates much early colonial writing is highly critical of the Indian way of life (Kehoe 1981). Such negativism not only views Indians as inferior, but as undeserving of the land they inhabited. A recurrent theme is that their life was conducted without toil, which was considered by many European observers not to be a matter of choice, but one of indolence. Such opinions were reinforced in 17th-century Native New England by the absence of ploughed fields, enclosed spaces, networks of roads, permanent architecture and other markings of value that European colonists associated with rightful ownership of land. According to these ideological, and inherently Eurocentric, notions of land tenure (Cronon 1983, p. 56), the Indians' failure to 'improve' land which was endowed with such great natural riches and transform it into wealth more than justified the colonists' claims. The legitimacy of their claims, particularly as exercised in the early colonial period, is rarely questioned or challenged in the framework of colonial archaeology.

In contrast to colonial archaeology, archaeological studies of acculturation are focused specifically on the material culture of Native America. Emphasis is placed on investigating the effects of culture contact as manifested in the interchange of cultural traits, and in the emergence of European social and cultural dominance. In modelling these transformations in native Indian societies, there is an assumed logical and rational progression from all Indian culture traits to none. This linearity makes the nature of the responses to culture contact and colonialism seem entirely predictable. It implies that Indians could be easily persuaded to adopt new items or alter their traditional ways of life. Given this sort of response, the end point to the transformations experienced by Indian societies is inevitable – assimilation into the dominant society. Given the multitude of responses that could have been elicited by the culture contact situation resulting from European colonial settlement, and the manner in which these might be reflected in or commented upon in material culture, acculturation studies offer an overly simplified view of 17th-century native America.

As an approach to the study of post-contact native history, acculturation studies can be traced to the common experiences and interests of anthropologists who had participated in Indian land claims research beginning in the 1930s. This research stemmed from complex litigation involving hundreds of millions of dollars in which a United States congressional commission engaged the services of anthropologists to determine whether specific tribes occupied relevant lands (Axtell 1978). Among archaeologists, similar interests led to the publication of several statements in which they developed a general system of classification for categorizing culture contact situations and the modifications to native material culture resulting from it (Wauchope 1956). An example of the latter is a system of classification proposed by Quimby and Spoehr in the early 1950s. Their approach to the study of post-contact native assemblages and their assumptions about material culture have served as basis for much subsequent archaeological research on native societies during initial contact and in later centuries.

In this system of classification, there is a division between items of European origin (or those of European-derived form) and native artefacts. Within each division, different categories represent a sequence of progressive alteration in material elements resulting from culture contact. Implicit in this system of classification is the assumption that the material record is the manifestation of the process of acculturation 'from the time of initial contact with the West to the time of assimilation' (Quimby & Spoehr 1951, p. 107).

In a later revision of the Quimby-Spoehr model by White (1975), not only were explicit inferences drawn between the material and the non-material realms, but it was proposed that quantification of the frequencies of European artefacts (or those incorporating some European-derived element) would provide the archaeologist with a rough index of the degree to which the native society was transformed. Higher proportions of these items relative to traditional ones would indicate a preference for these items, a willingness to abandon native industries in order to secure them, and a higher degree of accommodation to the changes resulting from European colonial expansion.

This attempt to study the historical processes affecting native America in a more processual way, as well as others that have followed in this vein (e.g. Fitting 1976, Thomas 1985, Williams 1972), have emphasized quantification, and have borrowed heavily from modern systems theory and White's (1958) ideas on technological efficiency, energy and evolutionary change. In Fitting (1976), for example, a numerical index was devised to express the relative efficiency of native tools versus their European counterparts in order to assess the degree of internal changes experienced by the native society. Using this index, it was proposed that an iron tool was equivalent to 20-odd stone tools and that it would take some 60 native-made ceramic pots to do the job of one good brass kettle (Fitting 1976, pp. 328–9). The implication is that the acquisition of more efficient European tools would enable Indian groups to cope more effectively with the natural environment and make them more like European colonists. And a more European-like Indian was, after all, a better Indian.

Thus, a common theme runs through both the traditional acculturation studies and the more processual ones. It depicts the gradual transformation of 17th-century Native America into a Euroamerican society. Indians are cast as active consumers and copiers of European goods, but also as passive recipients of the European brand of colonialism. It is their society and their culture that are the open systems, not that of the colonists. By emphasizing the emulation of European artefact forms and technologies, Indian behaviour is depicted as being essentially imitative (Trigger 1980). This assessment precludes any consideration of Indian initiatives in regard to material culture, and by implication any pertaining to economic, social or political matters.

This characterization of Indian responses to European expansion masks many of the ideological and economic confrontations that were created by colonial expansion in native America. Instead, it emphasizes the dependency of Indian consumers without exploring the accuracy of this assumption. Contrary to the expectation that the trappings of European material culture would seduce the natives irrevocably (e.g. Brasser 1978), Indians could seldom be persuaded to buy more than the necessities of traditional life or to use items in other than traditional ways (Axtell 1985, p. 4). Yet, by using numerical indexes and by quantifying the relative proportions of Indian to European artefacts, there is the presumption that the desire to acquire material goods and accumulate wealth was characteristic of Indian society much in the same way that it was of European society in the post-1500 period (cf. Cronon 1983).

This position is untenable. Not only did European objects themselves change meaning as they were transferred from one culture to another, but the ways they functioned once within the context of Indian social interactions differed. This is not to say that material things did not play important roles in Indian societies, such as in affording power and prestige, but that the manner in which they served to produce and reproduce these were different. In 17th-century New England, for example, the accumulation of personal items elevated the status of the European colonist among his (or her) peers, whereas the dispersal of wealth and the transference of gifts among friends and potential allies was important to Indians. Therefore, quantification may not only be irrelevant to assessing the transformations experienced by Indian societies, but instead it may tell us more about our attempts to present their acceptance of the economic principles which guided European expansion in eastern North America and which set in motion the systems of domination inherent in capitalism.

Similarly, arguments about the technological superiority of European material culture reveal assumptions about progress and evolution that are evident in many contemporary archaeological studies of process (cf. Miller & Tilley 1984). These assumptions posit the primacy of techno-environmental factors in accounting for social transformations, ignore social imperatives, and essentially deny the importance of historical processes in explaining change. As such, these generalizations about the relative utilitarian value of European versus Indian objects has no special relevance to Indian people, to their histories, or their current political struggles. By analysing the data in this manner, the interests of Euroamerican society rather than those of Indian people are served. By imposing our values on 17th-century Native America, we are creating the impression that these Indians are like us, and because they are like us, they are not separated or excluded from the colonial past, but assimilated into our view of it. This allows us to hide the fact that although Indians made accommodations to, and even participated in, the changes introduced by the expansion of capitalism, they also resisted them. Moreover, by saying that they are like us, we are dismissing the actions taken to dominate them.

Although there are exceptions to the observations that I have made, these do seem to represent overwhelmingly the dominant approaches that have influenced archaeological interpretations of 17th-century Native America. Each of these frameworks – colonial archaeology and acculturation studies – supports an ideology of conquest that not only justified the occupation of native America in the 17th century, but continues to serve as a basis for subverting the rights of Indian people today. In colonial archaeology, this is accomplished by ignoring Indians, and dismissing the content and the import of their interactions with European colonists. In acculturation studies, it is done by emphasizing how Indians became assimilated into Euroamerican colonial society, rather than their struggles against it. Whether through justifiable conquest or gradual assimilation, Indians are portrayed as the willing subjects of European colonialism as it was exercised in 17th-century America.

## Towards an archaeology of native resistance

In attempting to construct a different history – one of 17th-century native resistance against colonial domination – we are presented with a challenge: how can such histories be written since so little has been recorded about these efforts or about the people who were involved in them (cf. Handsman and McMullen 1987)? The position taken in this chapter is that these histories *can* be written. Using the archaeology of 17th-century Native America as an Indian commentary on the events and developments that affected native peoples' lives, work, and relations with others, it is possible to detect actions taken to express frustration, dissatisfaction, and even contempt of the systems of inequality being imposed upon them.

Just what Indians chose to comment upon and how they chose to express it through material culture, however, remains largely unexplored in the historical and archaeological literature. Nevertheless, it is expected that these political statements were very much a part of the mundane aspects of everyday life and death as were the relations and conditions inherent in the new phase of capitalism that was evolving in 17th-century America. A recent attempt to explore the archaeology of resistance is discussed next to illustrate how archaeology may help us to understand these historical processes in 17th-century Native New England.

By all accounts, tensions between Indians and European colonists mounted over the course of the 17th century. Once the latter had successfully embedded themselves in New England, their settlements grew into villages and urban ports, forests were cleared for farmland, and open space was increasingly contained within fixed property boundaries (Cronon 1983). Not only were systems of production transformed, but systems of government emerged through which they attempted to construct new systems of inequality. Their tactics of domination varied. Ranging from legal deceit to tribute collection and religious conversion, these tactics were intensified in the middle decades of the 17th century as were the ideological rationalizations that accompanied them (Jennings 1975, Salisbury 1982).

During this period the New England colonists began to direct their efforts of complete political and social domination toward the Narragansetts. The largest and most powerful tribe of the region, their core territory occupied a highly coveted parcel of land, roughly 400 square miles, in what now comprises the south-western third of the state of Rhode Island (Dunn 1956, pp. 68–9). Narragansett country was such a special object of contention that much, if not all, intercolonial affairs were in some way shadowed by it (Jennings 1975, p. 179).

The European colonists' motivation in gaining this piece of real estate was fuelled not by the region's natural riches, but instead by their desire to contain and control the Narragansetts whose hegemony extended over a much wider geographical area. At times during the 17th century, their jurisdiction encompassed the entire western shore of Narragansett Bay; territory to the north and west of their homeland; an area to the east occupied by a band of the Massachusett; and to the south, Block Island and the eastern end of Long Island (Chapin 1931, Simmons 1978). Although they claimed lands situated at their western frontier, their domain did not extend over rival groups like the Mohegan-Pequots in what is now the state of Connecticut (Simmons 1986, p. 14).

It is doubtful whether the full story could ever be reconstructed. As with most colonial history, partisan observers wrote to serve their own best interests and in doing so have omitted from the written evidence how the Narragansett Indians struggled to preserve their independence. Yet, despite this exclusion, there are some indirect insights to be gained by considering the tactics used by the European colonists to bring them into submission. Among these tactics, the demand for tribute seems to provide an important set of clues for learning about the processes of domination, but also those of native resistance. By demanding annual payments from the Narragansetts and by imposing 'fines' for what were perceived to be transgressions against colonial authority, the European colonists attempted to shift the balance of power in the Narragansett Bay region in their favour.

These demands for tribute were payable in wampum: small, native-made shell beads of almost standardized size and shape that were used in negotiating the fur trade and had come to be valued as legal tender among the colonists (Speck 1919, Weeden 1884, Willoughby 1935). Although the amount of wampum demanded by the colonists was often exorbitant, it is doubtful whether their concerns were governed purely by economics. The colonial government, in fact, seems to have increased its demands for wampum tribute from the Narragansetts when wampum had begun to lose its value as currency due to the influx of silver from the West Indies and the decline of the New England fur trade (Vaughan 1979). Thus, rather than being simply a measure taken to enhance the coffers of the colonial government and promote their commercial ventures, the demand of tribute seems to have been a ploy used to humiliate the Narragansetts and force their submission to colonial rule.

As a tactic of domination, the demand for tribute by the colonial government was a very interesting part of the strategy to control native New England. At one level, it undoubtedly had an impact on the organization of work and the relations of those involved in the production of wampum. Although it is not known how extensively these demands would have pervaded the division of labour between men and women or the scheduling of activities, it is likely that some restructuring would have been required since as a manufactured product, wampum involved high labour costs. A fathom of wampum containing anywhere from 240 to 360 individual beads (Vaughan 1979, p. 221) took at least a week to produce. The rate of productivity of purple wampum is estimated to have been about half of that for white beads, because the hard-shell clam (*Mercenaria mercenaria*) used in preparing the blanks for the purple beads was more difficult to process than the whelk (*Busycon sp.*) used for white wampum (Ceci 1982, p. 100). Given the large quantities of wampum demanded by the colonial government, often in the range of several thousand fathoms (Beauchamp 1901, p. 350), meeting these payments would have inflicted a heavy toll on native labour, especially in light of the demographic disruptions experienced by the Narragansetts in the middle decades of the 17th century (Robinson, Kelley & Rubertone 1985).

Perhaps even more insidious was the effect that the colonial tribute system was intended to have on native politics. In order to understand this, one has to consider the nature of government among the Narragansetts. Like other New England groups, the Narragansetts were ruled by a hereditary chief or leader, known as a sachem. Although colonial observers often characterized their system of government as 'monarchical' (Williams [1643] 1936, p. 140), its institutions and customs were unlike those of European nation-states (Jennings 1986). It was a system of government based on persuasion and consensus, rather than command and threat of force (Simmons 1986). If a sachem failed to satisfy the leadership needs of the ruled, then the latter could transfer their allegiance to another sachem. According to one 17th-century account, 'Their sachems have not their men in such subjection, but that very frequently their men will leave them upon distaste or harsh dealings, and go and live under other sachems that can protect them: so that their princes endeavor to carry it obligingly and lovingly into their people, lest they should desert them, and thereby diminish their strength, power, and tribute would be diminished' (Gookin [1792] 1970, p. 20).

The tribute referred to in this statement was presented to a sachem in acknowledgement of an agreement involving mutual obligations. Although the relationship implied was reciprocal, there were grades and degrees of obligation involved (Jennings 1975). In many cases, these tributary agreements were between the Narragansetts and less powerful groups who sought their protection or leadership, or some other benefits from the relationship. Narragansett sachems, for example, received tribute from those to whom they granted hereditary and temporary use rights to land (Simmons 1986, p. 13). Likewise, they are said to have received tribute from groups seeking rights to participate in the fur trade (Salisbury 1982). What the Narragansett sachems gained from these 'pacts' was the opportunity to extend their domain and enhance their access to tribute. This tribute was presented usually as gifts of wampum, although other goods such as corn, game, furs, and fish also were transferred. Regardless of its form, the presentation of tribute, like other aspects of behaviour among New England Indians, was largely a voluntary act (Axtell 1985).

In the context of these exchanges, wampum's value was more symbolic than monetary. Functioning as tribute, it served as an important mode of communication that facilitated understanding between tribesmen in the system of native politics (Jacobs 1949). Wampum, in fact, was the primary artefact of negotiation. Its presentation confirmed diplomatic alliances and established tributary agreements between groups. In the latter, the payment of wampum acknowledged the authority of a sachem. Without this vote of confidence, a sachem's power was diminished since it was the flow of wampum that enabled a sachem to engage in negotiations aimed at promoting social solidarity. In these negotiations, much of the wampum acquired as tribute, or for that matter through other means, was either liquidated or recirculated. It was exchanged as gifts in establishing new alliances with the living; it was dispersed on ritual occasions or sacrificed in special ceremonies in order to appease the dead and the spirit world (Simmons 1986). In a society based on consensus and persuasion, the ability to conduct these negotiations was a major factor in a sachem's leadership.

Given the character of the Narragansett political system, the imposition of tribute payments by the colonial government had serious implications. By demanding tribute, the colonists divested it of the quality of a voluntary offering, and transformed it into a tactic aimed at enforcing submission to colonial authority (cf. Jennings 1975, p. 193). By attempting to extract much of the wampum used in negotiating intertribal and intratribal social relations, native politics would have been undermined. In particular, the demand for wampum would have affected Narragansett leadership since it would have taken away the very commodity that was essential to a sachem's influence in 17th-century Native New England. As discussed, this influence was not so much based on the perpetuation of individual differences in accumulated wealth (Simmons 1986, p. 58), as on the ability to contribute wampum and other valuables to ceremonies and diplomatic exchanges.

In the light of these impacts, the questions to be considered are: how did the Narragansetts respond to these demands for tribute; and what, if any, tactics did they employ to fend-off these efforts by Europeans to force their submission to colonial authority? In this intense struggle for power, the Narragansetts were not devoid of resources to defend themselves against these offensives; nor were they incapable of mounting initiatives to elicit counter-responses by the colonists. They not only had keen insight into their own best interests, but also possessed the kind of social and political tenacity that enabled them to convert hostile enemies into loyal kinsmen (Axtell 1985). Among all New England Indian groups, the Narragansett exhibited undaunted confidence in their religious beliefs and adhered to ritual practices with unrivalled intensity throughout the 17th century (Simmons 1986). Armed with these defences, the Narragansetts devised strategies that were aimed at defeating their would-be conquerors, and challenging their demands for tribute.

Some of the tactics which they used to express their frustration and dissatisfaction with the colonial tribute system are alluded to in historical sources. Among them are a variety of non-violent actions such as delays in meeting tribute payments owed to the colonial government; recourse to the law, notably subscription to the English crown rather than colonial authority; and diplomatic manoeuvres. Some of the latter actions seemed to have been aimed at fostering tribal alliances in order to promote pan-Indian unity and resistance against colonial domination. There are, however, other dimensions of Narragansett resistance that have gone unrecorded in written documents, but are instead encoded in the archaeological record. In considering this line of evidence, we have access to unwritten statements which may be read as a critique of the injustices inherent in the colonial tribute system.

In examining the archaeology of 17th-century Native New England, one is struck by the paucity of wampum that has been recovered, in spite of the large quantities which were said to have been in circulation at the time. Although the small quantities of wampum from Native New England sites might be interpreted as indirect evidence for Indian compliance with the colonial government's demand for tribute, evidence from a recently excavated mid-17th century Narragansett Indian cemetery (Robinson et al. 1985) can be interpreted otherwise. Relatively large amounts of finished wampum beads (n=2390) recovered from the burial ground reveal that wampum was being taken out of circulation by placing it in the graves of the dead. Interestingly, the wampum occurred not as caches of loose beads, but were incorporated into single and multiple strands, or woven into intricately patterned bands, that were distributed among only a few graves. Ninety-five per cent of the wampum recovered from the burial ground was found in four graves out of a total of 47 undisturbed interments.

Although this evidence contradicts long-standing archaeological opinions (e.g. Speck 1919, Willoughby 1935), which hold that the social and political functions of wampum were lacking or at best undeveloped among coastal Algonquian – non-Iroquois – groups like the Narragansett, it could be questioned whether the ritual consumption of wampum in burial constitutes a conscious act of political resistance against the colonial tribute system. I would argue that it does. Comparative evidence from another 17th-century Narragansett burial ground dated about a generation earlier (see Simmons 1970) helps elucidate the points of the argument. It should be noted that the material assemblages from these two burial grounds comprise the only sources of archaeological information available for this period of Narragansett history.

In contrast to the later burial ground, which is believed to have been in use between 1650 and 1670, the earlier one (abandoned no later than 1658) had very little finished wampum placed in any of the 59 graves as offerings. There were only 52 tubular shell beads reported and identified as wampum. Twenty-five of these beads were found in a grave described as the most richly endowed in the cemetery, possibly that of a Narragansett sachem (Simmons 1970, p. 84). The remainder of the finished wampum beads were recovered in the grave of a young child. Compared to the paucity of finished wampum, a number of graves contained caches of partially finished wampum blanks, shells in various stages of the reduction process, and metal drills used in perforating the beads as offerings. Presumably, these comprised the tool kits of individuals engaged in wampum production and were interred with the deceased at the time of death.

At the later burial ground, there were significantly greater amounts of finished wampum beads, and few items that could be directly associated with its production. On the basis of this evidence, it is possible to draw inferences about Narragansett resistance to the colonial tribute system. It is proposed that the increased amount of wampum in the later burial ground, especially in the graves of only a few adolescents and juveniles, reaffirmed Narragansett leadership and tribal authority via acts of negotiation with the ancestors. The ritual consumption of wampum served as a material expression of the connections between the generations, and between the living and the spirit world. If it is assumed that these graves are those of individuals in the recruitment pool of the royal lineage of the Narragansett sachems, then the use of wampum in this context may have acknowledged adherence to the socially prescribed rules which governed hereditary authority (see Campbell & La Fantasie n.d., Chapin 1931). Given the Europeans' demands for tribute and the act of submission which it implied for the Narragansetts, the ritual consumption of wampum in these burials is interpreted as an unwritten statement of political resistance: it symbolically upheld Narragansett tribal authority, and at the same time took quantities of wampum demanded as tribute by the colonial government out of circulation.

Political struggles, both intercolonial and intertribal, were part of the dynamics of 17th-century Native New England. This can be inferred indirectly from the actions taken by the European colonists and from the archaeological evidence as illustrated in the example discussed in this chapter. As an act of negotiation with the ancestors, and with the living, the ritual consumption of wampum in 17th-century Narragansett burials is interpreted as a reaffirmation of tribal authority and the rule of the sachems. Viewed in this way, the ritual use of wampum challenged the role of colonial authority in Native New England. By ignoring that these struggles for power and other political actions were part of 17th-century life, we deny that native societies have political histories. In so doing, we fail to recognize that Indian people today have a legitimate claim to the past.

## Acknowledgements

I am indebted to Russell Handsman, William Simmons, and others who commented on earlier drafts of this chapter. All offered important suggestions and caused me to rethink the logic of my position. Without the support and co-operation of the Narragansett Chief Sachem and the Tribal Council, my research on 17th-century Narragansett politics would never have been actualized. The excavations conducted at the mid-17th century Narragansett cemetery (RI 1000) in 1982 and 1983 with their participation yielded information that continues to serve as a source of inspiration.

## References

Axtell, J. 1978. The ethnohistory of early America: a review essay. *William and Mary Quarterly* **25**, 110–44.

Axtell, J. 1985. *The invasion within: the contest of cultures in colonial North America*. Oxford: Oxford University Press.

Beauchamp, W. 1901. *Wampum and shell articles*, Bulletin 41. Albany: New York State Museum.

Brasser, T. J. 1978. Early Indian–European contacts. In *Handbook of North American Indians*, vol. 15, B. Trigger (ed.), 78–88. Washington, D.C.: Smithsonian Institution.

Campbell, P. and G. La Fantasie n.d. *Sachems and sanaps: a genealogical investigation of the Narragansett Indians in early Rhode Island, 1524–1676*. Providence: Rhode Island Historical Society.

Ceci, L. 1982. The value of wampum among the New York Iroquois: a case study in artifact analysis. *Journal of Anthropological Research* **38**, 97–107.

Chapin, H. 1931. *Sachems of the Narragansetts*. Providence: Rhode Island Historical Society.

Cronon, W. 1983. *Changes in the land: Indians, colonists and the ecology of New England*. New York: Hill and Wang.

Deetz, J. 1977. *In small things forgotten: the archaeology of early American life*. New York: Anchor Press/Doubleday.

Dunn, R. 1956. John Winthrop, Jr. and the Narragansett country. *William and Mary Quarterly*, **12**, 68–86.

Fitting, J. 1976. Patterns of acculturation at the Straits of Mackinac. In *Cultural change and continuity*, C. Cleland (ed.), 321–34. New York: Academic Press.

Fitzhugh, W. 1985. Introduction. In *Cultures in contact: the impact of European contacts on native American cultural institutions A.D. 1000–1800*, W. Fitzhugh (ed.), 1–15. Washington, D.C.: Smithsonian Institution Press.

Gookin, D. [1792] 1970. *Historical collections of the Indians in New England*. Reprint, J. Fiske (ed.), Towtaid.

Handsman, R. 1983. Historical archaeology and capitalism, subscriptions and separations: the production of individualism. *North American Archaeologist* **4**, 63–79.

Handsman, R. & A. McMullen 1987. An introduction to woodsplint basketry and its interpretation. In *A key into the language of woodsplint baskets*, A. McMullen & R. Handsman (eds.), 16–35. New Haven, Connecticut: Eastern Press.

Jacobs, W. 1949. Wampum, the protocol of Indian diplomacy. *William and Mary Quarterly* **6**, 596–604.

Jennings, F. 1975. *The invasion of America: Indians, colonialism and the cant of conquest.* Chapel Hill: The University of North Carolina Press.

Jennings, F. 1986. The comprador syndrome. Paper presented at the Department of Anthropology, Brown University, Providence, Rhode Island.

Kehoe, A. 1981. Revisionist anthropology: aboriginal North America. *Current Anthropology* **22**, 5032–517.

Leone, M. 1982. Some opinions about recovering mind. *American Antiquity* **47**, 742–60.

Martin, C. (ed.) 1987. *The American Indian and the problem of history.* Oxford: Oxford University Press.

Miller, D. & C. Tilley 1984. Ideology, power and prehistory: an introduction. In *Ideology, power and prehistory*, D. Miller & C. Tilley (eds), 1–15. Cambridge: Cambridge University Press.

Quimby, G. & A. Spoehr 1951. Acculturation and material culture-I. *Fieldiana: Anthropology* **36**, 107–47.

Robinson, P., M. Kelley & P. Rubertone 1985. Preliminary biocultural interpretations from a seventeenth century Narragansett Indian cemetery in Rhode Island. In *Cultures in contact: the impact of European contacts on native American cultural institutions A.D. 1000–1800*, W. Fitzhugh (ed.), 107–30. Washington, D.C.: Smithsonian Institution Press.

Salisbury, N. 1982. *Manitou and Providence: Indians, Europeans, and the making of New England, 1500–1643.* Oxford: Oxford University Press.

Simmons, W. 1970. *Cautantowwit's house: an Indian burial ground on the island of Conanicut in Narragansett Bay.* Providence, Rhode Island: Brown University Press.

Simmons, W. 1978. Narragansett. In *Handbook of North American Indians,* Vol. 15, B. Trigger (ed.), 190–7. Washington, D.C.: Smithsonian Institution.

Simmons, W. 1986. *Spirit of the New England tribes: Indian history and folklore, 1620–1984.* Hanover, New Hampshire: University Press of New England.

Speck, F. 1919. The functions of wampum among the Eastern Algonquian. *Memoirs of the American Anthropological Association* **6**, 3–71.

Thomas, P. 1985. Cultural change in the southern New England frontier, 1630–1665. In *Cultures in contact: the impact of European contacts on native American cultural institutions A.D. 1000–1800*, W. Fitzhugh (ed.), 131–61. Washington, D.C.: Smithsonian Institution Press.

Trigger, B. 1980. Archaeology and the image of the American Indian. *American Antiquity* **45**, 662–76.

Vaughan, A. 1979. *New England frontier: Puritans and Indians, 1620–1675.* New York: W. W. Norton & Company.

Wauchope, R. (ed.) 1956. Seminars in archaeology: 1955. *Memoirs of the Society for American Archaeology* **11**, Salt Lake City, Utah.

Weeden, W. 1884. *Indian money as a factor in New England civilization.* Johns Hopkins University Studies in Historical and Political Science, 2nd series, vii–ix, Baltimore, Maryland.

White, J. R. 1975. Historic contact sites as laboratories for the study of culture change.

*The Conference on Historic Sites Archaeology Papers* **9**, 153–63.

White, L. 1958. *The science of culture*. New York: Grove Press.

Williams, L. 1972. Fort Shantok and Fort Corchaug: a comparative study of seventeenth century culture contact in the Long Island Sound area. Unpublished PhD dissertation, Department of Anthropology, New York University, New York.

Williams, R. [1643] 1936. *A key to the language of America*. Reprint. Providence Rhode Island: Rhode Island and Providence Plantations Tercentenary Committee.

Willoughby, C. 1935. *Antiquities of the New England Indians*. Cambridge, Mass.: Peabody Museum of Archaeology and Ethnology.

Wolf, E. 1982. *Europe and the people without history*. Berkeley, California: University of California Press.

Yentsch, A., J. MacDonald & R. Ehrlich 1980. What species of Indian are you? Encounters between the museum public and museum interpreters. Paper presented at the American Anthropological Association Meetings, Washington, D.C.

# 3   History and prehistory in Bolivia: what about the Indians?

CARLOS MAMAMI CONDORI

(translated by Olivia Harris)*

## Introduction

It might be assumed that Bolivia is a nation with a homogeneous national culture, solidly based on a common historical heritage, in which there are no serious national or ethnic contradictions. However, in Bolivia some 70 per cent of the population is Indian, a term which embraces many different linguistic and cultural groups, of which the largest are the Quechua, the Aymara, and the Guarani. All the Indians have suffered colonial oppression since the arrival of the Europeans, but in spite of this, Bolivia is presented by our oppressors as a free nation, whose citizens are 'free and equal', and in which civil liberties exist.

Until the Agrarian Reform of 1953, the Indian was not even considered a person, and did not have even the most basic civil rights. Since the so-called 'National Revolution' of 1952 there has been some attempt to neutralize Indian opposition by extending us some of these rights. We were 'integrated' on condition that we renounced our cultural heritage, which was supposed to be relegated to the museums, alienated and converted into a mere souvenir of a dead past.

This chapter is written from the perspective of the colonized Indians. We are struggling to free ourselves, to become ourselves. There must be many errors, which we hope you will forgive: only in the last 30 years have our people had real access to literacy and everything else that could be called science or 'universal knowledge'.

## Bolivian archaeology, legitimator of colonialism

In an article in *América Indígena* Rivera criticizes the many failings of Bolivian archaeology, including lack of professional training, inadequate analysis, and ideological manipulation which ignores the Indian descendants of the people who built the monuments studied by the archaeologists (Rivera 1980, pp. 217–24). Nothing has changed since that article was published, except for the recent establishment of a degree in Archaeology at La Paz University.

The systematic study of archaeology in Bolivia goes back only to 1952.

*Department of Anthropology, Goldsmiths' College, London.

Before that it was the domain of a few antiquarians and interested foreigners who attempted a first systematization of their researches and observations. It was the triumphant National Revolutionary Movement (MNR) which in the person of one of its young militants first took seriously the task of archaeological research. In this sense the 1952 revolution was the most serious attempt by our white colonizers to form a Nation; archaeology had an important role in this project, since it had the job of providing the new nation with pre-Spanish cultural roots. The object of their concern was to integrate pre-Spanish archaeological remains into the 'Bolivian' cultural heritage, and at the same time to integrate the Indian population into the stream of civilization (another of the main nationalist projects).

Carlos Ponce, the ideologue of Bolivian archaeology, makes a statement that reveals clearly the aims of the Bolivian nationalists:

> It must be obvious to everybody that the Indian peasants of Bolivia, Perú and México are related to the high civilizations of pre-Spanish times. Although centuries have passed since the Spanish conquest many traces of the former culture remain. In spite of the intensive production of non-indigenous cultural forms, there is a solid cultural nucleus of pre-Columbian origins and a continuity of traditions. The archaeologist in countries of indigenous ancestry must then decipher the profound roots of the people and *the very foundations of the nation* [my emphasis]. In sum, the archaeologist can by no means hide away and engage with his discipline as though it were cold and detached.
>
> (Ponce 1977, p. 4)

In spite of this pronouncement Ponce is in fact obsessed with creating through archaeology the source of national identity in the sense of white-dominated republican Bolivia, and he does not hesitate to use archaeological data in a manner directly opposed to such statements of principle.

The case of Tiwanaku is the most obvious example. This major site was the centre of one of the Andean 'cultural horizons' between the 6th and 10th centuries. Since it is located in Bolivia near Lake Titicaca, Ponce treats it as the source of Bolivian national identity. He therefore refuses to acknowledge that Tiwanaku was influenced by cultural inputs from the Pacific coast (i.e. what is today Peru) in its early phases, and only admits links between Tiwanaku and the coast in the late expansive phases when Tiwanaku was the centre of an empire (phases 4 and 5 in his periodization). Ponce's distortion goes to extremes; he even claims that 'Bolivia as a nation is witness to the past' (Ponce 1977), whereas Bolivia is a country which actively *oppresses* the Indian majority of its population.

This nationalist archaeology, in spite of its continuous protests against imperialism and external influence, is firmly rooted in a Western ideological framework and as such carries a strong colonialist ideological load. Take the case of the two Portugals (father and son) who belong to the Ponce school. They claim to have 'discovered' archaeological remains, which the Aymaras have known for centuries. In the wake of such achievements Portugal writes of Tiwanaku as follows:

> Tiwanaku evokes the fields and roads which must have led to settlements situated in the altiplano – the immense space which is the theatre for the extraordinary spectacle of its ruins. It has a special appearance for the traveller or visitor as the outline of a great deserted city, the memory of times long past which call to mind the greatness of other cities of the ancient world: the fortress of Nineveh, the undeniable walls of Babylon overcome by Cyrus, king of the world; the famous palaces of Persepolis, and the fabulous temples of Baalbec and Jerusalem.
>
> (Portugal 1975, pp. 195–6)

This quotation reveals the deep insecurity of the mestizos who constantly seek points of comparison with the great centres of European and Asian culture in order to identify our past with other empires which perhaps had little in common with ours in terms of social and political organization.

The Portugals are intoxicated by this colonialist spirit; they take no notice of the original cultural context of our archaeological sites, and simply rename places whose names a long oral tradition has preserved, as if this was enough to credit them with their discovery. Thus the ruins of *Qalasayaña* (Aymara: lit. upright or standing stone) were changed to *Q'allamarka*, meaning 'origin of the city'. This name fitted their interpretation better, that these ruins were the beginning of Tiwanaku. *Intin Qala* near the sacred Lake Titicaca was also renamed. The name means 'stone which contains sun'; the Portugals called the ruins 'Inka seat' because their shape was like a chair or seat. One after another, 'gallows' and 'baths' of the Inkas appeared in their fever for names, which do nothing to clarify the organization of ancient Andean society and economy.

All the nationalist denunciations of outside domination, all their stress on internal development, have only led to the development of a sort of Monroe Doctrine: they take possession of what is not theirs in order to lay the foundations of their 'nation' in a past which does not belong to them and whose legitimate descendants they continue to oppress.

This appropriation of the eloquent material remains of our past is nothing new; it has been occurring in different ways since the early days of Spanish rule. Tiwanaku was used as a quarry first to build houses for the Spanish in the town of the same name; then its huge worked stones were transported to La Paz in order to build the Presidential Palace, and finally they were used for the railway bridges on the La Paz-Guaqui line. Plundering takes a different form these days; monoliths are carted off on the demands of their 'discoverers' to decorate squares and private houses in the city, for example the Plaza del Stadium and Posnansky's house. The expropriation is not only symbolic but also material: they have built earthworks round the ruins so that today we can no longer get in to Tiwanaku. The Aymara people have to pay an entrance fee to visit the ruins as tourists where they listen to invented accounts of the meaning of our history. The archaeologists completely ignore the fact that for our culture the site is sacred. It is a *wak'a*, a place where our ancestors lived and through which they communicate with us in various ways.[1]

## Archaeology, prehistory and history

If our independent historical development had continued, the discipline of archaeology would today be studied with seriousness and scientific rigour. Not only would there be fewer gaps in our knowledge, but since we understand the social and cultural practices which are still alive in our society we would be able to interpret better the central features of the social, economic, and religious-political organization of antiquity.

The traumatic fact of colonial invasion changed our contact with the sacred sites of our ancestors. It was claimed that they were places of 'devil worship'; thus leaving us with only a mythological understanding both of our past and the material remains of the past.

The archaeological ruins left by ancient cultures are not inert or dead objects: they have a reality which actively influences our lives both individually and collectively. They are the link with a dignified and autonomous past in which we had our own government and were the subjects of our own history. In short, they are the source of our identity. This is why many of these sites are held to be links with the past. In many areas the Indians believe that the *gentiles* – that is, our pre-Christian ancestors – still live and walk about in the ruins.[2] We are thus able to live with our ancestors and share our world with them. By day we live in a foreign time system, and by night we are reunited in secret with our own past, our own identity.

These ruins and the myths that they generate, are considered sacred (*wak'a*) but we believe that they are not the same as all the beings called *wak'a*. For example the sacred mountains (*achachilas*) are also thought to be *wak'a*, but are linked directly to religious practice, whereas the ruins are treated in a way more similar to how Western society honours outstanding citizens. Ruins are as it were historical *wak'a* related to social circumstances. An example of this can be seen in my own community in Pacajes Province. There is a ruin called Inka Uyu – a pen in which according to tradition Inka herds were kept. Today the community invokes its help when we have economic difficulties, or conflict either with neighbouring *ayllus*[3] or with the State. We make regular offerings, particularly of sweets, fat, and *q'uwa* (an aromatic plant burnt as incense); and in times of crisis we hold a llama sacrifice (*wilani*). Ruins also play a part in rituals connected with the agricultural cycle. For example, in the newly revived festival of Inti Raymi at the winter solstice (21 June) in Tiwanaku we perform propitiatory rites, including llama sacrifices, in order to affirm our faith in the re-establishment of Tawantinsuyu.[4]

Those who have studied the 16th-century anti-Christian millenarian movement of Taki Onqoy suggest that such rites were an escape from Spanish-dominated space and time (e.g. Curatola 1977). This is incorrect, since our colonial oppressors did not effectively wrest from us our control over space. Time on the other hand is another matter: we need to regain control of our own historical time and end the foreign domination of our history. I do not believe that this counts as 'escapism'. As for ritual time, the writings of Eliade can help us to understand the issue. He states: 'All liturgical time consists in making alive in the present a sacred event which took place in a mythical past at "the beginning" ' (Eliade 1959). His next sentence on the other hand does not fit our experience so well. He writes: 'To participate in a religious festival implies leaving normal durational time' (1959). It seems to me that the Aymaras do not need to leave normal durational time, since Bolivian colonial domination is so ineffective that it can be seen as a sort of enclave with partial control only in the cities.

The city is the centre of colonial power par excellence. Nonetheless in the case of La Paz it is in practice dominated by Aymara shamans or priests (*yatiris*, in Aymara literally 'he who knows'). These *yatiris* challenge the power of the official Catholic church from the calvary chapels where they perform their rites. Even the upper classes go to consult them when they have personal or family problems, revealing in this way their fragile sense of identity, and equally their fragile dominion over the country as a whole.

In these ways Indian society constantly reaffirms its links with the past through myth and ritual on both a daily and a calendrical basis. One could argue that in the *ayllus* and in the Indian neighbourhoods of the cities we live in a different time, one in which the 'sacred' and the 'profane' are united. This experience of time is interrupted only by the superficial contact we have to make with our oppressors.

For all these reasons it will be clear that the relationship we have with the material evidence of our past goes beyond a simple 'positivist' attitude which would treat them as mere objects of knowledge. Rather, they are for us sources of moral strength and a reaffirmation of our cultural autonomy. This is why the archaeological *wak'as* are surrounded by a mythical aura and are the object of individual and collective rituals. This proves that the attempt of the colonists to turn our culture into 'devil worship' has failed, and we are still able to approach them with respect, when we seek guidance or healing. The rites and offerings to the *wak'as* are acts of reaffirmation.

Let us compare this attitude with the one adopted by Bolivian archaeology. The statements by Ponce make clear its aims and position. According to him, the mission of archaeology is:

> to provide ancestral roots for the national culture. In the case of a people which is testimony of the past, therefore, archaeology uncovers the alienation in national consciousness *and regains legitimate possession of pre-Spanish antecedents*. [my emphasis]
>
> (Ponce 1977, p. 6)

The use of the term 'antecedents' reveals clearly that for Ponce History only begins with the European colonial invasion.

Historians are no different in their conception of the history of native peoples.

When Adolfo de Morales[5] was admitted to the Bolivian Academy of History in June 1986, one of the other academicians (who is a history lecturer in La Paz University) announced firmly in his speech of reply:

> Here and now we must once again emphasise that Bolivian history began 451 years ago with the arrival of Diego de Almagro and his advance guard to the banks of Lake Titicaca and from there across the altiplano. What happened before is prehistory, or at best protohistory.
>
> (Siles 1986)

The message of both archaeology and history in Bolivia is clear: the evidence of our past, the age-old historical development of our societies and the Indians are for them only prehistory, a dead and silent past.

Prehistory is a Western concept according to which those societies which have not developed writing – or an equivalent system of graphic representation – *have no history*. This fits perfectly into the framework of evolutionist thought typical of Western culture. All we can say by way of reply is that writing was only one among many of the great inventions which regulated both relations between human beings, and with the natural and supernatural worlds. While it has the advantage of leaving traces for posterity, writing is not the only, or even necessarily the best, form of knowledge and transmission of a society's historical experience.

On the other hand, we know that in Tawantinsuyu there were specialist historians, as there are today in our Indian communities. Even a chronicler openly hostile to our forms of social organization was forced to register the indigenous means of recording history:

> In addition there used to be, and still are, particular historians in these nations whose craft is inherited from father to son. We must also mention the great diligence of Pachacuti Inca who called together all the old historians from each of the provinces subjugated by him and of many others in this country. He kept them in Cusco a long time questioning them about ancient times, the origins and the notable things in the whole country. And when he had properly ascertained all the most important elements of their antiquities and history, he had everything painted in order on great wooden boards, and arranged a large room in the Temples of the Sun where they placed these boards decorated with gold. They were like our libraries; he established learned people who knew how to interpret them and tell their meaning. Nobody could enter the place where these boards were except the historians themselves or the Inca unless by express permission of the King.
>
> (de Gamboa 1942, p. 54)

This specialist, independent development of a historiographical tradition, universalized as 'official history' under direct State control, stagnated and went backwards as a result of the colonial invasion. In a way, we were condemned to inhabit prehistory, and to know our own past only in a clandestine way in the darkness of the night, that is, by oral tradition, which is transmitted from one generation to the next, and especially by myth, which has become the vehicle for our history and archaeology. These academic disciplines as practised by our oppressors treat us as part of prehistory, and undoubtedly they see in myth one more example of our 'backwardness'. We cannot, however, afford to abandon myth since it is a form of knowledge of our past, and a deposit of our own modes of thought and historical interpretation. Myths form the main basis of our historiography and philosophy of history.

## The myth of the world ages: liberty and order in our autonomous history

History, not only in the (Andean) Indian version, but also as a universal human concept and heritage, can be understood as a process of transforming and ordering the internal relations of society and the relations between society and nature which nourishes it.

In the mythical account of the world ages (pacha) independent Indian society passed through four distinct ages.[6] The first, the time of darkness (ch'amakpacha) was the origin of human life. That long night of birth has left no record; it develops without internal differentiation in total darkness (ch'amaka, tuta). This age was succeeded by the sunsupacha, the age of silliness or the nebulous age of childhood. Human beings were not distinguished from animals and other creatures of nature, and animals intervened actively in social life. We are still living out the consequences of many of these interventions today. In the sunsupacha a distinction between society and nature also begins to emerge.[7] It is the time of confrontation between humans and animals, revealed in many myths which show how society and nature re-establish a new balance.

An example of this is the myth of the 'Son of Jukumari', a type of bear which inhabits the tropical frontiers of the Andean world. The bear gathers wild pepper (ulupika) to exchange with humans and has a son by a girl whom he seduces. The boy when he grows up is extraordinarily strong, and kills people with a flick of his finger. He is able to defend himself against the attempts of the local people to get rid of him, but in the end he is killed in the forest. All versions of this myth end with the question: 'What would have happened if the Jukumari's son were still alive?'

The first two ages are obviously mythical. They are followed by two more which represent civilization and include more directly historical elements. The third age or pacha is that of the chullpa, the population living before the expansion of the Inka state which practised burials known by the name chullpa. These people practised agriculture and had domesticated animals; they left behind burials and remains of pottery and metalwork, and also numerous food plants which are thought to be the predecessors of those grown today. Thus the q'apharuma is the previous form of the potato, ajara of quinua grain, and illamankhu of kañawa grain.

They were succeeded by the culminating moment of the *inkapacha*, a time when humans, personified in the Inka himself, ordered both society and space. For example, one myth tells how Mount Illimani grew too tall and was threatening to unbalance the earth; the Inka decided to put a stop to its growth so he made it fall down and sent the highest peak to the western part of the cordillera, where today it has become the volcano of Sajama. The Inka age is also remembered as an age of plenty, of agricultural production and social order. Nobody died of hunger, there was enough of everything and the earth's wealth was at the disposition of humanity. When anybody committed a wrongdoing the Inka as a punishment made them pull up *wichhu* grass, and under it silver appeared. People also say that the huge buildings of the Inka period were created as a result of his power over nature: he gave orders and the stones moved into place of their own accord.

This independent historical development, representing a progressive ordering and differentiation of human society, was violently brought to an end when foreign forces burst onto our civilization and invaded Tawantinsuyu. The Inka was killed by the Spanish and order was broken and eroded. This event is also recounted in myths: the Inka used his control over natural forces to order the sea to enclose the Spanish. The Spanish were saved by the treachery of an Indian; this enabled them to take the Inka king prisoner, and to justify their rule because he was unable to read the letter brought to him from the King of Spain by the soldiers. Before he died the Inka ordered that all the wealth should be hidden, and put all his cities, fortresses, and sacred places under a spell. As a result they are all underground and frozen in time. The spell will last until Indian society frees itself from its oppressors.

## *Jichhapacha*: the present colonized age

While historiography was rigorous, scientific, under the Inkas, the rupture that resulted from colonization condemned our forebears to orality and illegality. Myth, an 'underground' means of transmitting and reflecting on history, was used to keep alive our memory. In Andean thought, there is a concept – *pacha* – which unites the two dimensions of space and time; *pacha* was unified so long as our society controlled both dimensions. Colonization meant for us the loss of control over time, that is over history, but not over space; one of the ways we think of our fight against the rupture of colonialism is through mythical thought, for example our aim is to reunite time and space in the unity of *pacha*.

Although our lands suffered one incursion after another under the colonial order, we still basically control them and thus our own space. History on the other hand was stopped in its tracks: Tawantinsuyu was cut off in 1532 and history will only recover its coherent course by going back in time to when that rupture occurred, truncating our historical development. This in turn can only be achieved within the forms and spaces in which our collective life is lived, the *ayllus*. *Ayllus* are the social units on which Andean society is based; although quite fragmented today they remain the vital centre of our cultural and social life, of our relationship with nature and with our forebears.

What has occurred in the course of the long period of colonialism? Have we just become part of nature, part of the land? Have we just vegetated? The answer is no; in a clandestine way *pacha* and the historical development of our autonomous time are maintained. From the moment of the colonial rupture, Tupac Amaru I and all the Incas of Willkapampa took up the struggle to recover continuity of time, and preserve the unity of *pacha*.[8] Since then, intermittently anticolonial movements flower on the surface, like flashes in which we momentarily regain control over our history and our identity as historical subjects. This process continues through movements like that of Tupac Amaru II, the Katari brothers, Zárate Willca and Santos Marka T'ula, violently bursting into the world of civilization in an attempt to overturn and thus restore the course of history.[9] In the most recent bursting forth (1952–3) we managed to destroy the feudal estates and restore our identity as historical subjects, but in that case only as individual subjects. Meanwhile Bolivian historiography merely treats us as a background – part of the landscape – except during times of war when we become useful as cannon fodder, for example the Chaco War (1932–5).

## Chukir Qamir Wirnita: savagery and freedom versus civilization and colonial subjugation

Let us follow the lead of myth in order to examine the ways in which the Indians confront the colonial order. The myth of Chukir Qamir Wirnita tells of an event that supposedly occurred in colonial times, but it is also reproduced again and again in contemporary history. The myth is well known in my community, which is located along the frontier between the high Andes and the tropical forest to the east.

Chukir Qamir Wirnita was the daughter of the most noted citizen of a Spanish town, which like all colonial towns was an enclave within a large territory beyond its control. Although many suitors came to court her, she accepted the suit of one called Katari, which in Aymara means snake. This personage appeared as a human being (as in the age of *sunsupacha*) – a fair-skinned Spaniard with elegant clothes and covered in jewels. He only came at night, and by day after visiting her would slither back as a snake to sleep in his cave (*chinkana*). The girl's parents realized that she was being wooed by a stranger and tried to find out who he was. By a trick they discovered that he was a snake living deep in the most dense part of the forest. (As is well known, for Christians the snake is the personification of the devil.)

However, the affair between Katari and the Spanish maiden had already gone far, and she was pregnant. Her children were also born as snakes, and her parents decided to burn these offspring of the devil and exorcise their daughter. But when they tried to do so they were cast under a spell. The area which had been controlled by the Spanish was invaded by snakes who brought darkness to the light of day. Ever since the town has remained under this spell. When an

Indian goes there without bad intentions Wirnita herself looks after him, but people who go there in search of gold or to try and undo the spell lose all their wealth. The bewitched town is guarded by snakes and the Spanish and whites try to set off the church bells by firing their rifles in order to break the spell and return to civilization.

Other versions of this myth say that the snake children of Wirnita still live in particular church towers, for example, in Sicasica, Peñas and San Francisco in La Paz. All these places are of central importance to Aymara colonial history.[10] In the case of La Paz there is a belief, or a hope, that one of these days the whole city will be bewitched by the *kataris*, that is, that civilization will be invaded and taken over by darkness and 'savagery'.

This myth is constantly re-created. For example, between August and October 1979 people said that a new Wirnita had appeared in the town of Viacha and she had given birth to her children in the public hospital in La Paz. The news was even broadcast on the radios, although they added that since it was only a 'superstition' no one need worry about it. Nonetheless, many people went in search of her and many claim to have seen her. People said that the city of La Paz would soon be bewitched by the *kataris*. The fact is that in November of the same year, the whole country was convulsed by a series of peasant mobilizations of which the most radical centre was among the Aymaras of the altiplano. Road blocks were established and lasted over two weeks, repeating in a way the seige of La Paz by Tupac Katari in 1781. No agricultural produce could reach the city and people were terrified by the prospect of an Indian invasion. These events are another indication of the historical power of myth. The ideological climate of anticolonial resistance and the hope of victory over our oppressors contributed to this historic mobilization of the Aymara peasantry, and was an important ingredient in this apparently spontaneous action.

## Cyclical vision of history

It seems clear that a cyclical vision of history is typically found in societies affected by profound crisis. This it seems is why Toynbee (1946) offered a cyclical philosophy of history at a time when the West was plunged in crisis and looking for some divine plan to save it from the Depression of the interwar period. It also explains Carr's (1961) refutation of Toynbee at a time when Europe was emerging from the mire (see also *Who needs the past?*, also in the One World Archaeology series).

Since 1532, Tawantinsuyu has been in crisis. It seems likely that our concepts of history have not always been cyclical, and that Indian culture developed this vision under colonial domination as a defence mechanism and as a means of recovering its historical destiny. In any event, it is clear that colonial oppression has been a major factor in shaping our own ideology.

While our process of development started from darkness (the first age of *ch'amakpacha*), the arrival of the colonial power forced on us a foreign light which turned our own light to darkness. For this reason, as can be seen in the myth of Chukir Qamir Wirnita, the victory of darkness over light is also the victory of our own freedom over a light which for us has meant oppression and disorder.

Our freedom movements are therefore orientated around the theme of return, and of the positive value of 'savagery' as a means of liberation from colonial oppression. The leaders of Indian movements give up their civilized Christian names and adopt names which to Western eyes conjure up the spectacle of the devil. Often they become snakes in order to uproot a 'civilization' which is pernicious and chaotic. For example, of the leaders of the great uprising against the colonial order in the late 18th century, those of the Chayanta region already bore the surname Katari; Julian Apaza, leader of the uprising round La Paz took the name Tupac Katari, and José Gabriel Condorcanqui, the leader in the Cusco region, was called Tupac Amaru (*amaru* also meaning snake in Quechua). At such times, often the use of Western clothes is forbidden by Indian insurgents (see for example Lewin (1957) in the 18th century, and Condarco (1977) for the Aymaras at the end of the 19th century).

But return is not simply going backwards; it means the recovery of our independent history. Since colonial times the wheel of our own history has not moved on; time has stagnated, damaging and imprisoning us. We wish to move on in pursuit of our own vision, a vision which is both in the past – before 1532 – but also in the future. For this reason it is essential to return to the past. This does not mean to push the wheel of history backwards, but that we ourselves set it turning once again.

This idea of history, rooted in the experience of anticolonial resistance, can be clearly illustrated by means of two concepts, one which we have used throughout this chapter – *pacha* – and a second, *nayra*, meaning both the eye and the past.

## Pacha as time/space

Let us start with the most concrete uses, such as the seasons: *jallupacha* means the season of rains (Aymara: *jallu*, rain); *juyphipacha* is season of frost, *awtipacha* dry season, and *lapakpacha* the season of scarcity. These seasons are linked to agricultural tasks and to different spatial locations (sowing, harvest, making *ch'uñu*, journeys to other climatic zones), and they follow on from each other through the annual cycle. *Pacha* refers to a specific time: *ukapacha* means that time, that period. *Ukapachay ukhamanx*: at that time things were like this.

Longer time periods, and historical stages which refer to less specific time-spans, are also expressed by the concepts of *pacha* as we have already seen in discussing the mythology of world-ages. According to Szeminski (1985) these ages each last a millenium; for Chukiwanka (1983) they are spans of 500 years. Each span has a spatial referent or *suyu*. In Chukiwanka's reckoning we are today living in the fifth world-age, which is the age of disorder and chaos. It will soon be ended, and will be replaced by a cyclical return to the independent temporal order of Indian society.

*Pacha* can also designate a spatial orientation. The sky can be called *pacha*;

when it is cloudy we say *pacha q'inayataway*, and as a joke we call very tall people *pacha k'umphu*, which means 'holder-up of the sky'. Probably through the impact of Christian ideas the cosmic division of space acquired a value distinction; thus *alaxpacha* is heaven, the upper space, and also the most venerated; *akapacha* is the world we inhabit, and *manqhapacha* is hell or the underworld.[11]

Another well-known context in which the concept *pacha* is used is the living space of *pachamama*. White Bolivians translate this concept as 'the earth mother', but according to Aymara tradition it is related more to the principles of fertility, nourishment, and protection, and is a cosmic category distinguished from the physical earth (known in Aymara as *uraqi*). *Pachamama* has a relation of correspondence and reciprocity with Indian society, offering food as the fruit of labour, which for us is a source of pride not a curse. The agricultural cycle is marked out by ritual offerings and libations to *pachamama*. The sowing is a propitiatory rite, a feast both for humans and for draught animals, which are decorated with vicuña skins, flowers, and flags. *Qhachwa* and *anata* are ritual dances performed to ensure a good harvest and offered to *pachamama* at specific moments in the agricultural calendar. In August too there are rituals in order to renew the reciprocal relationship with *pachamama*. This celebratory and festive spirit has been turned into 'devil worship' by Christianity, so that today the month of August is said to be the 'devil's month', a time when the earth's mouth is open and hungry for sacrifices.

Then there is *akapacha* which means both the present time and the space inhabited by humans, the 'here and now'. It can be called 'our space-time' (*jiwaspacha*), which also means 'we ourselves'. Thus the term *jiwaspacha* expresses the unity between humans and the space around them, in a harmonious relationship which was broken by the chaos of colonial time.

## Nayra

In its basic and restricted sense this word means the eye, the organ of sight, but it also means the past. The past is as it were in front of our eyes. By contrast the word *qhipa* which means literally the back, is used to refer to time after, i.e. the future. We thus reach a concept of time in which the future is behind our backs and the past before our eyes, both in time and space. The present brings together this conjunction between past and future, and between space and time.

A phrase which vividly expresses this is *qhiparu nayaru uñtas sartañani*. Literally it means 'let us go backwards looking in front of our eyes', but translated meaningfully it is 'let us go into the future looking into the past'. The authorities of the ayllu, when they hand over office to their successors, end their speech of advice to the new authorities (*iwxa*) with this phrase. To look into the past, to know our history, to know how our people have lived and struggled throughout the centuries, is an indispensable condition in order to know how to orient future action. *Pacha* and *nayra* thus incorporate notions of both past, present, and future. The two words together (*nayrapacha*) mean the past, former time, but former time is not past in the sense of dead and gone, lacking any renovating function. *Pacha* and *nayra* imply that this world can be reversed, that the past can also be the future.

If we were to talk of an Aymara philosophy of history, it would not be a vision of forward progress as a simple succession of stages which develop by the process of moving from one to the next. The past is not inert or dead, and it does not remain in some previous place. It is precisely by means of the past that the hope of a free future can be nourished, in which the past can be regenerated.

It is this idea which makes us believe that an Indian archaeology, under our control and systematized according to our concepts of time and space, could perhaps form part of our enterprise of winning back our own history and freeing it from the centuries of colonial subjugation. Archaeology has been up until now a means of domination and the colonial dispossession of our identity. If it were to be taken back by the Indians themselves it could provide us with new tools to understand our historical development, and so strengthen our present demands and our projects for the future.

## Notes

1  *Wak'a* is a concept of the sacred which embraces the works of humans as well as the deities. Thus Mount Illimani which dominates the city of La Paz is a *wak'a mallku*, which in Aymara means high god. Below Illimani in rank come other intermediate deities in more accessible, even everyday, locations which are called *katxasiri* and may be individual as well as collective. Finally there are the *illas* materialized in an object which may be kept in the house or carried around. 'Historical' *wak'as* on the other hand are not deities nor created by deities, but are the work of human hands.

2  A point confirmed to me recently in an interview with two Bolivian archaeologists – Roberto Santos and Juan Faldin – from the National Institute of Archaeology (INAR).

3  *Ayllus* are the basic units of Andean society; in the Aymara region they are in principle endogamous and territorially based.

4  Tawantinsuyu is the Quechua name for the Inka state, meaning literally the 'four divisions'.

5  Adolfo de Morales is known mainly for his genealogical researches in the Archivo General de las Indias in Seville, where he concentrates on demonstrating the noble ancestry of members of the Bolivian ruling elite. As a result of his 'researches' it has been 'proved' that almost all of them are direct descendants of El Cid!

6  The concept *pacha* has multiple resonances in Andean languages. These will be discussed below (see the final section of this chapter).

7  *Sunsu* is a Spanish word – *sonso* – which has been incorporated into Aymara. It may have replaced the Aymara term *q'inaya*, which means a cloud or fog, and is used to refer to children in that they lack the faculty of reason. If this is the case, it would support my argument that the early mythical ages reflect the stages of human growth.

8  The Andean forces of resistance to the Spanish withdrew under Manco Inka to the forests of Willkapampa (written Vilcabamba in Spanish) after their unsuccessful seige of Cusco (1536). The Inka state in Willkapampa maintained its resistance to the Spanish until 1572, when Tupac Amaru, the nephew of Inka Atawallpa, was captured and beheaded.

9 Tupac Amaru II and the Katari brothers were leaders of the great Indian uprising of the late 18th century. Zárate Willka led the Aymara forces against those of the Bolivian republic in the so-called 'Federal War' of 1899 (see Condarco 1984); Santos Marka T'ula led a massive resistance movement against the attack on Indian land rights in the first decades of the 20th century (see THOA 1984).

10 Sicasica was the birthplace of Zárate Willka; Peñas was the centre of his resistance to the republican armies; and San Francisco was the first 'Indian church' built after the city of La Paz was founded. It remains a neighbourhood particularly dominated by the Indian population.

11 See also Bouysse-Cassagne & Harris (1987) for a further discussion of the concept *pacha*, and Platt (1983).

# References

Bouysse-Cassagne, T. & O. Harris 1987. *Pacha*. En torno al pensamiento aymara' in *El pensamiento andino en al Qullasuyu: tres reflexiones*. La Paz: HISBOL.

Carr, E. H. 1961. *What is history?* London: Macmillan.

Chukiwanka, K. 1983. *Marawata. Calendario Indio*. La Paz.

Condarco, R. 1977. *Origines de la nacion boliviana: interpretacion, historico sociologica de la fundacion de la republica*. La Paz: Instituto Bolivano de Cultura.

Condarco, R. 1984. *Zárate el 'temible Willka'*. La Paz: Urquizo.

Curatola, M. 1977. El movimiento del Muro Onkoy. *Allpanchis*. **10**, Cusco.

Eliade, M. 1959. *The sacred and the profane*. New York: Harcourt Brace.

Gamboa, S. de, 1572. *Historia de los Incas* [1942]. Buenos Aires: Emecé.

Lewin, B. 1957. *La rebelión de Tupac Amaru*. Buenos Aires: Hachette.

Platt, T. 1983. Religion andina y conciencia proletaria. *Qhuyaruna y ayllu en el Norte de Potosí*. HISLA II. Lima.

Ponce, C. 1977. *El INAR: su organización y proyecciones*. La Paz: Instituto Nacional de Arqueología.

Rivera, S. 1980. La antropologiía y arqueología boliviana: límites y perspectivas. *América Indígena* **XL** (2). México.

Siles, J. 1986. Respuesta a Adolfo de Morales. *Presencia Literaria*. 15 June, La Paz.

Szeminski, J. 1984. *La utopía tupamarista*. Lima: Universite Católica del Perú.

THOA, 1984. *El indio Santos Marka T'ula, Cacique Principal de los Ayllus de Qallapa y Apoderado General de las Comunidades Originarias de la República*. La Paz: Universite Mayor de San Andrés (Taller de Historia Oral).

Toynbee, A. 1946. *The study of history* (first 6 vols abridged by D. C. Somervell). Oxford: Oxford Unversity Press.

# 4 Made radical by my own: an archaeologist learns to accept reburial

LARRY J. ZIMMERMAN

I have been called a troublemaker and rumoured to be the mastermind behind an Indian group seeking reburial. I have been totally ignored when my experience and assistance might have been useful. I nearly lost the editorship of *Plains Anthropologist* because of my views. I have been called an 'Indian lover,' a puppet, a sellout, a radical, and a malcontent. Of all the labels, the only one I will accept is that of 'radical', and that, not really because I want to. I have had a hard time accepting the role of a radical, because it is not really in my nature. But, I have been made radical by my own, by archaeological colleagues and their actions.

I did not come to this course by accident, hidden motive, or inherent personality flaw. I was pushed into it by colleagues who little understood my motives and the concerns of many Indian people. And, I think, these colleagues little understand themselves and their own discipline in terms of the effects of their actions and discipline on the lives of people.

My intent in this chapter is to examine the processes by which I became radicalized, or as I prefer it, how I came to accept reburial as scientifically, professionally, and personally ethical.

## Are we anthropologists or just archaeologists?

During the early years of the 1970s, when I received most of my graduate training, we were bombarded by the hucksters of the new archaeology whose preachings stated that what we were doing was anthropology. I sincerely came to believe that this was true, though the lessons were not always easy. Two events coalesced to bring me to a level of social consciousness about my profession.

Perhaps the most important experience came with the first lecture I ever gave. As a teaching assistant I lectured on Australian Aborigines, but continually made the excuse, 'Well, I'm an archaeologist and not really concerned with this material'. From then on I began to recognize that I had obligations that were somewhat more complex than digging holes in the ground and analysing artefacts. Not the least of these were obligations to people, especially those we studied. I understood what my professor, Nancie Gonzales, meant when she urged me to be 'Anthropologist First'.

At virtually the same time, the first of the reburial incidents occurred in Iowa. An Indian skeleton was found on the edge of a white pioneer cemetery being relocated for a highway. State Archaeologist Marshall McKusick removed the Indian bones to the laboratory in Iowa City for study, and the white remains were exhumed by morticians to be reburied immediately. An Indian woman, Running Moccasins (Maria Pearson), contested the differential treatment of the bones. I was given the responsibility for examining the grave goods associated with the burial. A metal box crumbled in my hands, and as the dirt was peeled away, a bone-handled iron awl and a bone comb were revealed. I remember thinking that though the material was meagre, the items must certainly have been precious to the woman who used them. Though I had dug burials before, this was the first time I remember thinking about the skeletons as people rather than as objects. That moment was the beginning of a conscience about digging burials. It is worth noting that my feelings about the grave goods plagued me for so many years that they went into a recent short story (Zimmerman 1986a).

I also discovered several attitudes of colleagues which have appeared often in the years that followed. My fellow students just could not see what the 'fuss' was about. Running Moccasins was a Sioux and culturally only remotely related to the burial which was assumed to be Potawatomie. She had no right to be concerned. McKusick was adamant that he would not turn over the bones to some radical Indian group and that Iowa law gave him responsibility for the bones. It took a court order to get the bones reburied. I simply failed to understand why he fought so hard and why my colleagues used what I considered to be a 'silly' argument when the matter was obviously of such concern to the Indian community in Iowa.

This was the first time I had come into contact with the idea that Native Americans were at all concerned about burials. It was the first of countless times I heard archaeologists rely on what Meyer (1985) has called 'the argument from lineage', that the Indian has no right to the bones unless he is of demonstrable genetic kinship, language which appears in the current Society for American Archaeology (SAA) policy statement on reburial. Nor is it the last time I have heard archaeologists rely on arguments of law.

The incident was the impetus for the Iowa reburial law which received considerable attention in Deloria's book, *God is red* (1973). It was certainly also important as an inspiration for some of my views. I do consider that hindsight is operating here. I do not believe in any way that I then saw the situation as a matter of ethics. I relate the incidents only to provide perspective on a nascent ethical sense.

## Are we academic racists?

I have seen the contradictions between an individual as archaeologist and anthropologist operate many times between the early 1970s and now, and have come to believe that this may be a fundamental source of our problem in dealing with Indians on reburial. Somehow because we feel that our own database is threatened, we are unable to use the approaches of anthropology to examine our own discipline, and that somehow disables the operation of anthropological ethics. In turn, we are led to be both self-protective and self-delusive. We end up making statements and carrying out actions which seem extremely ethnocentric (and sometimes even silly) when viewed from the outside.

We do not like to have our practice and ideals compared. When someone like me or Tom King points out the contradictions between the ideals and reality of archaeology, we become the target for scorn and labelling. That tends to increase our radical responses. A few examples might suffice. The first was the most devastating experience of my career, an incident which nearly caused me to quit archaeology.

## The Society for American Archaeology, 1982

In August 1981, I had just finished with the reburial of the nearly 500 victims of the Crow Creek massacre. We were roundly criticized by physical anthropologists (see Buikstra 1981, Willey 1981), but by working with the Crow Creek Sioux and the Arikara in a straightforward fashion we developed a great deal of trust. That trust brought me into contact with numerous Indian people concerned with the reburial issue. I simply had not realized the intensity of the feeling about the issue which I assumed had cooled since the early 1970s. Probably the most important person I met was Jan Hammil, now director of American Indians Against Desecration (AIAD). She told me that because of the Crow Creek precedent, AIAD wanted to 'target' South Dakota and make it a model state.

During a year, we worked to understand the limitations of our views. She showed me that co-operation could work to mutual benefit when we became involved in the Yellow Thunder Camp case. The Sioux were quite willing to use cultural resources management in their federal court case against the Black Hills National Forest. South Dakota archaeologists had had little success in changing what we considered poor Forest Service management until the Indians joined us.

Because of our relative success with the Forest Service, Hammil asked me to accompany a group from AIAD and the American Indian Movement (AIM) to the annual meeting of the Society for American Archaeology in Minneapolis. I was to present the positive aspects of working with Indians and to suggest that the executive committee postpone any action on an essentially antireburial resolution they were considering. I agreed because the importance of having someone from within the profession to assist in presenting an Indian view seemed clear. A paper was prepared for distribution at that meeting (Zimmerman 1982).

I went to the meeting with Hammil, Bill Means from AIM and the International Indian Treaty Council, and several other individuals. Hammil and Means presented a short statement, and mine was distributed and briefly discussed. The discussion seemed open and friendly, and we left the meeting feeling very positive. The next day was one of the most crushing of my life; I learned about academic racism.

In the morning, I happened to be standing in the lobby near a board member present at the meeting and overhead her discussing the meeting with a colleague. Her words I remember well. She said, 'I sure had to swallow a lot of blood last night in the meeting with the Indians'. I was somewhat chagrined and commented to Hammil that perhaps all had not gone as well as we thought. As late afternoon came I walked back to the hotel and met Hammil and the president of the SAA walking toward me in animated conversation. The latter denounced me as a troublemaker. Hammil later told me that she had been talking with executive committee members much of the day and that, in spite of our efforts, they planned to pass a resolution that evening. I talked with one committee member who was very unreceptive and noted that he could not care less about what Indians thought. In my paranoid fantasies, I could see my career going 'down the tubes' because I was now identified with the Indians. In the end, the committee was convinced to postpone consideration of the resolution (they passed one the next year and rescinded it six months later). I could not believe that my colleagues could be so patronizing and indeed, racist. I thought seriously about quitting the profession.

Though I failed to see it at the time, there was humour in it all. When I commented to Hammil that I had never been yelled at by anybody so important as the president of the SAA, she quipped, 'Well, I told you if you stuck with me I'd take you right to the top'. Though it did not seem humorous at the time, I remember well seeing the president, no small person himself, confronted in the lobby of the hotel by a mammoth Indian (later identified to me as Clyde Bellecourt). Bellecourt walked up to him and said 'Don't say anything bad about Zimmerman. He's our friend.' I felt from those moments on that I had shifted fundamentally toward a position more sympathetic to reburial.

The 1982 SAA meeting taught me the most about my profession and its realities. Our first concern is protecting our own turf. Our concern for those we study is minimal, and persists as long as it does not interfere with what we do. Though I have said it in another paper (Zimmerman 1986b), I believe we are sometimes very racist as a profession. We do not like to hear ourselves called that, and I am certain that racism is not our intent. But from the perspective of the Indians we most certainly are, at least by the implications of our actions. We use every tactic in the book to protect the great archaeological myth we call 'DATA'. But outsiders, in this case the Indians, can see our realities. When someone points out the contradictions we get angry.

Just about everything that has happened since the Minneapolis meeting only reinforces lessons learned there. The plenary session recently held in New Orleans is certainly a fine example, and from the outside the session looks farcical. I know that many of the Indians and archaeologists involved feel they were duped by an executive committee which had already made up its mind on a reburial statement, which in more elegant and exalted terms is essentially the antireburial resolution passed at the Pittsburgh meeting. Because of their planned actions, the paranoia of the executive committee at New Orleans must have been running high.

Rumours were floating freely around the conference that Dennis Banks and Means were going to disrupt it. I heard from several people that the executive committee had asked for additional security. Indeed, when we entered the room, there were two security men by the door looking us over. From the projection booth we were watched the whole time by a uniformed guard. When asked by Jan Hammil why the security was present, the president-elect of the SAA said they were worried about the more radical archaeologists disrupting the meeting. I did not know whether to be amused or insulted. I think (and hope!) the president-elect had perhaps really deluded herself into believing what she had said. Such delusion would not be out of character for any of us.

## Who controls the past?

One of our most damaging delusions is that we are the only ones who can know the past of the American Indian. Some have used it to pervert anthropological ethics. Clement Meighan's (1985) recent commentary in the *Anthropology News-letter* is a case in point. Meighan's major assertion seems to be that extinct cultures have a right to have their story told and that Indian demands for limitations on excavation and analysis prevent that story. He says, 'If archaeology is not done, the ancient people remain without a history and without a record of their existence'. He continually refers to the cultures as extinct, a peculiarly archaeology-centred view. He seems to believe that there is no cultural continuity between the Indians we excavate and contemporary tribes. Indeed, as he implies, we have apparently convinced ourselves that, without us, Indians have no past. Others evidently see it the same way. In an article on the repatriation of Indian sacred items and skeletons (Floyd 1985) Carol Condie, chair of the SAA Native American relations committee, is quoted as saying 'it's good that Native Americans are starting to care about their pasts'. I can only comment that this also seems a peculiarly archaeology-centred view.

We like to think that we are carrying out a noble task, preserving the Indian past, but many Indians view it as another form of exploitation. Our approach treats Indians as artefacts of the past, and as Deloria (1973, p. 49) points out, 'The tragedy of America's Indians . . . is that they no longer exist, except in the pages of books'.

Why do we seem to feel that Indians are incapable of preserving their own past or that our view of the past is the only reasonable view? It might be better to subscribe to a more extreme version of Trigger's (1980, p. 673) view that archaeology can make an important contribution to the study of Indian history by freeing it from reliance on written sources that are largely products of Euroamerican culture. Yet, we remain frustrated by modern Indian groups' disinterest and disbelief in the results of archaeological study (Talmage 1982, p. 44). We simply must shake the view that we alone control the past. We must also pay attention to the fact that archaeologists and Indians sometimes view the world differently.

## Can there be different views of time and law?

I have now participated in or examined proceedings from approximately 15 meetings between Indians and archaeologists about reburial. And though I have examined the issue closely in a later chapter (16) in this book, it bears repeating in a simplified form here. I believe that archaeologists and Indians, especially traditional ones, do not communicate well about two key issues, the past and the law.

Archaeologists view the past as something comprised of linear starts and stops, something which must be excavated, and studied to be understood. For many Indians, the past simply is. It is continuous, and forms the present, and perhaps guides the future. It need not be studied because it is always with you. The law is similar. Archaeologists tend to view the law in terms of a method for the settlement of disputes. We use it to talk about abandoned cemeteries, precedents, and the like. Many Indians, though they sometimes use the white legal system effectively, view the law as something given by god or the spirits that is timeless and immutable by man. When we get into meetings with Indians, both sides can be using the same terms and simply talk right past each other. We are supposed to be the ones trained in cross-cultural matters, but we apparently have difficulty seeing the problem. Sometimes the sense of frustration from the communication difficulties is high, and ends with one side yelling at the other. Most archaeologists seem to fear the yelling, perhaps because they believe it demonstrates their failure as anthropologists. I find it interesting that the one request SAA president-elect Dincauze made of the audience at the SAA reburial plenary was that they act with 'civility'.

## Being yelled at is good for the soul

I think being yelled at by colleagues and Indians is probably good for the soul. I wish more of my colleagues could share the experience. The archaeological penchant for 'civility' tends to force what is in every way an emotional issue into an analytical framework. Anger, especially when one is the recipient, opens one's thinking. Just coming into contact with Indians helps.

I was amused at the Peacekeeper-American Indians Against Desecration conference we hosted at the University of South Dakota when an archaeologist from Illinois came up to my wife at the traditional Sioux feast held after the first day of the meeting. He told her that though he is in charge of a large museum with lots of skeletons, his view of Indians was forever changed because of the conference. These were, after all, the first live Indians he had ever met. He never realized that their feelings on the reburial issue were so intense. He thought it was all just politics.

I suspect that most archaeologists have had few opportunities to deal directly with Indians on the topic. I have had several chances, and although my life has been threatened by Indians and although Maria Pearson has chewed me up one side and down the other, my treatment by Indians has been better generally than my treatment by many archaeologists. Indians have generally been more respectful. I sometimes wonder, too, at the patience and persistence of Indians working on the issue. It is amazing that people like Jan Hammil keep trying to reach compromises with us. In working with her over the years, I know we have all tried her patience and that of her colleagues. However, that time is coming to an end, and we are facing stern tests in the United States because of our refusal as a profession to compromise. The pending federal legislation on reburial as recently reported (Society for American Archaeology 1986) is an example of where our intransigence can take us. I have no doubt that compromise will occur in the end. Does it have to be so hard to reach?

## Some conclusions

I hoped, by writing this chapter, to show how I came to the point of being easily able to accept reburial and, how, at least in some circles, I came to be viewed as a spokesman, indeed a radical spokesman, for reburial. In the end, I believe I have been made radical by my own; that my own colleagues have influenced and structured my attitudes more than Indians or some more nebulous set of personal and professional ethics. My colleagues have brought me face-to-face with the structural contradictions of our profession's ethics and probably, my personal ethics. They are largely responsible for moving me from being neutral about reburial to supporting substantial compromise on the issue, if not finally realizing that reburial should be commonplace, and part of our normal practice in the treatment of all human skeletons.

Here I found the fundamental paradox of anthropological ethics. We are largely in this profession for what we can learn about people, and as Turnbull (1983, p. 16) has suggested, perhaps mostly what we can learn about ourselves. We happen to have developed a concept called cultural relativism which says that one worldview is no better than another, and that must include our own as archaeologists. We have attached this to an ethics code which says the rights and wishes of the people we study supersede our own research needs. Not withstanding attempts by people like Meighan (1985) to say that our primary obligation is to the people of the past, I have come to realize that contemporary Indians do have a say in all this. My ethics code says I should place their needs before my own. Yet, access to the past is my own survival. How do I proceed when I must weigh the ideal of my professional ethics against the realities of my own need for data?

I have no easy answers, but only ask that colleagues cease to delude themselves about their own motives as they develop opinions about the reburial issue. I ask too, that they avail themselves of every opportunity to talk and deal directly with Indians about the matter, rather than somehow trying to protect themselves with the mystical, but flimsy, cloaks of 'science' and 'objectivity' as they circle the wagons around the ivory tower. In terms of both scientific and humanistic potential, much is to be gained by becoming 'anthropologists, first!'

# References

Buikstra, J. 1981. A specialist in ancient cemetery studies looks at the reburial issue. *Early Man* **3**(3), 26–7.

Deloria, V. 1973. *God is red*. New York: Delta Books.

Floyd, C. 1985. The repatriation blues. *History News* **40**(4), 6–12.

Meighan, C. 1985. Archaeology and anthropological ethics. *Anthropology Newsletter* **26**(9), 20.

Meyer, L. 1985. Philosophical problems in the conflict over sacred sites and objects. Paper presented at the annual meeting of the American Anthropological Association, Washington, D.C.

Society for American Archaeology 1986. Federal reburial legislation approaches. *Bulletin* **4** (3), 4.

Talmage, V. 1982. The violation of sepulture: is it legal to excavate human burials? *Archaeology* **35**(6), 44–9.

Trigger, B. 1980. Archaeology and the image of the American Indian. *American Antiquity* **45**(4), 662–76.

Turnbull, C. 1983. *The human cycle*. New York: Simon and Schuster.

Willey, P. 1981. Another view by one of the Crow Creek researchers. *Early Man* **3**(3), 26.

Zimmerman, L. 1982. Indians, archaeologists, and bones: cooperation and compromise in South Dakota. Paper presented to the Executive Committee of the Society for American Archaeology, Minneapolis.

Zimmerman, L. 1986a. Redwing. *The Anthropology and Humanism Quarterly* **11**(1), 19–20.

Zimmerman, L. 1986b. A perspective on reburial from South Dakota. In *Proceedings: conference on reburial*, P. McW. Quick (ed.), Appendix Document 2. Washington, D.C.: Society for American Archaeology and Society of Professional Archaeologists.

Zimmerman, L. J. 1989. Human bones as symbols of power: aboriginal American belief systems towards bones and 'grave-robbing' archaeologists. In *Conflict in the archaeology of living traditions*, R. Layton (ed.), ch. 16. Unwin Hyman.

# 5 On the problem of historicist categories in theories of human development

ANGELA GILLIAM

> If everything is historical, and Papua New Guinea had agriculture 9000 years ago – before Europeans – why didn't we discover them instead of vice versa?
>
> (Overheard at the University of Papua New Guinea, 1980)

In no way is a hierarchical relationship more pronounced than in who describes what is 'modern' or 'backward', 'primitive' or 'civilized'. Of equal importance is the relationship between those who officially define such categories and institutions of economic and political control. In the jargon of today's times, the 'North' describes the 'South', although increasingly, peoples of developing societies are demanding the right to define the situation. More and more, they are boldly challenging received definitions of development, noting the direct relationship between how 'development' gets defined and those who benefit from this process.

For members of national minorities in Western – or 'developed' – societies, the situation is complex. On the one hand, in international contexts, they benefit from 'global unequal exchange'. On the other hand, domestically their national condition is reinforced by the same spurious definitions of 'development' and 'backwardness' that abound in the so-called scientific descriptions of Third World people in general. Dominated people anywhere are incapacitated and immobilized by demeaning descriptions of themselves, which are often legitimated by the cloak of 'scientific authenticity'.

The struggle to change society is engaged by those whose optimism is enhanced by a positive image of who they are and where they have come from, as a people. What is fundamental is a belief in the correctness of the principle of equality. Such optimism is built on a foundation of a science that looks horizontally, not vertically, at humanity and that is unencumbered by the mental entrapments and cognitive constrictions of the East–West struggle.

This chapter then, is the attempt by a member of a national minority group in the United States (and a member of the academic community with teaching experience in Papua New Guinea) to raise new questions about how the 'past', 'present', and 'future' are described.

The application of historicist principles in the study of society is crucial to understanding the direction of development – whether that development occurs by endogenous (internal) or exogenous (external) innovation and invention. One of the primary uses of a functional body of historicist theory is that it provides the frame of reference for periodization in a society. That is, it organizes the concepts surrounding 'stages of development'. For people in Papua New Guinea and other parts of the Third World, a consistent theory of developmental direction and historicist principles is vital since, more than in any other regions, these are the people burdened by Western concepts of 'primitive' and 'civilized'. They are also laden with unequal trade and labour relationships. As do other exploited workers of the world, Papua New Guineans want to be able to answer such questions as: Who are we as a people? Where did we come from? Why is our country so rich, yet the people so poor? Are we really like Europeans were 20,000 years ago? Leaders of liberation movements such as those in Africa understood the importance of those questions, because one of the first tasks to accomplish in the liberated zones was to give people a history of themselves that was liberating as opposed to one that ground them under. These histories invariably started with theories of origin and direction, and were written for a sixth grade reading level, i.e., the AFRONTAMENTO publications of the former Portuguese colonies in Africa, and produced in Lisbon.

Importantly enough, theories concerning societal periodization are central to both Marxist and bourgeois social science. Though there are distinctions to be made between the two perspectives, the purpose of this chapter is to demonstrate the continuing problem for the universal application of historicist theory, and the ongoing contribution Marxist analysis and practice gives to this question. In addition, historicist categories such as 'progressive', 'advanced', 'backward', 'developed' need to be uniformly defined on a much broader scale by scientists; that these terms are, more often than not, used ideologically is not sufficiently acknowledged.

What a South African anthropologist (Mafeje 1971) refers to as the 'ideology of tribalism' in the West, in which the social scientist is incapacitated from perceiving a group of people in broad, human terms, plagues bourgeois and Marxist theorists. One of the reasons that this occurs in Marxian theory is that historicist concepts about the stages of human development have yet to be universalized. In order for that process to occur, scientists from the contemporary polities which were formerly kin-based, small-scale systems, such as those in Papua New Guinea, must also contribute to the expansion and modernization of theories related to periodization in society.

All of this notwithstanding, it is clear that Marxism is the only intellectual construct that permits periodization or historicism to be corrected by contemporary science. The reason for this is due to the reality of the geopolitical contexts which influence intellectual production and scientific work, and within which this theory is produced.

The issue of human development in today's world and the Marxian definition of it cannot be separated from geopolitics, to wit, the struggle for peace and against the militarization of science throughout the world. In his work on the politics of science, Dickson (1984, p. 312) makes the observation that concern about scientific literacy for United States citizens on the part of the country's leaders is really geared towards pushing the people to accede to the directions United States science is taking:

> Greater scientific literacy was therefore encouraged not to promote greater questioning of these [political] decisions – a process that many industrial leaders felt had been carried too far in the 1970's – but the reverse: to generate a greater willingness to accept the conclusions of scientific experts.

Increasingly, a quasi-religious obsession with communism directs United States and other Western scientific endeavour, as well. Thus, anticommunism also dominates social theory. Yet modern times have seen the merger of two ideological constructs, racism and anticommunism, in the development of American social thought. Mitchell (1983) of the United States-based National Alliance Against Racist and Political Repression, has pointed out that racism is used to stop communism; anticommunism is used to stop the advancement of equality. That is, when the Third World people begin activating an alternative definition of development for themselves, their presumed right to see themselves as equals is challenged. Much of the Western world sees the struggle for equality as signifying 'communism'. Therefore, as Curtin (1981, p. 59) maintains, the historiographical changes in the study of African and other Third World societies must create a situation in which the 'ultimate decolonization [of the mind] will . . . come from a merger of the anti-Eurocentric revolt and the anti-elitist revolt'.

The 'Soviet expansionism thesis' then, is the quintessence of racism, because it implies that none of the world's darker peoples would perceive of themselves as equals were it not for 'outside agitation'. The spectre of Soviet influence has become the rationale for military response to Third World peoples' calls for 'liberté', 'egalité', and 'fraternité' (the 18th-century principles of the French Revolution) for themselves. The analysis of a United States anthropologist, the late E. Leacock, demonstrates why this is a logical geopolitical paradigm of capitalist societies.

> Historically then, capitalism has been inseparable from racist brutality and national oppression throughout its history . . . thus class exploitation and racial and national oppression are all of a piece, for in their joining lay the victory of capitalist relations.
>
> (Leacock 1979, p. 186)

In such a situation it is unavoidable that science becomes a more ideological function of the 'East–West' issue, and, in today's world, this serves not only functions of class, but of racialism as well.

Thus, many of those Western social scientists who have defined periodization and the stages of human development have theoretically arranged it so that European-derived culture and physical type represents not only the most evolved, but also the absolute zenith in human development. A Papua New Guinean researcher (Takendu 1978, p. 155) puts it this way: 'How is the process of development explained: from a progressive or a terminal point of view?' The unspoken issue is how the definitions of people as 'native', 'primitive', 'simple', and 'savage' have been used as a justification and rationale for the continued expropriation of a people's land and resources, and the maintenance of cheap labour to engage the plunder. Papua New Guinean anthropologist Iamo (pers. comm. 1985) stated unequivocally that merely putting quotation marks around the word 'primitive' is no solution because it still moulds the reader's cognitive interpretation of that society. Beyond the limitations of the ideology of tribalism or primitivism for Western researchers is the impact that it has for Third World scientists. In the words of Nigerian political scientist Bala Usman (1979, p. 219), 'To what extent has the use of English words like "tribe", "ethnic group", "modern" prevented the English-speaking (and thinking) African from grasping the real nature of his social existence?' These aforementioned words form part of the lexicon of historicist categories, which comprised much of the 'white man's burden' ideology of the colonial past. Yet this ideological construct still continues to plague the abilities of humans in Western society to 'see' other cultures.

The field of anthropology has a unique responsibility for the narrow optic through which the world perceives many Third World cultures. Knowledge about Africa or Oceania has often gone largely through the epistemological conduit of anthropology. Rarely have Papua New Guineans, for example, had sufficient access to the various forms of international media in order to define themselves to the world. This one-way observation has a history in the social sciences where there has been a tendency to only see 'traditional society' and never life under capitalist domination. A Nigerian anthropologist, Onoge (1977, p. 33), called this the 'functional amnesia of functionalism' in Western anthropology. Diamond et al. (1975) also ask:

> How do we assess the knowledge claims of a discipline which writes accounts of 'culture' abstracted from the contexts of capitalism and imperialism, racism and domination, war and revolution?

Irrespective of what one would venture as answer, it remains fact that periodization of the world's cultures has occurred within the field of anthropology. And even those anthropologists who would study the élites of the world-system rarely investigate the ideological association – indeed the superstition and myth – that Westerners reproduce regarding their own societies.

It was Onoge (1977, p. 34) who said that the excesses (of predominantly 'armchair' Victorian evolutionists) had rendered historicizing suspect among early fieldworkers. But the ills of value-laden historicism can be traced to Hegel. A Soviet scientist (Olderogge 1981, p. 272), complained that Hegel 'divided the peoples of the world into two kinds: historical peoples, who had contributed to the development of mankind, and non-historical peoples, who had taken no part in the spiritual development of the world'. Had not Hegel said 'the history of the world travels from East to West, for Europe is absolutely the end of history, Asia the beginning' (Onoge 1977, p. 34)? Though one can ponder that statement as a prophetic version of nuclear holocaust, the truth is that until the world is in a situation to permit historical reinterpretation and reconstruction from those thinkers and scientists of so-called 'non-historical peoples', historicism and periodization will remain counter-productive at worst, or incomplete at best, as a tool for understanding human development. Indeed, the function of this process would be for non-Western peoples to not only describe their own societies, but to demystify the so-called developed ones. As Iamo says (1983), 'if conventional [Western] sciences do not adequately explain our cultures, whose do they explain?' Iamo, whose doctoral research concerns the struggle for shelter in the United States (1986), ponders the possibility that such Papua New Guinean studies as his own do not affect mainstream theories, but remain peripheral to the field. A Papua New Guinean historian (Waiko 1982) points out a similar dilemma:

> If the person who has acquired a Western language and knowledge of the methods of Western scholarship writes about his people, then he extends the boundaries of the foreign culture . . . nothing is returned to the people who are the subjects of the scholarship.

True science is committed in word and deed to oppose this fragmentation of the scientist from the developmental processes of his or her own people which is antihistorical and produces stagnation. In short, it represents a dissolution, if you will, of the dialectic of history, because the interpretation of reality is encased within a series of myths which must remain constant.

Waiko, as much as any Papua New Guinean intellectual, has challenged definitions of development by participating in the confrontation of his village with a Japanese multinational timber company (Waiko 1979). How could the traditional Binandere concept of development – 'sinenembari' – which sought to preserve the forest, be the same as that of the transnational corporation, which wanted to cut down the trees? Indeed, in the process of struggle around these issues, the Binandere transformed their language and resuscitated obsolescent words such as the one for 'fish trap', which was modernized to mean 'dependent capitalism' (because the fish are forced to the top of the trap).[1]

True science then must never be imprisoned within ethnocentricity. The uniqueness of reality lies in its diversity. What capital does not appreciate is the unique and diverse nature of humankind. This diversity, however, does not imply multiple directions. Thus it is not a signal to embrace cultural relativism, which has often functioned as ideological accommodationism. For example, if ritualized and totemistic warfare is part of a given culture (i.e. the United States), do humans have to accede to it as a 'progressive' part of the human cultural response? No. To appreciate the universal is to appreciate the sum of many 'uniquenesses' within a concrete direction. The relationship between the unique and the universal is the nexus of Marxism. Marxist scholars must move from the particular to the general in the process of equilibration. This is the essence of synthesis. And to regard any synthesis as permanent is conservative and reactionary.

Science in its best form is the common heritage of humankind. To try to sell intellectual production or force commoditized ideas on people is to take away the value of these concepts for true development. Until scientists demystify and universalize the true origin of human civilization, they contribute to the prolongation of the anticivilization of humankind. Indeed, the exiled Kenyan writer Ngugi wa Thiong'o (1981) refers to the current state of perpetual warfare and inhumanity in Western societies as 'social cannibalism' – evidence of unrelenting backwardness, not civilization.

Lenin (1975, p. 531) has said that no researcher describing social relations in a class society 'can help taking the side of one class or another'. The researcher's connections to power and property both within and without the society being studied have to be taken into account. African revolutionary Cabral maintained that 'class suicide' was necessary for petit-bourgeois intellectuals actually to participate in shaping liberating definitions of human development. In discussing the particular socioeconomic formation of Guinea-Bissau, Cabral explained that culture reflects a people's socioeconomic level:

There are certain types of economic life and geographical environment that produce certain types of songs . . . whether in Africa, Asia or America.

(Cabral 1975, p. 75)

Here, we see an African thinker using the Marxian paradigm scientifically to explain the condition of his people. Yet, unanswered by Cabral, but certainly a debate raging on the African continent is this: As people control their environment more efficiently, does that mean they concomitantly give up their traditional cultural forms? Does 'revolution' mean abandoning traditional music or dress? In addition, Cabral (1969, p. 129) maintained that it was necessary to 'respect the tribal structure as a mobilizing element in our struggle [especially] the cultural aspects, the language, the songs, the dances'. If the transformation of socioeconomic formations is the 'logic of the historical process', then a key question is what part of culture does a society keep? Who and what determines what is moving forwards or backwards?

This question is raised in a different way in Mozambique. The women in the country are challenging the notion that traditional customs such as 'lobola' (bride price) should be a part of future Mozambican society (Urdang 1985, p. 340, 1988). However, this does not mean that an issue such as bride price is seen by men or women as universally 'backward'.

For example, in his analysis of bride price in Papua New Guinea, Lohia (1982) asserts that bride price exchange regenerates Eastern Motuan village economies far more than do 'development' projects proposed and supported by national government. The implication of this discussion by Lohia is that in capitalist-affiliated countries like Papua New Guinea, the social reality is such that though bride price is anachronistic in one socioeconomic formation, it can be progressive in another. Though the elimination of bride price is necessary in order to engage the march towards equality, in neocolonial societies certain atavistic processes can become sufficiently transformed to serve positive functions.

Religion is one area in which the concepts of 'backward' and 'progressive' become contentious issues for science. Western social scientists have sometimes attached much importance to monotheism versus polytheism, for example, as a reflection of social evolution and human development. However, the construct of attributing power to the supernatural is characteristic of both monotheism and polytheism. Scholarly examination of processes like magic, religion and witchcraft in non-Western societies is not scientific unless the researcher continually utilizes a parallel process by applying the same principle of inquiry to the corresponding process in Western cultures. Thus, if the Fundamentalist tenets of 'the Rapture' – a state of glory between death and Heaven, characterized by an almost blinding light – represent ideological and enthusiastic anticipation of the coming of the nuclear holocaust, then this is a part of a concrete stage in capitalist development.[2] It is also unequivocally antiscientific and anti-intellectual; evolution in a 'primitive' direction. What Cabral told his people about the belief that spirits reside in lightning is relevant for United States citizens preparing for the 'Rapture'.

> We must build a society on a scientific base; we can no longer afford to believe in imaginary things.
>
> (Cabral 1975, p. 84)

And, according to Soviet social scientist Petrova-Averkieva (1980), what distinguishes Marxist historicism from unilinear evolutionism is the recognition of revolutionary leaps, retreats, and zigzags. Hence, it is dialectical to recognize that the official United States policy is promoting a state of retreat from the forward thrust of true development, 'Star Wars' technology notwithstanding.

If science in the West, and particularly the United States, can be conditioned by its foreign policy, so too must one acknowledge that Soviet foreign policy support for racial equality and the principle of non-racialism has had an impact on the intellectual production of the Soviet Union. A dialectical understanding of Papua New Guinea enabled Soviet ethnographer, Tumarkin, to make this astute observation about that country:

> The PNG, like many other recently liberated states, is faced with the necessity of choosing the path of its further development, as the traditional communal structures are disintegrating and the question of what they are to be replaced with – private farms or collective methods of farming, and in the first place cooperation – is becoming an increasingly urgent one.
>
> (Tumarkin 1978, p. 223)

This is not, however, to say that Soviet science has not made errors in interpreting Third World reality and applying historicist analysis. Witness the error made by Soviet linguist, Kapantsyan, during the great Soviet linguistics controversy in 1950. In discussing the theories of linguist N. J. Marr, Kapantsyan (1951, p. 43) asserted that the pronunciation in the languages of certain regions in Africa proved the backward state of these peoples. But can historicist theory be applied to phonology (accent) in the same mode that it can be applied to the lexicon (vocabulary), especially since it is clearly the lexicon of a language that reflects the transformations in the productive base? Soviet linguist, Chikobava (1951, p. 11), made a unique and vital contribution to the study of historicity in language when he demonstrated during the same debate of 1950 that to apply historicist categories to parts of speech other than lexicon led to racism. In this he reinforces Waiko's already-stated position that a people can, and must, reactivate traditional vocabulary for new needs. Nothing could be more dialectical. It is one way to build in linguistic accessibility for the people, all of whom need theoretical tools to explain their own condition and the socioeconomic formations under which they live. Linguistic accessibility is vital for theoretical accountability. Woichom, a Papua New Guinean researcher, criticizes the promotion of 'expertise' and Western scholarly reputation at Papua New Guinean expense; this process he refers to as 'scientificism'.[3]

As a result of this scientificism, there is a dissolution of the dialectic of development and progress. The United States has become the centre towards which everything else in the world is supposed to gravitate. The struggle in the world is a desperate attempt by the world's people to resist this pull whether internally within the United States, or externally.

Since science has become commoditized as an item of consumption in the West rather than as an item of investment in dominated societies, the exploited cannot productively use many of the scholarly analyses developed about their societies. When Third World societies have attempted theoretically to merge the issue of access to resources with that of the struggle against racism, they have often been accused by the intellectual representatives of the capitalist classes as 'politicizing' science. This is connected to the United States government's position regarding the withdrawal from Unesco, for example, and demonstrates the relationship between 'science' and the call for a New World Information and Communication Order in which the studied or observed would participate in defining the situations which govern their lives. More than anything, it speaks to the need to teach science according to authentic national needs. Otherwise, science remains merely cultural capital in the hands of an elite which dispenses knowledge to the lesser privileged in ways designed to maintain the economic status quo. According to Mozambican anthropologist Figueiredo Lima (1977, p. 15), 'the major error of [presumably] civilized people is to presume they are much more than they really are, and that the black person is much less than he really is worth'.

In any event, Petrova-Averkieva (1980) maintains that 'Western ethnographic writings often contain statements about the inapplicability of Marxist historicism to the study of primitive society'. What this chapter affirms, however, is that not only will the theoretical contributions of Third World scientists universalize Marxist historicism, but the dialectic of development and progress will enable the world's peoples to better understand the real choices of the current historical moment. But this understanding is made all the more difficult when the very definitions of development are exclusionary rather than inclusivist of the world's peoples.

Waiko has been cited in Gilliam 1984 as maintaining that even progressive or Marxist thinkers do not acknowledge traditional Papua New Guinean definitions of development; they are not even considered, rather just ignored as though they never existed. The challenge to Marxist intellectuals is clear.

A similar challenge to theories about kin-based societies was seen in the film produced by an Ecuadorian federation of Amazonian villages, *The Sound of Rushing Water*. According to Horowitz, the film's director, the Shuar people commissioned a 'public relations' film to reach out to non-Shuar peoples, given the extent of negative feelings in Ecuadorian society about Indians.[4] In one compelling scene, the narrator asserts that the Shuar people can discern the problem of class conflict in the settler society. They say they would like to align themselves in that struggle with others, but that even the poorest of the poor settlers see the Shuar as little more than animals. One singular reason for this perception is that the articulation of class conflict in Latin America often does not account for the power of racist theories in that articulation. It is Eurocentricity in the articulation of class struggle. Mafeje (1981) in fact says that in order to overcome this 'the absent must be made present' in social theory. Indeed, Mafeje calls 'for a theory of mediation', i.e. incorporation into social science thought categories, which are European-derived, of that which has been excluded.

The important difference between bourgeois and dialectical formulations about stages of development is that in the former construct, 'backwardness' is primarily associated with physical type (phenotype) whereas socioeconomic formations form the basis of dialectical materialism. The distinction is critical, and is the essence of internationalism, in theoretical and geopolitical terms. Marxists have often referred to small-scale systems as reflecting temporary backwardness, a backwardness defined by technology. This is where Gellner (1980, p. 82) errs in his interpretation of Semenov's view about the 'differences of level of development, and referring to the obligations of global leadership which this carries with it'. Semenov's position on unilinear progression through time by human society does not imply a 'mission civilisatrice' or 'white man's burden' (1980, pp. 29–58). Those latter theoretical formulations relate to the permanence of backwardness – a backwardness rooted in physiology. This is the permanent ascription of immutable retardation and is the basis of racism, which Vidyarthi attributes to the misuse of Darwinism.

Racism as the belief in the *natural* superiority of a group is . . . recent. It developed in parallel with the colonial expansion of the Europeans and found its scientific justification in social Darwinism, an unwarranted extrapolation from the theories of Darwin.

(Vidyarthi 1983, p. 150)

And it is Semenov (1975) in an earlier work who puts the blame for misunderstanding the contradiction of development on the 'simplified evolutionist interpretation of Marxist theory'. The further confrontation to the 'unwarranted extrapolation' of Darwinist theories that Vidyarthi refers to is the internationalist and dialectical updating of the concepts of development and 'moving forward' in time to a better material condition.

There is no question but that theories of the stages of human development have often served to reproduce the need for external domination. The ethnocentric presumption that 'contact' and colonization by Europeans started the path forwards from the Stone Age is dysfunctional as an intellectual construct. It is counter-productive to discuss people as 'primitive' because it reproduces their alienation and prevents them from discussing historical periodization in ways that facilitate their confrontation with colonialist biases about 'development' and 'modernization'. The primary members of an inferiorized (a structural process in the organization of the state, and which does not imply 'inferior') culture who can casually discuss the imposed 'backwardness' of their society are the petty bourgeoisie, who usually feel that the inferiorization does not pertain directly to them. Even then, the existence of an organized system with clear and possible goals of change promotes such analysis about 'our historically backward society'. Mafeje makes a similar point:

> It takes *organization* to bring together mass subjective commitment and scientific knowledge in such a way that their full potential is realized.
>
> (Mafeje 1978, p. 82)

It is because the major geopolitical pole of Marxist thought – the USSR – is already engaging this task, that it is primarily in the socialist world then that the theories of development and societal direction have become a source for people to use as tools for moving their societies forward. Western societies, led by the United States in particular, have seemingly chosen to fight this aspect of the movement towards equality, and have instead opposed such tendencies as being inimical to their national interests. Thus, the West has surrendered to Soviet internationalism the struggles for equality in the contemporary world. More-over, the internationalist goals within Soviet life as such are agents for promoting further social development within the Soviet Union itself.

In his discussion of Western Marxism, Anderson (1976) asks: how can inter-nationalism be made a genuine practice, not merely a pious ideal? One definite way is to make Marxist theory accessible to those who would utilize it as an instrument of intellectual liberation. Yet Marxist theory often serves functions of class or hierarchization when it is removed from those who do not have access to institutionalized education. Marxist theory – even perhaps this chapter itself – is often trapped by its discourse when it is removed from the discipline of struggle. The language of Marxism is thus often used as a social marker of élite education systems. In many societies, the people resent a discussion of the 'masses' problems' that they cannot comprehend. Too often Marxist theoreticians split hairs, a process which reflects the increasing powerlessness of people to intervene positively in the determination of their own destinies. This serves the status quo and the established order, which thrives on conservatism and other forms of non-action. The dialectic fails when the laws of scientific inquiry are formulated by intellectuals for their own consumption. Kahn & Llobera (1981) have noted that the Marxist tradition (among Western intellectuals) is rich because it interprets, extends and systematizes the work of Marx. But that is not sufficient. Marxist laws must be applied in not only contemporary struggles, but also in the description of those struggles.

It is important to note that African liberation movements found solace in Marxist theory because it not only enabled the discussion of structural, techno-logical arrest as related to the mode of production, but was also accompanied by concrete internationalist support from other socialist societies.

Furthermore, the incorporation of traditional knowledge from small-scale systems can contribute much to the 'dialectic of progress'. It is Waiko of Papua New Guinea who insists that the ecological success of small-scale Pacific cultures is not accounted for in conventional historicist theory (1979). Indeed Wad reinforces this contention.

> Traditional knowledge can have immense value for self-reliant develop-ment but has often been suppressed by modern science and technology.
>
> (Wad 1984)

In addition, viewing contemporary kin-based and small-scale systems as being inhabited by the Europeans' 'contemporary ancestors', to use the phrase coined by Mercier (1966, pp. 54–5), helps to locate those cultures in some ahistorical orbit.

Soviet ethnographer Bromley once observed, 'Everything in society is historical'.[5] However, Third World social scientists whose commitment is to the elimination of domination of their people are shedding even further light on Marxian historicity. Indeed, rationality in Marxist theory will be enhanced by the contribution of the historically observed to the epistemology of historicist observation.

Such a process is vital not only because it will eliminate the OTHER – the outsider – in the social sciences, but because it will enable the entire world's peoples to resist the centrifugal, absolutizing pull of militarization in today's world. Increasingly, this resistance leads to a polarization throughout the world between pro-apartheid forces and anti-apartheid ones. More and more, irre-spective of the previous limitations of historicist theory, Marxist theory has led to the development of an inclusivist, non-racialistic science for a civilized future. It is the historical responsibility of human beings in the Western cultures to understand that inclusion of the previously excluded – whether as scientific theory or broader participation in state power – is not a threat to authentic civilization. As once was observed on the Free Speech Bulletin Board at the University of Papua New Guinea, 'Wearing high heels is *not* civilization'.

# Notes

1 Waiko's discussion of linguistic transformation in Binandere language took place during a guest lecture on 4 March 1980 to the students of the Language and Development course at the University of Papua New Guinea.
2 An analysis of this issue was the theme of an independent radio production by Joe Cuomo for WBAI-FM radio in New York City on 8 May 1984. The name of the programme was 'Ronald Reagan and the Prophecy of Armageddon'.
3 This terminology was used by J. Woichom in personal communication with the writer in pre-publication response to an article entitled, *Language and 'development' in Papua New Guinea*. (See References under Gilliam.) In employing the word 'scientificism', Woichom used a term that Argentine mathematician, Varsavsky, had also utilized to describe a 'scientific market' that Third World scientists do not control, yet were expected to join. (See References under Varsavsky.)
4 The information about *The Sound of Rushing Water* was provided by B. Horowitz in a personal communication in 1975. The address of the federation as depicted in the film is Federación Shuar, Sucúa, Morona Santiago, Ecuador. The film is available for rental in the United States from the University of Pittsburgh, Audio-Visual Department, or the University of Wisconsin at Madison, Audio-Visual Department.
5 This comment was made during an interview with the writer during the Tenth International Congress of Anthropological and Ethnological Sciences in New Delhi, 1978. At that time, Yuri Bromley was the director of the Institute of Ethnography of the USSR Academy of Sciences.

# References

Anderson, P. 1976. *Considerations on Western Marxism*. London: New Left Books.
Bala Usman, Y. 1979. *For the liberation of Nigeria*. London: New Beacon.
Cabral, A. 1969. *Revolution in Guinea: an African people's struggle*. London: Stage I.
Cabral, A. 1975. *Análise de alguns tipos de resistência*. Lisbon: Seara Nova.
Chikobava, Arn. 1951. On certain problems in Soviet linguistics. In *The Soviet linguistic controversy*, J. Murra, R. Hankin & F. Holling (eds). pp. 9–19. New York: Columbia University Press.
Curtin, P. D. 1981. Recent trends in African historiography and their contribution to history in general. In *General history of Africa I: methodology and African pre-history*, J. Ki-Zerbo (ed.). pp. 54–71. Paris: Unesco; London: Heinemann; Berkeley: University of California Press.
Diamond, S., B. Scholte & E. Wolf 1975. On defining the Marxist tradition in anthropology: a response to the *American Anthropologist*. *Critique of Anthropology*, Autumn.
Dickson, D. 1984. *The new politics of science*. New York: Pantheon.
Figueiredo Lima, M. H. 1977. *Nação Ovambo*. Lisbon: Editorial Aster.
Gellner, E. 1975. The Soviet and the savage. *Current Anthropology* **16**(4), December.
Gellner, E. (ed.) 1980. *Soviet and Western anthropology*. London: Duckworth.
Gilliam, A. 1984. Language and 'development' in Papua New Guinea. *Dialectical Anthropology* **8**, 303–18.
Iamo, W. 1983. History of some anthropological ideas: a field statement. Unpublished

paper, Department of Anthropology, University of California, Berkeley.

Iamo, W. 1986. In search of justice and shelter in Mix-Town, USA. Unpublished PhD dissertation, Department of Anthropology, University of California, Berkeley.

Kahn, J. S. & J. R. Llobera 1981. *The anthropology of pre-capitalist societies*. London: Macmillan.

Kapantsyan, Gr. 1951. On certain of N. Marr's general linguistic theses. In *The Soviet linguistic controversy*. J. Murra, R. M. Hankin & F. Holling (eds). pp. 42–5. New York: Columbia University Press.

Leacock, E. 1979. Class, commodity and the status of women. In *Toward a Marxist anthropology*, S. Diamond (ed.). The Hague: Mouton.

Lenin, V. I. 1975. *Collected works: volume II*. Moscow: Progress Publishers.

Lohia, R. 1982. Impact of regional bride price on the economy of Eastern Motu villages. In *Post-independent economic development of Papua New Guinea*, P.A.S. Dahanayake (ed.). Port Moresby: Institute of Applied Social and Economic Research.

Mafeje, A. 1971. The ideology of 'tribalism'. *Journal of Modern African Studies*.

Mafeje, A. 1978. *Science, ideology, and development: three essays on development theory*. New York: Africana Publishing Company.

Mafeje, A. 1981. On the articulation of modes of production: review article. *Journal of Southern African Studies*, October.

Mercier, P., 1966. *Histoire de l'anthropologie*. Paris: Presses Universitaires de France. [Quoted in *Marxism and 'primitive' societies*, Terray, E. 1972, New York: Monthly Review Press.]

Mitchell, C. 1983. In personal communication.

Ngugi wa Thiong'o 1981. *Writers in politics*. London: Heinemann.

Olderogge, D. 1981. Migrations and ethnic and linguistic differentiation. In *General history of Africa I: methodology and African prehistory*, J. Ki-Zerbo (ed.). pp. 271–291. Paris: Unesco; London: Heinemann; Berkeley: University of California Press.

Onoge, O. 1977. Revolutionary imperatives in African sociology. In *African social studies*, P. Gutkind & P. Waterman (eds). pp. 32–43. London: Monthly Review Press.

Petrova-Averkieva, Yu. 1980. Historicism in Soviet ethnographic science. In *Soviet and Western anthropology*, E. Gellner (ed.). pp. 19–27. London: Duckworth.

Semenov, Yu. I. 1975. [Published response to E. Gellner, The Soviet and the savage.] *Current Anthropology* **16** (14), December.

Semenov, Yu. I. 1980. The theory of socio-economic formations and world history. In *Soviet and Western Anthropology*, E. Gellner (ed.), 29–58. London: Duckworth.

Takendu, D. 1978. Social research and the problems of resource use and development. In *Paradise postponed: essays on research and development in the South Pacific*, A. Mamak & G. McCall (eds). Oxford: Pergamon.

Tumarkin, D. 1978. Soviet ethnographers on the islands of Oceania. *Social Sciences* (Moscow) **9**, (2).

Urdang, S. 1984. The last transition? Women and development in Mozambique. In *A difficult road: the transition to socialism in Mozambique*, J. S. Saul (ed.) New York: Monthly Review Press.

Urdang, S. 1988. *And still they dance: women, destabilization, and change in Mozambique*. New York: Monthly Review Press.

Varsavsky, O. 1977. O cientificismo. In *Ciência e in-Dependência*, S. Anderson & M. Bazin (eds). Lisbon: Livros Horizonte.

Vidyarthi, L. P. 1983. On race and racism: a new look at old questions. In *Racism, science and pseudo-science*. pp. 51–9. Paris: Unesco.

Wad, A. 1984. Science, technology and industrialization in Africa. *Third World Quarterly* **6** (2).

Waiko, J. 1979. Land, forest and people: villagers struggle against multinational corporations in Papua New Guinea. Unpublished paper delivered at the IV Pacific Congress, Khabarovsk, USSR. 20 August 1979.

Waiko, J. 1982. Be Ji jimo: a history according to the tradition of the Binandere people of Oro province in Papua New Guinea. Unpublished PhD dissertation, History Department, Australian National University Canberra.

# 6 The burden of an encumbered inheritance upon the study of the past of Madagascar

JEAN-AIMÉ RAKOTOARISOA

(translated by Marianne Dumartheray)

It is no longer a question of lamenting our ancestors, the Gauls, in Madagascar, even if such rubbish was taught for dozens of years in our schools. Today such statements appear more of a joke, and contemporary researchers do what they can to eliminate from textbooks those paragraphs which asserted our assimilation with the 'mother country'.

However, it must be noted that 25 years after our 'independence', although the words have certainly disappeared, this is not always the case with the ideas behind them. Archaeology, a necessary component in the study of the past of Madagascar, has already been the object of a series of controversies. To speak of archaeology in a country which lacks even the material to build its history, was meaningless in the eyes of many sceptics and even for some scientists. This is why archaeology has not always occupied the place it deserves, and has been recognized officially as a scientific subject only for the last 20 years. The Malagasy archaeological team, composed of geographers and historians, has been functioning since 1973, and comprises approximately ten researchers.

## A scandalous imbalance

Most studies dealing with the past in Madagascar were conceived, written, and published by foreigners whose main concern was to satisfy their own interests and those of their own country. Overtly or not, their aim was most probably to supply the metropolitan state with facts which might be used in the future exploitation of Madagascar. The scientific value of the work of certain authors has been unanimously recognized, but even they exhibit the general tendencies characteristic of the period.

The first type of research recorded fragmentary folkloristic descriptions of the customs and habits of the 'indigenous' population of Madagascar, not forgetting to mention the exotic side. They sometimes also made ill-considered generalizations, extrapolating from the experiences of the author in a given region to the whole of Madagascar. This attitude, well understandable for the period, has been the cause of numerous mistakes which continue to encumber the work of modern researchers.

It is generally admitted that the most serious bias is in the blatant disproportion between the number of works published and the historical periods covered. More than half of the available documents concern the 19th and 20th centuries; a great part deal solely with the colonial period, yet this lasted for only 60 years (see Fig. 7.1).

Some importance has been attributed to problems relating to the origin of the Madagascans. The arrival of the Austronesians has been emphasized, thus undervaluing the Arab and African contributions. This aspect of Madagascar's past continues to generate polemic, turning attention away from the prime objective, which is to fill the gaps in the record of our prehistory. At present, we have a very limited knowledge of the periods prior to the 16th century, apart from the rare glimpse of light on the establishment of the trading posts controlled by Arabs and Islamized peoples between the 12th and 14th centuries. Beyond the 11th century we reside entirely in the realm of suppositions and hypotheses. Very few scientists have, then, taken an interest in the first millenium of Madagascar's past. Yet this period, extending from the 5th to the 15th centuries is of prime importance. Most researchers have concentrated their efforts either on the origin of human settlement in Madagascar or on the recent past (see Fig. 7.1).

## To re-establish the balance, or to strive for a diploma?

The imbalance may be explained in several ways. Early researchers may well have paid little attention to the prehistoric periods, but why is it that modern researchers have not taken pains to fill the ten-century gap? National researchers are just as much victims, consciously or otherwise, of this bias. Nearly a quarter of a century after 'independence' it has not yet been possible to reorientate studies towards Malagasy history because of a series of apparently insuperable problems.

For many Malagasy researchers the main objective is to finish their thesis and get a diploma, if possible according to the criteria of the old metropolitan university system. It is easier for national historians to work on recent periods of time, particularly the colonial period, because they offer the most immediately exploitable facts. They have contributed the greatest part of our archives and our libraries. To venture to write a thesis on data still to be collected (recording oral traditions, conducting archaeological excavations) presents a certain number of risks and demands too much time. To study Malagasy prehistory necessarily implies a much longer period of preparation before award of the diploma which is synonymous with promotion.

In spite of their sincere will to redress the situation, most national researchers have therefore been obliged to complete the work of their late mentors. Modern versions of certain concepts prevailing during the colonial period pervade their work.

It was part of colonial strategy to show up criteria of division in society. There are researchers today who, while they recognize the damaging effect of

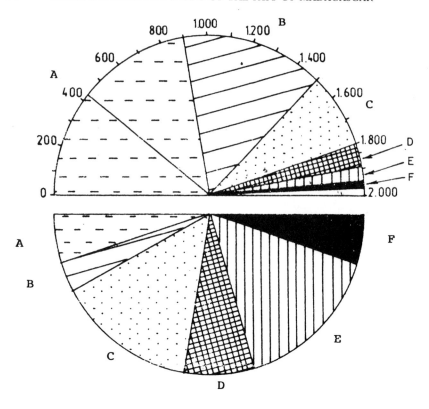

**Figure 7.1** Disproportion between the duration of phases of Madagascar's past (upper half) and the number of published studies on each phase (lower half).

*Key*

A Period before the 10th century AD: human occupation of Madagascar uncertain prior to 5th century AD; first waves of Austronesian settlement occur between 5th and 10th centuries.

B 11th to 16th centuries AD: the proto historic period. Last waves of Austronesian settlement; arrival of the Arabs and other Islamized populations.

C 17th to 19th centuries AD: period of native kingdoms; first contact with Europeans.

D 19th century prior to colonization.

E 1895–60: colonial period.

F 1960–86: post-colonial period and birth of a republic.

such a practice, either continue to work on subjects intended in part to prove the authenticity of a particular group or region as compared to the rest of the country, or encourage their disciples to do so.

To recognize this we need to look again at the list of diploma dissertations or theses presented over the last 20 years. The greater number begin by contending that the region or group which is the object of the study constitutes a unique entity in the context of the whole country. It is asserted that on no account must analogies or similitudes be seen with their neighbours. Do we have here a genuine search for identity, or merely a trauma inflicted by the colonial experience?

## Archaeology and received ideas

Certain contemporary archaeologists engage in still more dangerous research practices. Social classes exist in Madagascar as elsewhere, and the colonial power did not hesitate to make use of them. This is perfectly comprehensible; but there is very little justification for the present practice, among archaeologists, of continuing to look only for material proofs of class distinctions when working on a site, and assimilating data without justification to the model of a society stratified into nobles, bourgeois, and slaves. According to their logic, everything, from spatial organization of a village to technological innovations, can be explained only with reference to this hierarchy. Under the pretext of using new survey, excavation, and dating methods, they seek evidence to support questionable hypotheses. At least these hypotheses have been committed to writing. There is a great temptation, in this case, to follow the work of one's predecessors without questioning it.

Where recent archaeological finds indicate the inaccuracy of certain assertions, it is not always easy to gain recognition for the new data. Traditional literature, for instance, accepted without question that the South of Madagascar had been inhabited for a maximum of three to four centuries. Recent archaeological research in the South has revealed not only the presence of human occupation since the 12th century, but also evidence of intense external trading activity. The same is the case for the use of iron. Traditionally it has been said that iron did not appear in Madagascar until the 16th century, during the reign of Prince Andriamanelo (1540–75). His victory over the Vazimba, the first occupants of Madagascar (considered to be mythical figures), is attributed to the use of spears with metal heads. According to tradition, rice fields were more speedily constructed with the aid of *angady* (the long-bladed spade which is the main tool of the Malagasy peasant). Recent archaeological finds have proved without any doubt that iron has been known by the Malagasy since the first phase of occupation.

Concerning eating habits, official mythology credits introduction of the eating of beef to Prince Ralambo (c. 1575–1610). Archaeological excavations have shown, however, that the Malagasy did not have to wait for the good will of this prince to enjoy eating beef. On the contrary, it is quite clear that the use of iron and the consumption of beef preceded the two princes, Andriamanelo and Ralambo. The facts are now scientifically demonstrated. It would, however, be imprudent to emphasize these facts as they jeopardize the legitimacy of the princes' accession to power and, thereby, that of all their descendants. Examples of this nature can be multiplied at will, especially those concerning staple agricultural products such as rice: the victorious prince is often regarded as a genial innovator.

## Ethnicity, politics, and behaviour

The problems discussed do not necessarily arise from contradictions between received ideas and the findings of archaeology. They can also be explained to a great extent by the very attitudes of Madagascans who fail to throw off the weight of their colonial heritage. Certain statements, not always justified but often repeated, continue to be considered by the Malagasy themselves as symbols of their authenticity. Ethnic or political groupings are in the throes of acquiring a quasi-sacred and therefore untouchable character, much like the taboos recommended by the ancestors. Everyone knows how much these divisions in the community have been artificially elaborated. Yet, who would dare to question the frontiers of African States today, knowing the risk of triggering conflict? In Madagascar, it was once pronounced that there existed 18 clans. Now people actually identify themselves with these ethnic groups. This tendency is now so deep rooted that a political balance could not be reached without taking the 18 clans into consideration. During the colonial period, a 19th clan was added. It should be noted that the representatives of this clan were numerous in the first government of the Malagasy Republic!

Studies of behaviour in Malagasy society show once again the damage caused by the colonial heritage. Many find it embarrassing to admit their African affiliation, but are prepared to speak with pride of their Arab or Austronesian origin. Several explanations can be found for this tendency. We can perceive here the transposition of an ideology which associates technological superiority in astronomy, irrigation methods, mathematics, and so forth, with supposed ethnic groups. In Madagascar, the Arabs and the last wave of Austronesian immigrants arrived with the most recent technological innovations of the time. They were thus able to impose their mode of production, as well as their political organization, upon earlier settlers. It is impossible to explain this domination in terms of innate ethnic superiority. In fact the case of the Austronesians well illustrates the absurdity of such a doctrine since the last arrivals excelled over the first even though there can be no doubt that they came from the same stock.

## Possible solutions

The means finally to rid ourselves of the hold of our colonial past exist. What is needed is the individual and collective will to acquire a truly independent spirit and to accept an objective reconsideration of our past.

This choice not only demands much self-sacrifice on the part of researchers, but also requires substantial material and financial support, which are not always available.

One solution is to invite outside co-operation, but this is risky unless certain precautions are first taken. Conventions must be set up by officially recognized institutions. No decision should be implemented without the consent of all parties. It should be recalled that the nationality of those concerned can be neither a criterion of acceptance nor of refusal. Only the technical value and quality of the researcher will be taken into account. Experience has shown that indigenous researchers tend to put their personal interests before those of their country. It would be much more profitable to co-operate with foreigners whose primary objective is to fill the gaps in our knowledge and enlighten those aspects of our past which are still obscure.

International co-operation can, however, only partly solve the difficulties in the quest for the past. Archaeology provides only part of the expertise, but is not in itself sufficient. Other disciplines must be called upon if the country is not to be steeped into a new set of false assertions, to be perpetuated by future generations.

# 7 Archaeological and anthropological hypotheses concerning the origin of ethnic divisions in sub-Saharan Africa

PANCRACE TWAGIRAMUTARA

(translated by Marianne Dumartheray)

## Interaction of culture, ecology, and biology in the genesis of African cultures

### The problem

In previous publications the author has shown that we cannot refer simply to linguistic data, nor to human biological data alone, in order objectively to explain the ethnic bases of primitive social formations in interlacustrine Africa in general and Rwanda in particular (Twagiramutara 1980a, b). In this chapter, and through an examination of several studies, we ask whether ethno-archaeological information can be useful in our quest. We direct discussion to the interrelations which, over a period of time, have arisen between ecological, economic, and cultural phenomena. We also consider the possible effect of such interrelations upon the emergence and development of the socio-ethnic categories under consideration.

### Nature and culture

Archaeological research in Black Africa in general, and Rwanda in particular, is unfortunately still in its early stages. Research shows, however, that this region was the scene of a series of climatic changes which, alternating from very early times between arid and rainy periods, contributed to diversified modes of production. These studies show that during a period between 18,000 and 12,000 B.P., a large zone of the African continent stretching from the Mediterranean coast to Nigeria and to Chad suffered a particularly dry period (Rognon 1976, Faure 1980). They further show that the succeeding period, between 14,000 and 8000 B.P., was a phase of great humidity, which brought about a considerable elevation and extension of lakes and local rivers in low altitude zones.

Researchers have shown that, as a result of the increase and extension of the level of Lake Chad, Lake Rudolph, Lake Victoria, Lake Tanganyika, and other large fluvio-lacustrine basins around 9000 B.P., a number of populations who had until then been nomads, commenced a process of at least partial sedentarization, establishing themselves in the vicinity of these basins (Cornevin 1966, Sutton 1974, Phillipson 1977, Said 1980, Noten 1980).

At the end of this humid phase, the African continent again endured a progressively drier climate, characterized around 4000 B.P. by a general lowering of the levels and reduction in extent of the lakes and rivers referred to above. Minor fluctuations are dated by some authors to around 3000 B.P., by others to 2500 B.P. Since then, the aridification of the Sahara and many other African regions had been accelerated.

How did these climatic changes affect the modes of production of the successive indigenous populations who occupied these zones?

None of the studies cited allow us at this stage to explain how some of the populations undergoing progressive sedenterization acquired the techniques of domestication. Can we imagine that this phenomenon came about as it did in certain regions of the Near East? Studies concerning certain Near Eastern sites show that it is precisely during this preagricultural phase that the dog and sheep were domesticated. These studies also show that domestication of plants and of certain known thieving animals such as the goat and the cow probably took place at around the same period, between 8000 and 5000 B.P.

The available ethno-archaeological data thereby allow us to infer that 5000 years ago the Sahara was sufficiently well watered to be inhabited by livestock-rearing and agricultural populations who also practised hunting and fishing, just like those populations who were wandering across other relatively high regions of East Africa at that time. These data also show that the progressive drying up of the African continent appears to be one of the factors likely to have contributed to the migration of Saharan populations at this time towards other more hospitable regions.

However, a great number of these populations moving South from the Sahara to the Sahel were forced, by the new social and cultural environment into which they entered, to adopt specific, dominant modes of production. What is more, archaeological studies from different regions of interlacustrine Africa show us that around 3000 to 2000 B.P. populations characterized by the practice of agriculture, livestock breeding, and pottery manufacture already existed in these regions.

Anthropological studies show that certain elements within indigenous ethnic groups have at different times adopted different modes of production, whereas others of the same groups persisted with one or another dominant mode of production (see below).

## The processes of culture change

Authors such as Noten (1980) and Porteres & Barrau (1980) have clearly shown in the context of Black Africa, how man has had, from the start, to adapt to various specific micro-environments, each with its own climate, flora, and fauna, and in so doing how populations responded in various ways to the conditions created by the diversity of these micro-environments by developing distinctive cultures. Porteres & Barrau also point out that the origin, diversification, and the development of cultivation and husbandry were closely related to local soils and vegetation, the types of plant originally exploited, and the nature of the food and other resources these yielded. If the natural milieu played an important, even a preponderant role, in the genesis of farming and husbandry, it was however not the only factor, for these processes also implied the intervention of culture. 'Men, in the course of their migrations and movements, carried with them their techniques, their modes of perception and interpretation of the environment, their ways of conceiving and using space, etc. They also brought with them a whole series of attitudes and behaviours generated by their rapport with nature in their initial habitat' (Porteres & Barrau 1980, p. 726). Let us try to explain how these two kinds of fact contributed to the genesis of cultivation and pastoralism in Black Africa.

## The origin and development of the techniques of animal domestication

It is fairly well known that during the pluvial phase already mentioned and the dry period that followed, the Sahara and sub-Saharan regions were populated, in certain environments, by social groups that had modes of production undergoing diversification. There were, on the one hand, social groups characterized by a mode of production based predominantly on fishing, hunting, and gathering. Elsewhere, there were social groups who, in addition to activities linked to a predatory type of economy, would little by little develop the domestication of animals such as the goat, sheep, and cow. It is therefore possible that social groups which first attempted domestication were amongst those who lived for a long time in the heart of relatively high regions (above 500 metres altitude) of the Sahara and East Africa. Such was the case for social groups who, around 11 000 and 7000 B.P., had already domesticated the sheep and cow in certain regions of moderate altitude in the Sahara and East Africa. Torrential rain precluded this practice in mountains and other elevated zones. A further instance is provided by social groups who practised domestication of goats, sheep, and cattle around 6000 B.P. in sites neighbouring Es Shahaeinab and de Kadero (Sudan).

Climatic fluctuations may well have contributed to a greater and greater diversification of both geographical environments and modes of production. The balance which had existed during the period of heavy rains had been generally favourable to a fishing and gathering economy. As the new dry period set in this balance was upset. After 6050 B.P. a new balance, favourable this time to breeding and agriculture, seems to have been inaugurated.

## The inauguration and development of techniques of plant domestication

It is quite possible that those social groups who first attempted to domesticate wild plants were those who had long lived near rivers subject to annual floods in zones which, with the onset of a drier climate, become progressively desertified, or in regions near lake sides or swamps in the heart of relatively dry zones. The river Nile offers an example of the former possibility, Lake Chad an example of the latter.

It is also possible that the domestication of food plants was speeded up by the progressive improvement of agricultural tools and farming methods, which helped to increase production. Crafts are evidenced by potsherds and tools such as iron axes and hoes which allowed clearance of greater areas and their conversion to arable land.

Archaeological evidence from these regions shows that by 4000 B.P. they were occupied by populations who had already entered a cultural phase characterized by the practice of agriculture, animal breeding, and the manufacture of diverse types of pottery.

We know further that during the 4th millenium B.P. a number of populations located at sites situated between the Cross and Benue Rivers on the modern border between Nigeria and the Cameroon, progressively abandoned exogenous plants, turning to the domestication of local types such as sorghum and millet, which were better adapted to the local environment. This seems likely to have enhanced their prosperity, and the influence of populations living in certain areas of this part of Africa was extending by 3000 B.P.

With regard to the particular case of Rwanda, the first Iron Age (with associated pottery) had until recently been dated to between 2200 B.P. and 1800 B.P. The second Iron Age was dated to the 8th century AD onwards.

Recent archaeological data have shown that by 2865 B.P. Rwanda was populated by iron workers using small blast furnaces and that bricks were being made.[1] It is quite possible that such improvement in the manufacture of iron tools was combined with parallel developments in agriculture and animal breeding, as was the case in other parts of sub-Saharan Africa.

It is, moreover, likely that certain social groups, according to local circumstances, progressively specialized in either crafts or agriculture, hunting and gathering or stock rearing. Other groups may progressively have combined a number of these activities.

In brief, Africa in general and Black Africa in particular has been inhabited by a diversity of cultures from the Neolithic onwards. Whereas certain social groups continue to carry out a predominantly predatory economy orientated essentially to hunting and gathering, other groups become more and more involved in agricultural production (Sutton 1980, p. 521).

Finally, for other social groups we observe the development of domestication of sheep, goats, cattle, and other species (Anfray 1968, Sutton 1980, Porteres & Barrau 1980).[2]

## Culture and society: the articulation of biological and cultural processes

### The phenomenon of reversibility

The evolution of these formations should not be envisaged as unidirectional. The phenomenon of reversibility must be considered. While one local population changes in one direction, others may, at the same time and for different reasons, evolve in other directions (Lévi-Strauss 1973).

Authors such as Godelier, Clastres, and Lathrap have shown that a number of hunter-gatherer societies of the American forests constitute false archaisms. Far from being the last representatives of prehistoric hunter-gatherer groups, they are what is left of advanced agricultural groups that have been driven back from river banks into the wooded hinterland by other agricultural communities and reverted to hunting and gathering (Godelier 1974).

Other social groups came to lose the practice of agriculture and went over exclusively to fishing. For example, the 'Toffinu' of Benin (formerly Dahomey) are said to be erstwhile agriculturists who, fleeing before the raids of slave hunters in the middle of the 18th century, took refuge in the centre of Lake Nokoue where they established a lake-dwelling society. 'They had to invent everything, readjust their common effort to live and survive, achieve the collective elaboration of fishing techniques: a new vocabulary, tools, processes, rites, . . . all the know-how, . . . the whole socio-cultural system of solidarity from which the "Toffinu" ethnic group of lake-dwelling fishermen was born, whose members will be different from agricultural groups living on lake sides, such as the Aguenu' (Godelier 1974). Other studies evoke a similar process, this time for large cattle breeders who, for various reasons, came to abandon their dominant mode of production and adopted techniques orientated towards an agricultural economy in order to live and survive. This may be due to the presence of more numerous and stronger groups living alongside them who practised agriculture as their dominant mode of production. It is the social position of weaker and minority groups which fosters their integration into a neighbouring, dominant culture. The impact of drought also provoked a degradation of pastoral or agricultural activities or even predatory ones, forcing the social groups in question to adopt new practices to survive.

Douglas & Lyman report on similar transformations of ethnic identity in Latin America. Anthropologists studying Post-Columbian communities have found that where geographic and socio-economic mobility bring about certain changes in the mode of life, isolated individuals or whole populations have ceased to be Indian and become Ladino. In the same way, these authors continue, the anthropologist Leach (1954) has demonstrated that, in highland Burma, the ethnic categories Kachin and Shan designate two complex cultures which constitute the poles of a continuum along which a given group may in time be transformed, little by little modifying its mode of daily life (Douglas & Lyman 1976).

### Genetic change

In a previous study we have shown that ethnicity is the product of multiple factors linked to the interaction between man and his material and socio-cultural environment (Twagiramutara 1980b). A similar analytical approach may be found in the works of Ki-zerbo and Olderogge. Olderogge writes that ethnicity results from the interaction of multiple factors which cause progressive differentiation of inherited traits. Among these factors Olderogge includes gradual adaptation to the ambient environment: relative exposure to sunlight, temperature variation, ecology. He also notes that the migration of populations bearing different genetic heritages provide two possible sources of change: first through further genetic adaptation to the new environment, and secondly through intermarriage with other populations encountered as a result of the migration (Olderogge 1980).

Ki-zerbo puts forward a similar point of view when he argues that in the very distant past, small populations with elementary technology and culture spread into varied and increasingly dispersed ecological niches. Here they would have been subjected to very strong selective pressure to adapt to the local environment. Population growth, the improvement of techniques related to modes of production, conflict with neighbouring groups, migration and intermarriage would all have contributed to the emergence of ethnic categories (Ki-zerbo 1980).

## Rwanda: a case study

### The increasing significance of culture

Certain authors consider that the socio-ethnic categories of Central Africa constitute biologically distinct populations. Hence their analytical approach focuses on the separation and reproduction of such populations. This is done by positing ancestry in a primordial nuclear family who, for some reason, left their initial location to settle elsewhere. Sub-groups within such ethnic units are supposed to arise from population growth leading to segmentation into clans and lineages. Geographical movement is explained as the consequence of tension and conflict (see for instance Laeger 1939, pp. 48ff, Pauwels 1965, Murego 1975, pp. 9–30, Ndahimana 1979). In this way the dispersion of such social entities in ancient times is explained, whether it be within a small area of one country or across many countries of Central Africa. Many authors cite the example of the 'Abasinga' whose representatives are distributed through many regions of interlacustrine Africa. They are to be found nearly all over Rwanda (more or less concentrated according to the region), they exist in Zaire, in the regions of d'Ijwi (where they are called 'Mbiriri', 'Ishaza' . . .) and Itombwe (under the name 'Abarenge'), and finally in Tanzania in the region of Kigezi, under the name of 'Abarenge' (see Biebuyck 1973, Desmarais 1977, pp. 157–205, Smith 1979).

Interesting though such analysis may be, we consider it inadequate as an explanation either of the origin of cultural entities, or of the present multi-ethnic composition of most of them (for a critical analaysis see Desmarais 1977, pp. 151–200).

Other authors invoke the interaction of biological and cultural factors to explain the persistence and fusion of ethnic groups. According to this explanation distinct ethnic units become integrated under circumstances where opportunities for geographical movement are restricted, and there is limited scope for the exchange of material goods and information. In such contexts, when a localized, powerful group is in contact with a smaller, adjacent group for a certain length of time, population growth may promote the proliferation of cultural prohibitions which have the effect of maintaining boundaries between the respective ethnic groups. Were this the case, it might be expected that after a time the dominant group would succeed in imposing its vision of the world upon the dominated with a view to reordering social relationships entered into between members of the different groups. Eventually members of the dominated groups would come to see themselves as submitting to a common authority, and sharing descent from the eponymous ancestor of their group.

In other words, we wish to argue that different existing sub-groups within the populations assembled under a single authority progressively lose the various marks of their initial identity in favour of new identities imposed by the dominant social group. Assimilation and absorption takes place on both the cultural and the political levels. As a result, members of a given economic and political category end up considering themselves to belong to a single cultural entity.

Such processes may have been at work during the period when ethnic differences between the social categories 'Hutu', 'Tutsi', and 'Twa' were still present in the minds of the population of Rwanda, before political unification began, a process directed in turn by leaders of the Singa, Banda, and Nyiginya clans. Any individual integrated into a neighbourhood characterized by a predominantly agricultural mode of production was considered a Hutu, whereas any individual integrated in a neighbourhood characterized by a dominantly pastoral mode of production was considered to be a 'Tutsi'. Finally any individual integrated into an environment characterized by an essentially predatory type of production was considered to be a 'Twa' (Twagiramutara 1976, pp. 37–56).

We argue that the ethnic labels Twa, Hutu, and Tutsi were, then, simply a system of classification, a series of onomastic emblems, banners or symbols serving to signal identity among members of heterogeneous social units.

In reaching this conclusion we agree with Matejke (1984) who proposes that ethnicity is today primarily a historical and cultural phenomenon, rather than, as some authors contend, a biological one. Ethnic affiliation is generally attributed at birth and gradually becomes the source of a prescribed status. In certain African societies ethnic affiliation follows the patrilineal principle. In other African societies, ethnic affiliation is transmitted by descent through the female line. In a country like Rwanda both principles are found, and have today regained their traditional importance. As cultural phenomena based on inherited status within a culturally specific model of social organization, ethnicity can develop only as long as the members of social groups believe that such organizing principles offer an appropriate response to existential questions of identity with which they are confronted at a given moment and in a certain spatial context. Recent scientific research in Rwanda, Burundi, and neighbouring regions of interlacustrine Africa have shown that theories which treat ethnic groups as immutable derive less from indigenous perceptions than from cultural models introduced during the colonial period by European administrators. The idea that ethnic groups are racially distinct became a veritable ideological doctrine, political and cultural, diffuse and mobilizing. With time it has become implanted in the minds of indigenous populations. As a consequence ethnic cleavages are now perceived as facts of nature not to be called into question. In reality, however, biological and ecological factors were primarily of importance during early human evolution (Alard 1981). Increasingly cultural processes have displaced such factors as the major causes of ethnic differentiation (Loupamselle & N'bokolo 1985, pp. 11–38).

## Notes

1 Carbon 14 analaysis of recent excavations of blast furnace with bricks and coals in Gasiga/Masango (Rwanda) have shown that, around 685 AD, this area was peopled by groups using forges and making bricks. On the other hand, carbon 14 analysis from other furnaces made in the same period at Bulinga/Buramba (Mwendo) showed that similar production was carried out here in about 865 AD. These regions were already peopled by social groups with a similar mode of production.

2 Indirect evidence for agriculture is provided by the abundance of objects such as axes and hoes of polished stone, the presence of grindstones found in certain localities in the border regions between Kenya and Ethiopia, between Kenya and Tanzania, and in the region of the high plateaux of East Africa.

## References

Alard, D. 1981. Ecologie sociale et evolution: essai de synthese de travaux sur les rapports entre l'evolution biologique et l'evolution sociale. *Sociologie et societes*, **13**, 133–43.

Anfray, F. 1968. Aspects de l'Archeologie ethiopienne. *Journal of African History*, **9**, 345–66.

Biebuyck, D. P. 1973 *Lega culture: art, initiation, and moral philosophy among a Central African people*. Berkeley: University of California Press.

Cornevin, M. M. 1966. *Histoire del 'Afrique: des origines à nos jours*. Paris: Payot.

Desmarais, C. 1977. Ideologies de l'ancien Rwanda. Unpublished doctoral thesis, Department of Anthropology, University of Montreal.

Douglas, W. A. & S. M. Lyman. 1976. L'Ethnie: structure, processus et saillance. *Cahiers Internationaux de Sociologie*, **61**, 205–6.

Faure, H. 1980. Le cadre chronologique des phases pluviales et glaciaires de l'Afrique *Histoire Generales de l'Afrique*, **1**, J. Ki-zerbo (ed.), 409–34. Paris: Unesco.

Godelier, M. 1974. Anthropologie et biologie: vers une co-operation nouvelle. *Revue Internationale des sciences sociales*, **26**, 30–5.

Ki-zerbo, J. 1980. Theories relatives aux races et histoire de l'Afrique. *Histoire Generale de l'Afrique*, **1**, J. Ki-zerbo (ed.), 291–9. Paris: Unesco.

Laeger, L. de 1939. *Le Rwanda ancien*. Kabwayi.

Leach, E. R. 1954. *Political systems of Highland Burma*. London: Athlone.

Lévi-Strauss, C. 1973. *Anthropologie structurale deux*. Paris: Plon.

Loupamselle J. & E. N'bokolo, eds. 1985. *Au coeur de l'ethnie*. Paris: Ed. de la Decouverte.

Matejke, A. 1984. Le changement d'indentite ethnique: l'impact des nouveaux arrivants sur les Canadiens polanais. *Recherches Sociologiques*, **15**, 241–63.

Murego, D. 1975. La revolution Rwandaise. Unpublished thesis, Institute of Political and Social Sciences, Catholic University of Louvain.

Ndahimana, F. 1979. Les Bami ou roitelets Rwandais. *Etudes Rwandaises*, **13**, 5–20.

Noten, F. van 1980. Prehistoire de l'Afrique Centrale. *Histoire generale de l'Afrique*, **1**, J. Ki-zerbo (ed.) 581–600. Paris: Unesco.

Olderroge, D. 1980. Migrations et differentiations, ethniques et linguistiques. *Histoire Generale del 'Afrique*, **1**, J. Ki-zerbo (ed.), 301–20. Paris: Unesco.

Pauwels, M. 1965. Le système de parenté au Rwanda. *Annales del Pont. Museo Miss. Ethnologie*, **29**, 243–5.

Phillipson, D. W. 1977. *The later prehistory of eastern and southern Africa*. London: Academic Press.

Porteres, R. & J. Barrau. 1980. Debuts, developpement et expansion des techniques agricoles. *Histoire generale de l'Afrique*, **1**, J. Ki-zerbo (ed.), 727–43. Paris: Unesco.

Rognon, P. 1976. Essai d'interpretation des variations au Sahara depuis 40,000 ans. *Revue de geographie physique et de geographie dynamique*, **18**, 251–82.

Said, R. 1980. Le cadre chronologique des phases pluviales et glaciaires de l'Afrique (part 2). *Histoire generale de l'Afrique*, **1**, J. Ki-zerbo (ed.), 399–409. Paris: Unesco.

Smith, P. 1979. Personnages et legendes. Paper presented at the conference on the civilization of the peoples of the Great Lakes, Bujumbura, September 1979.

Sutton, J.E.G. 1974. The aquatic civilization of Middle Africa. *Journal of African History*, **15**, 527–46.

Sutton, J.E.G. 1980. Prehistoire de l'Afrique orientale. *Histoire generale de l'Afrique*, **1**, J. Ki-zerbo, (ed.), 451–86. Paris: Unesco.

Twagiramutara, P. 1976. *Rapport a l'espace, rapport social: étude de leur liaison*. Faculty of Economic and Political Science, Catholic University of Louvain: New series publication number 130.

Twagiramutara, P. 1980a. Anthropologie et linquistique. *Dialogue*, **83**, 56–74.

Twagiramutara, P. 1980b. La tolerance au lactose et la question du processus d'emergence des categories ethniques du Rwanda-Burundi. *Etudes Rwandaises*, **13**(2), 98–106.

Vercouter, J. 1980. Invention et diffusion des metaux et developpement des systèmes sociaux jusqu'au Vième siecle avant notre érè. In *Histoire generale de l'Afrique*, vol. 1, J. Ki-zerbo (ed.), 745–70. Paris: Unesco.

# 8 The role of language in African perceptions of the past: an appraisal of African language policies and practices

BONGASU TANLA KISHANI

In a sense, the irony of this chapter consists in discussing African languages in an archaeological context. It is popularly held that archaeology studies the arch-past, the proto-past, the ancient past, almost there where history ends or, at best, is at rivalry with it. Yet colonial ideologies and experiences seem to have successfully transformed African languages into some of the most peculiar archaeological objects: African languages continue to live a somewhat colonially initiated, now instituted, silent life in the apparent seclusion of their own hearths. The opposition between European and African languages in some semantic usages of today's African can illustrate this:

*Status of languages in Africa today*

| *African languages* | *European languages* |
|---|---|
| Unofficial, non-lucrative | Official, lucrative |
| Non-administrative | Administrative |
| Local, indigenous, regional | National, universal, world-wide |
| Vernacular, dialect, non-scientific | Language, scientific |
| Market-use ◄─────── Pidgins ───────► Lingua franca | |
| (mid-way) | |

'In addition, the very absence of a literary tradition led many Europeans to assume that the languages of Africa might be primitive in some way', according to Welmers (1971, p.564). As a result, today we need a new fillip of conviction and a lot of to-and fro-ing before we can persuade the speakers of these African languages of the dignity and scientific values of their own languages, let alone carrying out research, creative activities, government, etc.; in short, experiencing every linguistic phenomenon in, through and with African languages.

Consequently, African language research, policy, and practice need to remain, not only indigenous and African-centred in their orientations, but also, serviceable first and foremost to Africans, instead of being orientated, as if always on demand, to foreign exigencies. In other words, African language research which aims at alienation is far from fulfilling this task. Experts would readily admit that in most cases, not even African informants can benefit from, and make full use of, most African-conducted research. In this context, both long and short term enterprises in the field of African language policies and practices up to now linger on the borderline of creating alienating gaps between African generations. The passive role of an informant whom the *Oxford Advanced Learner's Dictionary of Current English* (1985) defines, not without some linguistic motivation, as 'a native speaker of a language who helps a foreign scholar who is making an analysis of it', merits a revision: the more so, as it is debatable whether an informant should always render his or her services only to 'foreign scholars'. Quite often, with the incentives to baptize African orality with the invention of writing, in the same manner as missionaries are wont to baptize Africans and lure them away from their African religions, many a researcher consciously or unconsciously turns Africans into passive observers rather than active participants in their own African languages. Nowadays, some Africans resist this passive role by having recourse to their active creating capacities in the modern media, in which orality and writing are only beginning to rediscover their complementary roles in the cassette and tape-recorder, television and film.

As a matter of fact, as far as the practical uses of African languages – most particularly their writing – are concerned, colonialism and neo-colonialism seem to have made a successful and final conquest. Thus, we are quite often obliged to assume that African languages are dead, though they are still in use, and consequently, to speak of beginnings when they have never ceased to exist. It was in this light that we wrote a Lámnso' poem entitled *Nsùyri Làm (In Praise of Language)* in an attempt to persuade the Nsó' to take up the writing of a language they have never ceased from speaking for centuries (see below). This, therefore, means that to utilize alphabetical writing in Africa is neither to replace nor rival centuries-old African cultural experiences and languages, but to put it at their services.

| | |
|---|---|
| *Nsùyri Lám*<br>Written by the author (10/6/85) | *In Praise of Language*<br>Translated from Lamnso' by Karl Grebe. |
| Eènó, Nso'! Ghá' ke'!<br>Vèsan sáasí ràn, a saṇ Lám Nso'o!<br>À bìṇ, a lòm, Kù ghá' ke'!<br>Ghá' ke' sìì wíy mày e ghàn ka? | Yes Nso! Beginning is hard.<br>Let's welcome the dawn, Let's write Lamnso!<br>Beginning is hard, always was, always will be.<br>Will it ever change? |
| Nyaa vèsán Nso'!<br>Moo a dev mvan yò' sì móo te kifa.<br>Ghán sí kùvsín ne<br>Á kúvsin nshùm, á kùvsín kidzán.<br>Bú' lamé dzè yú! | Nso, let's not neglect our language!<br>Carrying an arrow does not make you a hunter.<br>Times are changing.<br>The dance follows the drum.<br>The essence of language is understanding. |
| Nyaa vèsán Nso'!<br>A veè jav javìn, bo yìì fo la Nso' lám! | Nso, let's not neglect our language!<br>If language were given by man, what would our portion be? |

| | |
|---|---|
| Boŋ ka e shaà  lám a wíri? | Is there a greater treasure than a people's language? |
| Ee Lamnso' woo yír wan, | We call a child Lamnso, our-language. |
| Ee Lamnte' woo yír wan. | We call a child Lamnte, language-of-our-village. |

| | |
|---|---|
| Nyùy mbóm yii ŋwéy wíri lám á? | Does the Creator ever withhold language from a people? |
| Nyaa vèsán Nso'! | Nso, let's not neglect our language! |
| Bòŋlám woo yir wan | We call child Bonglam, nothing-is-better-than-language |
| À ŋgaà jà', à ngaà sham, | In scoff, in praise, |
| Bòn lám woo yír wan! | Bonglam is still the best name. |

| | |
|---|---|
| Bú' làmé dzè yú, bì'fì'tì! | The essence of language is the sharing of understanding. |
| Viwìr ve làm ví sì lán, | Today, the glory of Lam Nso |
| Bì' sáŋ, bì' súŋnín! | springs from writing, springs from speaking. |
| Lám menànné yú akoó. | Only the hunter understands the language of the prey. |
| A sì moo yee le, bòŋ moo yee shó! | A bird in the hand is better than a pigeon on the roof. |
| Vèsan saásí rán, a saŋ Lám Nso'o! | Let's welcome the dawn. Let's write Lam Nso! |
| Vèsan saásí rán, a saŋ Lám Nso'o! | Let's welcome the dawn. Let's write Lam Nso! |

On balance, the present ardent and massive use of European languages to the total or partial exclusion of African langues within the framework of African writing by Africans and/or non-Africans alike, seems irreversible. As such, it calls for a special concern. Apparently, it smacks of a language break in the African time continuum, and thus creates an unending hiatus between contemporary or future Africans, and their linguistic past, let alone the fact that for both British and Belgian (and even for the other) colonial powers, somewhere beneath colonial policy and the philosophy which engendered it, lay a sense of an unbridgeable cultural gap between themselves and their African subjects. In both cases, linguistic policy derived from a colonial philosophy which emphasized separate development for the different races in contact in Africa, and which has in the case of the British, a political counterpart in the theory and practice of indirect rule (Spencer 1971, p.541). So, though the practical problem of how to strike a balance in the choice between this use of colonially initiated European languages and African languages remains blurred in the mind of many Africans today, its solution certainly involves obvious political and practical issues which, at least for the present, can neither be easily answered nor dismissed. Indeed, some knowledge of the complexity of the facts in some cases prevents whoever delves into the problem from being too insistent. For, apparently, we cannot today, given our historical colonial experiences, ask African writers to give what they never received. African colonial educational systems for the most part offered little or no opportunities for a large scale practice and development of writing in African languages, arbitrarily dismissed as non-lucrative and considered incapable in those systems of being written, of promoting and transmitting science and civilizations, and of defining African countries; and consequently branded as dialects, vernaculars about to become languages in a colonially designed evolutionary movement which soon discovered its scientific emptiness.

In modern times, scholars have devoted closer attention to, and expressed concern about, this problem. But some of them, who often fail to discern the difference or make a simple clear distinction between cultures and language, in spite of their close links, have attempted to reinstate African cultures without defining and carving out corresponding practical and new policies for the future of African languages, more or less left destitute through colonial substitutions. 'Indeed, it may be said that during the forties and fifties the french African *évolué* was predominantly concerned with his cultural emancipation . . . There was less pressure upon French colonial officials to learn the local languages and more reliance was placed upon African interpreters (Spencer 1977, p.544). It should, however, not be forgotten that attempts at cultural substitutions through the policies of assimilation, indirect rule . . . failed simply because, even if it is true that language can to a certain extent help us to penetrate into the cultures of other peoples, it is impossible to use a different culture or language fully to comprehend the languages of other peoples and cultures. A replaced language then becomes a purely parasitic entity with nothing to offer, nothing on which to hang or implant its own being. The exclusive use of European languages in defence of African cultural past experiences, though proving how languages and cultures can thus be made at times to live apart, reduces and turns African languages and cultures into mere parasites vis-à-vis African cultures or languages. The need for more African-centred language and cultural policies in Africa today becomes very important in view of these living experiences which bear witness to the alienation of African languages from their past, and thereby also from their African cultures, civilizations, and peoples. Our present struggles cannot therefore be directed towards reinstating African cultures to the exclusion of African languages. These ideas can best explain some of the opinions which some Africans like Wali (1965 cited by Tanna 1974) had entertained against African literature in European languages, though later on writers like Jahn (1968) and Omari (1985) refute the criterion of language as a functional determinate in world literatures.

A different view was taken by Achebe who wrote:

> The African writer should aim to use English in a way that brings out his message but without altering the language to the extent that its value as a medium of international exchange will be lost. He should aim at fashioning out an English which is at once universal and able to carry his *peculiar* experience . . . What I do see is a new voice coming out of Africa speaking of African experience in a world-wide language.
>
> (Achebe 1975, p.61)

But, truly, due to the practical needs of the times perhaps, Achebe's implicit solution of this problem inclined to universalism as incarnated in and by European languages alone, presently the only worldwide languages. In this way, Achebe does not distinguish himself from the struggle to resuscitate integral African cultural experiences to the exclusion of African languages. Thus, consciously or unconsciously, he dismissed the advantageous role African languages have been playing within African cultural experiences as a whole and vis-à-vis

European languages. His idea of universalism smacks of cultural communications which betray and suppress the use of African languages under the pretext of portraying or exchanging African cultural experiences. On the contrary, such positions betray African cultures at the expense of African languages through the extraneous co-existence of African cultures perpetually recorded in European languages.

On that score, Césaire's conception of universalism becomes more convincing and practically more reliable:

> I have a different idea of a universal. (Provincialism? Not at all, I am not going to entomb myself in some strait particularism. But I don't intend either to become lost in fleshless universalism. There are two paths to doom: by segregation, by walling yourself up in the particular, or by dilution, by thinning off into the emptiness of the universal.) It is of a universal rich with all the particulars there are, the deepening of each particular, the co-existence of them all.
>
> (Césaire 1957, p.15)

The consequences of such a rectification enable us to dismiss the gratuitous opinion that universalism or internationalism reveals itself exclusively or at best in the languages written or spoken by a majority of women, children, and men. According to Césaire, we have to embrace the concrete realities with their contingent and non-contingent aspects. In other words, it is real anathema to divorce languages from the cultural milieux and, worse still, experiences which beget, nourish, and transmit them, under the pretext that we are anxious to pursue 'a medium of international exchange', as if that were the best and only way of becoming fully universal. Such a procedure only subjects us to the yoke of an unending alienation, since we are thereby condemned to pursue what Césaire appositely terms 'fleshless universalism'. The political identification of universal with European is essentially what is here at stake (Kishani 1976, p.112).

There is, therefore, no doubt that African cultural experiences and languages should continue to live as integral entities wherein the universal and the particular simultaneously reside. Any attempts to separate the one from the other can only result in multiple forms of alienation, historically well known as colonialism, neo-colonialism, or more specifically as the policies of indirect rule, assimilation and apartheid, let alone slavery.

Even within the fields of African spoken languages and of African writings in European languages, linguistic phenomena such as code-switching, unconscious interferences, borrowing, as well as all sorts of pidginizations clearly point to the failure of linguistic universalism in Africa. It is, therefore, nothing more than wishful thinking to pursue the make-believe of *uni*versalism (turning into one) as an attainable goal. What of internationalism? Genuine *inter*-nationalism does not substitute languages in order to achieve a worldwide cultural exchange. African literary writings in European languages, dotted as they are with African linguistic units of various dimensions, clearly prove the need for the presence of African languages at the level of a genuine international exchange. In other words, internationalism should mean an exchange of concrete African cultural experiences and languages as they happen in life. For, to use European languages to 'carry' African cultural experiences is not simply to betray, but to alienate them because these European languages will never express African cultural experiences in their true light or with the same fidelity of expression and creativity as the African languages themselves.

To echo Achebe's term it is *peculiar* to present African cultural experiences in this parasitic life of the alienated. African languages can only be or not be *universal* and *peculiar* when we measure them with foreign yardsticks. And the 'ideological pun or witticism here consists in pretending to aspire towards a future devoid of any links with the past beaming with all its peoples but already freed from their babel of languages' (Glucksmann 1978, p.356). Such ideological puns, which spurred Zamenhof (1859–1917) to conceive his utopian *Esperanto* as a way of hastening the advent of universalism, have been discerned and rejected by Diop, who writes of the exponents of such a view:

> To this category belong all the Africans who reason in the following way: we must cut ourselves off from the whole of this chaotic and barbaric past and join the technical world which moves at the speed of the electron. The planet will become unified: we must be part of the vanguard of progress. Science will soon solve the big problems and local, secondary preoccupations will disappear. We require nothing other than the cultures and languages of Europe, which have already proved their worth. In other words, they have adapted to scientific thought and are already universal.
> (Diop 1979, p.15, transl. Marianne Dumartheray)

Our concern with the role of language in the African perceptions of the past needs to liberate itself from such a futurism. For it is now time for us Africans to speak and write our languages instead of keeping them buried deep down in our pockets as if they were real archaeological, earthen data, for fear that we might be slowing down the advance towards an utopian future devoid of the plurality of languages and cultures, albeit reminiscent of them all. The African experiences of plurality should serve as a lesson to the rest of the world where such experiences have either never been known, lived or have, for ideological reasons, been kept dormant. A future devoid of the plurality of languages and cultures has never been, and will never be, without the annihiliation of the intermarriage between time, space and human minds.

Human time is at any moment, capable neither of annihiliation nor of manifesting itself as naked as it might at times appear. If the notion of time can neither be annihiliated nor lived nakedly, i.e. as pure succession without the slightest stain in the name of human experiences, then the idea of the past cannot be declared null and void. It should, on the contrary, be perceived as *the area of our lived res gestae*. Time past is clothed in the succession of events. As Wainwright expressed it (1982, p.131):

History, which is Eternal Life, is what
We need to celebrate. Stately tearful
Progress . . . you've seen how I have wept for it.

History? Which History?

Africa South of the Sahara had no history before the coming of Europeans . . . History only begins when people take a writing
(A.P. Newton, quoted in Akintoye 1975)

To this statement, the West Indian novelist, Condé, humorously adds with the
same vehemence of negative terms, though in jest and with a high technique of
romantic irony:

What are you talking about? Don't you know that History has never
bothered about Negroes! Because, and we have proof of this, they
weren't worth it. They've not left their mark on the Golden Gate nor on
the framework of the Eiffel Tower. Instead of saying their prayers in
Notre Dame or Westminster Abbey they worshipped bits of wood or
knelt to a snake (imagine, a snake, the very one that tempted Eve!) And
they called it Ancestor or God . . . you might think that all peoples have
a history; well, these people, no, they had none.
(Condé 1976, p.26, transl. Marianne Dumartheray)

In a way, the heart of the matter lies here. Some of the root causes of colonial
mentalities and ideological principles which stripped Africans from their rights
to history – rights which accrue from their insertion in time – and dispossessed
them of their lands, government, and languages, arose from this unfounded
ideological idea that history is related to writing as an effect to its cause, and
consequently, that culture is the prerogative of literature and literate societies.
As a result, without a system of alphabetical writing, Africans could only enjoy
a colonial consumer status in almost every domain, be it political, economic,
linguistic or cultural as a whole. And this to the extent that, today, most Africans seem to limit their creative initiatives solely within the magnetic fields of
European languages. In a way, within these European language usages, Africans
become passive, without any linguistic darings which constitute the forte of
those delectable capacities and prerogatives of native speakers and writers. And
in practice, Africans are therefore bound to stick often to systematic styles reminiscent of European metropolitan literary endeavours. And quite often, too,
some of these Africans continue to transpose these styles whenever they speak
or write in African languages. Linguistic borrowing, code-switching, and interferences based on European languages abound, and are even becoming a characteristic mark of the ways the present African Westernized élite and youth
speak in African languages. The sublime explanation of such a situation is that
most African writers and speakers of European languages find themselves subjected to a double norm of inheritance, and hence, of corrections: firstly, from

European metropolitan speakers and writers; and secondly, from African unilinguals or multilinguals who have equally upheld the traditional dynamism of speaking and even of writing in African languages.

In fact, by only subjecting themselves to European language norms, some Africans define themselves partially in terms of those European norms as poets, linguists, historians, mathematicians, lawyers, simply because of their capacities to speak and write only in European languages about their own cultures. But how can we, Africans, still claim to be experts of our respective disciplines, if these can only be carried out in European languages? Can we practise our various specialized disciplines with the same dexterity when we speak and write in our African languages? It is obvious that our positive, or negative, answers to these questions will determine our creative potential in African languages. But to our mind, it is almost irrefutable that, though it is problematic whether our expertise in and practice of a science can thus be limited to our knowledge and subsequent practice of the language which we use in expressing it (which the possibility of translation and the existence of multilinguals refute by their very *raison d'être*), these African forms of alienation in fact confine and subject Africans to a recipient status. Under such conditions they are bound to the constant and almost endless exercises and corrections of which Duponchel aptly observes:

> Under these conditions it is no surprise that the French spoken in Africa is badly known and its existence even denied. Thus, a regional expression in the works of Claudel, C.F. Remuz or Georges Sand is regarded as a matter of style and merits an explanatory footnote. An expression in African French is however considered barbaric, or incorrect. It is considered to be a question of grammar and worthy of reproach, even though it does not lead to incomprehension and is used in several countries . . . The status of a functioning language is never neutral. In Africa the situation is particularly complex.
>
> (Duponchel 1974, p.7, transl. Marianne Dumartheray).

On closer examination, Duponchel's worries are not unlike those of Achebe but, unlike Achebe's, Duponchel's affirmations help to illustrate the failure of a European language universalism within colonial and neo-colonial parameters. The exigencies of the persistent presence of African languages can be felt through the African use of the European languages. Consequently, to aspire towards such a utopian linguistic universalism would mean remaining blind to the presence of African languages, which still constitute and animate African cultural realities. Achebe, Duponchel and many others, Africanists especially, have thus been arguing from an implicit but unproven consensus or premiss that Africans are bound to use European languages at all costs, since historically, centuries of the slave trade, colonialism, neo-colonialism, and even apartheid, have lured Africans away from the use of African languages. In practice this amounts to the assertion of an irreversible cultural experience for the entire continent of Africans, and African languages can therefore only become preambles for European language studies.

As a matter of fact, the present status of African languages and cultures stems both from the superficial introduction of European languages in Africa and from their pretention to adequately reflect, interpret, and assume creativity in, for and through African cultural and linguistic experiences. Under such alienating conditions African languages can only be left to ossify as pure archaeological objects within their own soils, with nobody to speak or write them down. What is quite often forgotten is that the life of European languages as administrative, lucrative, official codes borders on the precarious, ephemeral status of second-class languages. If their historical and scientific usefulness has helped Europeans to know Africa in a way, their departure cannot be said to deny knowledge of the European World to Africans. Think of what is happening now in Tanzania between English and Kiswahili (Polome 1979); think of what happened with German in the Kamerun, Togoland, Tanganyika etc.; think of what is going on in Ethiopia between English, Italian and Amharic. Once German, previously a lucrative, administrative, and official language was ousted overnight from the former German colonies in the events of the First World War, Africans whose cultures and territories had been defined only in terms of German found their knowledge of German no longer marketable. Things would have been otherwise, had the Germans used African languages as the administrative, official, and lucrative languages in their colonies. At the moment, English is giving in to Kiswahili in Tanzania, whereas in Ethiopia, it is obvious that the winds are blowing in favour of Ethiopian languages, Amharic especially.

So no one can doubt the great need for more genuine language policies in Africa in favour of African languages and in favour of the apposite roles of European languages in Africa. Until now most African countries have surprisingly been keeping silent about policies in favour of African languages. Consciously or unconsciously, Fonlon, though speaking only in terms of the Cameroon Federal Constitutions, identified this silence in the following words:

> With regard to our native languages, the Federal Constitution and the constitutions of the Federal States are mute and there is no official policy in so far as these languages are concerned. This constitutional silence however, does not wipe out of existence nor weaken their influence: they are asserting themselves vigorous living realities, if not getting stronger . . . The cultural movement of which the Cameroon Cultural Review, Abbia, is the spear-head and mouthpiece, has taken the stand that Cameroon languages, at least the major ones, shall not die . . . De jure, Cameroon has become a bilingual State, but de facto, it is a highly diversified multi-lingual country.
>
> (Fonlon 1969, pp.27–8)

Although aware of the problem, Fonlon surprisingly and regrettably argued as if Africans had still to adapt their language policies within the parameters of European languages. Like other Africans of his generation, he was still apparently caught by the neo-colonial obsession in favour of 'One Country,

One language', though in a more subtle manner. Consequently, he seems disappointed by the absence of linguistic unity in African countries rather than suggesting practical means to embrace the multilingual African situations. Thus he wrote:

> In Africa, partly due to the failure of the great African Empires to consolidate themselves and expand and endure, partly due to the constant movement of peoples, and most especially, to four centuries of the ravages of slave raiding and trafficking, no languages, with the possible exception of Arabic and Swahili, at the African level, have been able to impose themselves as dominant media of wider expression. And thus, very few countries, today, in Negro Africa, can boast of linguistic unity. Nearly every independent African country, at present, is a patch-work of linguistic and ethnic groups.
>
> (Fonlon 1969, p.8)

Our principal argument here has been that there is a great need for African language policies to bring African languages out of the silence which colonial powers had inflicted upon them. Spencer (1971) rightly observed the way this silence was practised: 'One incidental but significant aspect of the language policies of almost all colonial governments in Africa was their reluctance to teach the languages of their European powers, even when their territories are adjacent. This effectively placed a kind of linguistic *cordon sanitaire* around each group of territories, linking them in language, as in trade and finance with the metropolitan community, and cutting them off from their neighbours.' In addition, colonial powers also shielded the Europeanized language élite from speaking African languages within their institutions. I remember a case in Nigeria where we were allowed to speak Latin but not Igbo or Hausa, which were and still are our own African languages.

Conscious of these facts, then, our views of African languages should become more positive, taking them to be a network rather than 'a patchwork of linguistic and ethnic groups'. What we actually need are practical solutions which can best embrace the multilingual reality of Africa, be they short or long term enterprises. In this way we can utilize even the artificial, colonially imposed linguistic boundaries to unite Africans more on the basis of African languages, instead of continuing to divide Africans through such boundaries. In other words, African languages should be given the status and be called upon to play the roles which are theirs in Africa and out of Africa. Instead of shunning African plurilingual societies through implicit or explicit acknowledgement of the thesis of universalism, there is need to welcome the plurality of African languages as a natural phenomenon wherever it occurs. The artificial nature of so-called linguistic unity has throughout history been responsible for forms of discrimination, segregation, and alienation. Warnier's (1980) study of the multilingual context within which the Cameroonian Grassfields-languages have been living for centuries, revealed how the speakers embraced a more or less generalized social multilingualism rather than having adopted a unique *lingua franca* in favour of the doctrines and practices of universalism.

The point we are making here is that Africans cannot continue to see themselves only through the mirror of European languages and forsake their own languages. Neither should they continue to have confidence in the make-believe that the writing of these languages or the policies which would uphold African languages will be better understood when they come from Europeans or from using European languages. Underpinning some of the assumptions of Westerners like Tempels was the idea that the Bantu cannot speak and write our European languages like us:

> We do not claim, of course, that the Bantu are capable of formulating a philosophical treatise, complete with an adequate vocabulary. It is our job to proceed to such systematic development. It is we who will be able to tell them, in precise terms, what their inmost concept of being is. They will recognize themselves in our words and will acquiesce saying, 'You understand us: you know us completely: you "know" in the way we "know" '.

> (Tempels 1953, p.36)

To judge from Tempel's own convictions, the reason which commits Europeans to this missionary task is not the existence of Bantu ontology alone. It is the European's mastery of the languages of culture, arbitrarily identified with European languages; and not with the Bantu dialects or vernaculars, presumably incapable of formulating an 'adequate vocabulary'. In other words, Bantu ontology becomes valid only when it is written in European languages, and at best by Europeans, the only competent speakers. Quite apart from the distortion which is implied in the use of European languages to interpret African cultural experiencs to the detriment or exclusion of African languages, is the fact that being a native speaker does not necessarily qualify speakers of a language to be its best writers or speakers.[2] The pertinent point here therefore is that from the days of the slave trade, through colonialism, neo-colonialism and apartheid, Africans have systematically been taught to minimize the use of African languages in the sciences, in government, and in the identification of their own countries. Quite often, this has meant luring Africans into language debates which are in a way foreign to them: the opposition between African Anglophones and Francophones when it comes to choosing and adopting certain policies in the Organization of African Unity sometimes gives the impression that the language opposition is no less external, and superficial than the opposition between African Catholics and Protestants.

So far, our main concern has been the corrupt status of African languages as seen through distorted ideologies, mentalities, and unscrutinized language policies and practices. From now on,

It is not in depraved beings
but in those who act in
accordance with nature that
we must seek what is natural.

(Aristotle, Politics, I.V.1254a)

## Towards more positive results: missionary efforts

On balance, the relentless efforts of some Westerners, researchers, scholars, missionaries, administrators, throughout the age of the slave trade, and colonial and neo-colonial times, have been directed towards locating more positive roles for African languages. To put the story simply, even until today missionaries have remained among the first to give African languages their due importance or to reinstate them as languages of civilizations and cultural experiences. This has been partly due to their avowed religious interests and, partly, because being more exposed to the daily lives of African languages, missionaries are more conscious of the usefulness of African languages within the cultures which feed, uphold, and transmit them more adequately into the future. Over the years they have been working with the aid of Africans to promote the use of African languages in writing.

Jesuit and Capucin missionaries pioneered the study of Bantu linguistics as far back as 1624, 1650, 1659, and 1697 with such outstanding publications as *Doutrina Christãa*, 'a little volume of 134 pages, prepared by three Jesuit priests, containing a catechism composed in Portuguese by Marcos Jorge and Ignacio Martinz, with an interlinear translation into Kongo produced by or under the supervision of Mattheus Cardoso, to whom goes the main credit for this historic work'; (Cole 1971, pp.2–3) and the first Bantu Grammar by Brusciotto de Vetralla in 1659 (Cole 1971). Other missionaries such as the Church Missionary Society whom Sigismund Wilhelm Koelle represented with his monumental *Polyglotta Africana* (1854) joined their ranks in the 1850s. Recently, this missionary-animated work has been adroitly undertaken and given a new fillip of scientific competency by the Summer Institute of Linguistics, whose main concern is to train Bible translators (Welmers 1971, p.566)

Yet, there are still numerous African languages which today possess neither a written grammar nor a literary work like the Bible. Alphabetical writing, introduced through Euro-Arabic African contacts in Africa, has not quite gone beyond its initial stage, even though 'it should be remembered that, in different parts of Africa – Yorubaland, Ghana, Swahili-speaking East Africa – vernacular literature flourishes. Anyone who has read a translation of Thomas Mofolo's *Chaka*, for instance, would have 'an idea of the beauty and wealth of some of this literature' (Fonlon 1963, p.41). In Cameroon, for example, many languages cannot even now boast of the triple missionary concern: *doctrine lessons/catechism, grammar* and *a bible translation*. For, though many Cameroonian languages had already figured in Koelle's *Polyglotta Africana*, they were not committed into writing back in their native soils until later. Neither did the slaves themselves, freed or not, who had assisted this linguist to constitute his monumental catalogue of over 100 African languages, manifest any other written documents of the kind, apart from those offered them through the charitable works of the missionaries. This paucity, in fact, was partly due to colonial language policies and practices, which tended to silence and minimize the use of African languages, and partly due to the unproven popular beliefs that some of these languages had scanty populations and would soon disappear, or that European languages were gaining ground in Africa.

> In areas where English is the official language, English-speaking missionaries frequently claim that most of the people understand English or that English is growing; one mission refused, about ten years ago, to permit one of its missionaries to devote himself to work on a language not previously investigated, on the ground that it was spoken only(!) by about 150,000 people and would be dead in a decade – a decade later it is still spoken by about 150,000 people, of course. Significantly, in areas where French is the official language, French-speaking missionaries tend to make a comparable claim: French is allegedly replacing the indigenous languages.
>
> (Welmers 1971, p.561)

German language policy in *Kamerun* did not quite dissociate itself from these ethnocentric claims and attitudes. The Germans worked for a long time on a selected number of Cameroonian languages like the Bali and the Duala languages which were to provide the preambles to the eventual smooth triumph of the German language itself. In fact, European colonial powers never set out to establish a language policy solely in favour of diffusing all the African languages. My interviews at Fumban and Kimbo' in the *Mvām* and *Nsó'* areas (Cameroon) in 1982, among the few surviving elders who had attended German schools, revealed that, even among non-native speakers, the Bali language was mastered before the study of German, which would have been longer in use, but for the coming of World War I. At the time of my interview, some of these elders spoke German as if from memory, due to lack of contact with the German-speaking world and to the fact that German had ceased to be marketable with the departure of the Germans from Cameroon. On the contrary, their knowledge of the Bali language which the Basel Missions had converted into a language for evangelization in the Grassfields of Cameroon, could not be doubted. They even narrated stories of pilgrim-like journeys which they undertake periodically to Baliland to strengthen and refresh their mastery of their quasi-religious language. In other words, both native and non-native speakers of the Bali language are more attached to this, an African language, than to German, the foreign, lucrative, and administrative language which had disappeared with the events of the First World War.

Tribute to missionaries? Yes, but with some qualifications. For genuine missionary contributions consist of a type of trial-and-error achievement, an affair of successes and failures. In other words, though missionary mentalities, attitudes, and practical efforts sometimes went marvellously ahead of their times, the absence of rudimentary knowledge in linguistics, or competence in the exigencies of African languages (tone analyses, noun classes, oral phenomena, etc.), as well as unavowed ethnocentric interests, contributed at times to their errors. Happily, they kept trying again. Some missionaries acquired fluency in African languages by luck, without knowing how, and were consequently unable to teach others. Thus, with or without organized instructions, quite often due to the poor mastery of linguistic techniques or due to the bias inherent in Western linguistic schools (tranformational, functional, generative analyses), the study of African languages suffered immensely. African languages were often written with alien language norms.

This reminds me of the futile efforts that Rev. A. Kerkvliet, a missionary of the St. Joseph's Missionary Society (Mill Hill), and many of us native speakers of Lámnso', undertook to produce *A Simple Lamnso Grammar* in 1967 without any adequate knowledge of linguistic techniques even though, spurred on by the anxiety to get started, we set out and wrote a first Lámnso' grammar. To put it simply, we were inspired more by written European language-grammars than by the analysis of Lámnso' itself. Consequently, a lot of linguistic data escaped our observation: contrast between diachronic and synchronic analysis, morphological and syntactic analysis, borrowing, verb-variations, noun classes, phonemic analysis with special emphasis on the tones, and so forth. Today I realize that our Lámnso' grammar was more complex than simple, due to our lack of a previous linguistic formation which could have enabled us to offer a grammar based on the actual analysis of Lámnso' rather than on a guess-work of impractical, partial rules. There are many points of similarity between *A Simple Lamnso Grammar* and a grammatical text, *Notes From Lamnsaw Grammar,* which was prepared by Bruens and later corrected by Phyllis M. Kaberry[3]: both wandered in the desert of linguistic ignorance in so far as a real analysis of Lámnso' was concerned, and based on their findings on their knowledge of existing European-language grammars. They both exhibit a great passion for what could not be found, such as articles.

Such mistakes and omissions have characterized the history of the written Lámnso' from the publication of *Polyglotta Africana* in 1854 until today. Generally, practical needs of our African, colonial oral contexts have taken precedence over the lack of knowledge of (African) linguistics. *Polyglotta Africana* in which Lámnso' seems to have appeared for the first time in writing in 1854 was, in spite of its reputation, an unrivalled pre-Saussurean linguistic monument and, consequently, presented a certain aspect of Lámnso' lexical units. German colonial jottings of Lámnso' were motivated by their practical uses such as war expeditions rather than by genuine linguistic purposes. The Catholic hymns, songs, sermons, and the catechism which appeared around 1920 were equally the works of laymen in the field of linguistics rather than of experts. They aimed at evangelization.

Our interviews with some of the Lámnso' teachers of the 1940s revealed that linguistic analysis of Lámnso was even then either unknown, or simply secondary to some of the practical needs of their times. Both Fáay Banka', alias

Benedict Somo, and Mr Sheey confessed that their main handicaps in teaching Lámnso' orthography were the difficulties of distinguishing such phenomena as lexical units in which the pertinent mark is the tone: *Tan*, poor, *Tán* cap, headwear, and *Tàn*, five. In the hands of later authors such as M.D.W. Jeffreys, this difficulty led to a jumbled, anglicized orthography, but it motivated P.M. Kaberry, whose monumental anthropological research among the Nso' had gained her the rare title of *Yaa Wóo Kóvvifam*, Queen of the Ruined Forest, to attempt *A Lámnso' Phonological Study*. Unfortunately she did little to publicize this work. Until the 1970s, therefore, some administrators were using little more than an anglicized rendering of Lámnso' vocabulary in their writings. Leading anthropologists and some Nso' authors either adopted it or followed a quasi-systematic orthography which was still not as thorough as that which Koelle had displayed more than one and half centuries earlier. Anglicizing orthographies of Lámnso' continued in the work of W. Zumbrunnen of the Basel Mission of Kishóong with his *Yoñri Lam Nsó* (1952–7), a quasi-phonetic pedagogical text, which, as pupils and informants, I still remember, we nicknamed *Lámnso' woo Kibay ki Táalá'*, Europeanized Lámnso', followed in 1968 by Rev. Clement Ndze's *Kinyo ke Cova D'Iria ke Kiya de 1917*.

In fact, until the early 1970s, the writing of Lámnso' tended to be more pragmatic than theoretical, ignoring, minimizing or simply keeping at bay pure linguistic analyses, even though such analyses would have facilitated the task of writing Lámnso' for the desired practical uses. The *Lámnso' Mass* which the Nso' seminarians studying at Enugu (Nigeria) translated in 1967, and *A Small Catechism in Pidgin and Lamnso* which the Cathoic Mission in Kimbo Town produced around the same period, were all motivated by the practical needs of those who could neither term themselves linguists nor, consequently, provide the desired linguistic thoroughness. What remains true, however, is that, with these practical aims in view, the Nso' were gradually embracing literacy as the needs and opportunities arose. The administrators in Kimbo' continued to take down notes and translate, especially in courts, Native Authority Offices, etc., from Lámnso'. In general, the Nso' English speaking literates wrote down Lámnso' with or without the use of an anglicized orthography, depending on their personal skills and the extent of English orthographical influences on them. It can, therefore, be concluded that the absence of a common orthography never prevented the Nso' literates, like any of their principal neighbours, from writing their language. Nevertheless, this common orthography was very much needed.

This was, more or less, the missionary contribution to the writing of Lámnso', until the arrival of Karl and Winnifred Grebe, Summer Institute of Linguistics experts, in Nso' in 1972. Once in Nso' the Grebes identified Lam Nso in relation to other African languages as a bantoid language of the Benue-Congo group, a subfamily of the Niger-Congo family (Grebe 1984, Grebe & Grebe 1975, p.5). In the same linguistic lines of analysis can be associated our own imperfect though historical study, *Etude du contract entre le Lámnso' et l'Anglais* which, in fact, was our first attempt to collect and explain Lámnso' loan words before 1970 (Kishani 1973, pp.43–76).

The Grebes have encountered some problems during the decade when they endeavoured to tackle the structure and writing of Lámnso' with the modern know-how of linguistics. These difficulties have been due in part to lack of foresight or to the misunderstanding on the part of some Nso' English language literates, and partly due to the exigencies of the current orthography for Cameroonian languages. Recently, thanks to the introduction of a current Cameroon language orthography in the early 1980s, some of the Lámnso' orthographical problems have not only been solved, but have also been revealed as common to most of the Cameroonian languages. Current Lámnso' studies will soon immerse Nso' culture in post-literary tools like the tape-recorder and the television. For the rest, anyone who has been acquainted with the high quality of the linguistic achievement of the Grebes and their collaborators, all of whom deserve our tribute here, would readily admit that their contribution to the promotion of the Nso' language and culture within a short span of time, has been partly due to factors like their linguistic know-how, and the collaboration of the Nso'. Lámnso' written literature has grown enormously. Provision of the necessary funds and, above all, a well-concerted language policy and practice, have also contributed to the success of the project.

We have argued that, in the Africa of both colonial and neo-colonial periods, policies in favour of African languages have been kept dormant, as is testified by their explicit omission from the constitutions of most African countries. Some of the statements of the OAU tend to support this situation. Ayi Kwei Armah, one of the leading Ghanaian novelists of our day, believes in a unified African language policy in which 'there is one central language which operates as the international medium, and around which all the smaller national and ethnic languages orbit'. In Armah's opinion 'the cultural order implicit in the OAU's sanctification of colonial boundaries means a continuation of colonial linguistic power. It is that reality that confronts African writers today.' And if these same writers 'are on record as favouring' his development of an overall African language policy in principle, Armah himself observes pertinently that 'there has been no concerted effort to bring the principle down to earth' (Armah 1985, pp.831–2. See also Hickey 1986).

Here again, we are faced with the absence of an African planned language policy for which writers like Obi Wali had wrestled and had decidedly solved in the 1960s in favour of African languages. Today many African writers have emphasized the importance of the use of African languages even to the extent of gaining a bad name from it, as in the case of Ngugi Wa Thiong'o and Micere Mugo who, according to Maja-Pearce, 'at the Conference on African Literature held at the Commonwealth Institute in November 1984' received nothing but 'hostility and abuse as one delegate after another sought to defend the writing of African literature in European languages' (Maja-Pearce 1986). But, since 'the vitality of African languages is patently evident for all to see' and a realistic language policy consists in offering African and non-African languages their apposite roles, the wisest course will be to abstain from promoting deceptive language policies and practices.

In other words, this means something other than what Maja-Pearce calls the 'final break with the West and the reorientation of Africa's perception away from Europe and back to Africa' (Maja-Pearce 1986). Why? Because, according to our way of reasoning, the real matrix and patrix of African languages and cultures have never been broken. Diop and many African and Africanist writers have ostentatiously refused to grow weary of affirming and recognizing the linkages which bind us with the ancient black Egyptian and present day African civilizations. The title of his book indicates this quite clearly: *Nations nègres et culture: de l'antiquité nègre Egyptienne aux problèmes culturels de l'Afrique noire d'aujourd'hui.* We cannot, therefore, talk of a break where there has never been a real cultural unity or wholeness. The apparent colonial and neo-colonial seclusion of Africans from their own languages through the use of some European languages has never meant a break in the continuum of the vitality of African languages. On the contrary, all our arguments are founded on this vitality and will lose their ground without it; it is thanks to them as part and parcel of African cultures and civilizations that the perception of the African past and present, and future can be adequately assured. To annihilate Africans is to introduce a break! The apartheid system has now placed itself in the vanguard, after the failure of the slave trade and Western colonial imperialism to accomplish a mission of annihilation or genocide.

In conclusion, therefore, our concern over African language policies and practices has not been mere words, empty of meaning. It envisages the future, practical uses of African and non-African languages in a new light. For Nga' Bi'fon II of Nso' revealed some truth when he asked the present writer how he could study Nso' culture in Europe. The Fon insisted: *Bòy a ye'ey lii Nso' fo Nso' e Lám Nso'*: Nso' culture is best learned among the Nso' and in Lamnso' (interview 1978). If colonial and neo-colonial history has kept most precious documents in foreign lands, it is not true that African languages can best be learned through foreign languages. In using African languages to study African cultures, civilizations, and languages, Africans can offer the best of their creative talents in their perceptions of the African past, as the African source of guidance, evaluation, and inspiration for the present and the future.

## Notes

1  Although the French version suggests that Tempels is worried about the 'intellectual formation', i.e. the academic presentation of Bantu ideas, he does not foresee the possibility of presenting these ideas in an academic manner in a Bantu language. Regrettably for his and our age, this possibility is still held in abomination. European languages are still the mirror through which Africans can see the faces of their innermost or ontological selves. Tempels who had worked among the Bantu as a missionary in the French-speaking world did not lose his language identity. No. He wrote his *Bantu Philosophy (Bantoe-Filosofie)* in his native language, the language of the people of the Netherlands, Dutch. But he would have gone one step further and ahead of his contemporaries, had he written his monumental work in one of the languages of the Bantu.

2    Examples like that of the novelist Joseph Conrad abound in human history.
3    We are very grateful to Mrs E.M. Chilver for the copy of *Notes from Lamnsaw Grammar* which she so generously handed to us.

# References

Achebe, C. 1975. *Morning yet on creation day.* London: Heinemann.

Akintoye, S.A. 1975. Nigerian contributions to Black history. *Nigeria Magazine*, **115–116,** 116–36.

Armah, A.K. 1985. Africa and the francophone dream. *West Africa,* 29th April 1985.

Césaire. A. 1957, *Letter to Maurice Thorez.* Paris: Presence Africaine.

Cole, D.T. 1971. The history of African linguistics to 1945. In *Current trends in linguistics: linguistics in sub-Saharan Africa,* vol. 17, T.A. Sebeok (ed.), 1–28. The Hague: Mouton.

Conde, M. 1976. *Herenakhonon.* Paris: 10/18.

Diop, C.A. 1979. *Nations nègres et culture.* Paris: Presence Africaine.

Duponchel, L. 1974. Le français d'Afrique: une langue, un dialecte ou une variante locale? *Dossiers Pedagogiques,* **13,** 7–13.

Fonlon, B. 1963. African writers meet in Uganda. *Abbia: Cameroon cultural review,* **1,** 39–54.

Fonlon, B. 1969. The language problem in Cameroon, an historical perspective. *Abbia: Cameroon cultural review,* **22,** 5–40.

Glucksmann, A. 1978. Ideologie et revolte. In *Histoire des ideologies.* F. Chatelet (ed.), vol. 3, 349–65. Paris: Hachette.

Grebe, K. 1984. The domain of noun tone rules in Lamnso. MA thesis, University of Calgary, Canada.

Grebe, K. & W. 1975. Verb tone patterns on Lamnsok. *Linguistics,* **149,** 5–24.

Hickey, R. 1986. Hausa as a lingua franca. *West Africa,* **3585, 3586.**

Jahn, J. 1968. *Neo-African literature: a history of Black writing.* New York: Grove.

Kishani, B.T. 1973. *Etude du contact entre le Lámnso' et l'Anglais.* Document de Licence, University of Paris V, France.

Kishani, B.T. 1976. African cultural identity through Western philosophies and languages. *Presence Africaine,* **98,** 104–30.

Maja-Pearce, A. 1986. *Loyalties.* Harlow: Longman.

Omari, C.K. 1985. Writing in African languages: towards the development of a sociology of literature. *Presence Africaine,* **133–4,** 19–27.

Polome, E.C. 1979. Tanzanian language policy and Swahili. *Word, journal of the international linguistic association,* **30,** 160–70.

Spencer, J. 1971. Colonial language policies and their legacies. In *Current trends in linguistics. Vol. 7: Linguistics in sub-Saharan Africa,* T.A. Sebeok (ed.), 537–45. The Hague: Mouton.

Tanna, L. 1974. African literature and its Western critics. *Abbia: Cameroon cultural review,* **27–8,** 53–64.

Tempels, P. 1953. *Bantu philosophy.* Paris: Collection Presence Africaine.

Wainwright, J. 1982. Thomas Muntzer (for David Spooner). In *The Penguin book of contemporary British poetry,* B. Morrison and A. Motion (eds.), 131. Harmondsworth: Penguin.

Wali, O. 1965. African literature and universities. *The Muse,* **2,** 10.

Warnier, J-P. 1980. Des precurseurs de l'ecole Berlitz: multilinguisme dans les grassfields du Cameroun au 19ième siecle. In *L'Expansion Bantoue,* L. Bouquiaux (ed.), 827–43. Paris: Société de Linguistique d'Afrique Occidentale.

Welmers, W.E. 1971. Christian missions and language policies. In *Current trends in linguistics.* Vol. 7: *Linguistics in sub-Saharan Africa*, T.A. Sebeok (ed.) 559–69. The Hague: Mouton.

# 9 A chapter in the history of the colonization of Sámi lands: the forced migration of Norwegian reindeer Sámi to Finland in the 1800s

MARJUT AND PEKKA AIKIO

## Introduction

There has been increasing controversy about the absence of objectivity in research. Researchers are human beings with their own individual, subjective backgrounds. Thus, research results are bound up with the researcher's theoretical background and methods. This lack of objectivity by the researcher is especially noticed by representatives of indigenous peoples. These representatives have seen that the so-called objective picture presented in the scientific literature of indigenous peoples has been created by researchers who see these indigenous people through the eyes of the conqueror.

The Venezuelan Riva Rivas described this situation quite accurately when giving a talk at the Fifth General Assembly of the World Council of Indigenous Peoples held in the Peruvian capital of Lima in July 1987. Riva Rivas (1987) presented the dual picture of how the conqueror sees himself and the conquered people. For example, the conqueror 'finds' or 'discovers' the indigenous people and their land, although the people themselves have thousands of years of history behind them. The conqueror comes from cities and represents nations, and the conquered people live in small villages and represent tribes in a tribal culture. Moreover, the conqueror sees himself as representing the noble ideas of a humanitarian people, and the conquered are seen as a splendid research object, the naive human being. The conqueror represents civilization, and he sees the indigenous peoples as uncivilized, primitive and barbaric. The conqueror has science on his side, the conquered can only present witchcraft. The conqueror leans on religion, and the conquered practise pagan rites and rituals. And of course, the land of indigenous peoples has always been seen as unclaimed wilderness, which can be freely occupied and exploited by the conqueror.

It is astonishing to realize that Riva Rivas' description fits very well with the reality of the Nordic Sámi people. Since the time of Tacitus and Procopius, Lapland, the home of the Sámi people, has been described as an exotic and faraway place. Huurre (1979) describes how Tacitus presented a civilized Roman perspective on the life of this nomadic hunting people: there is no agriculture. People live in non-permanent conical tents. Their clothing is fur and skins. The most important weapon is the arrow which is used in hunting. Iron is scarce and hence not often used.

The ethnocentrism presented in Tacitus' text has, since that time, become the archetype for describing the life of the Sámi. This ethnocentrism is dominant and can be seen in the ethnographic descriptions of Sámi villages, which are called Siidas. The Sámi people in this research are described as wandering nomads; migration followed the rhythm of nature and the seasons. This characterization was made possibly to misrepresent the fact that the Sámi village, the Siida, was an administrative areal unit according to the Swedish legal system. Within this system, the nomads had the legal right to own the land. Lapland has attracted tax collectors, merchants, explorers, and ordinary tourists. There are few if any areas in Europe described as intensively and as unrealistically as Lapland.

Archaeological research in northern Finland has been focused mostly on the non-nomadic agrarian culture. The prehistory of the Sámi has been studied by archaeologists at only five different sites (Carpelan 1985). This research into Sámi prehistory has been hindered due to lack of funding. Many remarkable discoveries have been found in 'emergency excavations' which were hurriedly carried out before the sites were destroyed, for example by the creation of artificial lakes for hydroelectric power dams. Archaeological finds discovered at Sompio in Finnish Lapland have uncovered the fact that the Sámi people already had established regular trading relationships both to the east with Russia and to the west with Sweden in the 1400s and 1500s (Carpelan 1987).

Research into legal history has brought forth much new information on the social and legal structure of Sámi society. This line of research was initiated by the Nordic Sámi Institute in the late 1970s. The Siida, previously described as an ethnographic community comprised of nomads with no desire to own land, has been redefined as a territorial entity where the Sámi, especially as nomads, had the right to own land according to the legal system in force (Korppijaakko 1985a). This right to own land by the Sámi living in the Siida has been re-recognized in the decision made by the Supreme Court of Sweden in 1981 (Bengtsson 1987).

The legal relationship of the indigenous people to the land has become a global concern. The ethnocentric definition of the indigenous peoples as only users and not as owners of land is seen to be an intentionally conscious effort to support the conqueror's view that these wide wildernesses have no owners.

This chapter describes the fate of one nomadic Sámi group from the late 1800s to the present. This reindeer-herding Sámi group was the victim of the border regulations between the Nordic countries, and so serves as a good example of how an indigenous people in Europe have been colonized and victimized by the process of colonization.

## The reconstruction of the Sámi village based on research into legal history

As late as 1750, Lapland, the land of the Sámi, was a common territory undivided by national boundaries. As a result, Denmark-Norway, Sweden-Finland, and Russia all attempted to extend their sovereignty over the area. Until the early 19th century, Swedish rule was dominant. Lapland was separated from the rest of the country by the so-called Lapland Boundary (Julku 1968, Korppijaakko 1985a). South of this boundary people lived by agriculture. North of this boundary was the area where the Sámi lived.

The Siida were large territorial units, and their boundaries were approved by public authorities. Hultblad (1968) has reconstructed the spatial location of Siidas according to conditions in the early 1600s (Fig. 9.1). Recent Finnish studies of legal history have succeeded in identifying some of the Siidas' ancient boundary cairns (Korppijaakko 1985a). The age of these cairns has been estimated by lichenometry. The Siida population was engaged in Sámi livelihoods, in other words reindeer husbandry, fishing, and hunting. The inhabitants of the Siidas were obliged to pay land taxes to the state. According to modern legal and historical studies, this process continued in Finland as late as 1924 (Korppijaakko 1985a). The Sámi way of land use in their Siidas fulfilled all the criteria of landownership.

The taxed lands of the Sámi could be traded, sold, distributed by inheritance, or given away. Consequently, the Siida fulfils all the conditions which we, in the west and Nordic countries, associate with the concept of real estate. This new legal reconstruction of the Sámi village is interesting not only because it differs from the traditional ethnographical description, but also because it gives a new legal status to the Siida. The legal status of the Siida is thus clarified, and we can see that in many respects, the Siidas were governed not only by Sámi customary law, but also by Swedish legislation.

## Lappekodicill – the Sámi Magna Carta

The Strömstad treaty of 1751 determined the first international boundary that was drawn through Lapland. However, before this border could be established, the King of Denmark-Norway, Frederick V, ordered that thorough research be made into the inhabitants and how and where they were using the land (Tikkanen 1966). On many occasions between 1742 and 1745, Schnitler (1929, 1962) undertook to interview the inhabitants of Lapland, both those permanently settled and those whose life was migratory. Obviously the Sámi who were interviewed under oath tried to answer carefully all the questions that they were asked, but the far-reaching implications of the questions were not clearly understood by them. The answers given indicate that they were not asked about the conditions of landownership for the taxed lands in the Siida.

Seen from the outside, the Sámi were considered to be politically weak and immature, even though they were completely at home in the subarctic

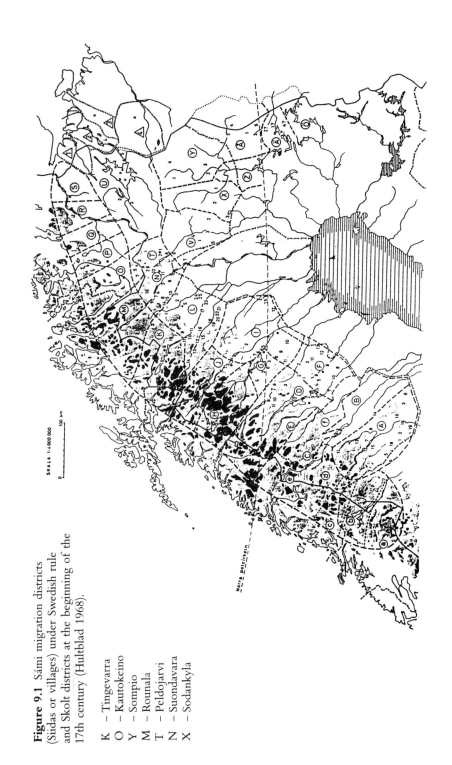

**Figure 9.1** Sámi migration districts (Siidas or villages) under Swedish rule and Skolt districts at the beginning of the 17th century (Hultblad 1968).

K  – Tingevarra
O  – Kautokeino
Y  – Sompio
M  – Roumala
T  – Peldojarvi
N  – Suondavara
X  – Sodankyla

SKALA 1:4 000 000

0          100 km

Norra polcirkeln

environment where their way of life required free seasonal migration between the inland forests and fells and the Arctic Ocean. Neither during the investigations for the Strömstad treaty to determine where to place the border, nor at any time since then have the Sámi striven to establish a national state of their own. This has caused serious difficulties for the Sámi, because the national boundaries crossing Lapland have divided the area into fragments. Lapland, formerly one area, was after 1751 shared by two and later by four countries.

In a section of the Strömstad treaty (called the Lappekodicill) it was affirmed that the Sámis still had the right to cross the border between Norway and Sweden with their reindeer and to use the land on both sides of the border. However, the obligation to pay taxes was limited to the paying of taxes either to Norway or to Sweden. The border line divided the Sámi people and the Siidas unnaturally in two. As a consequence, the Sámi were said to be citizens of either Norway or Sweden. The Strömstad treaty plays a very significant role in determining the rights of the Sámi and has been the subject of intensive investigation. For example, the Nordic Sámi Institute in Kautokeino, Norway, arranged a four-day research conference on this theme in September 1986. The conference was called 'The Lappekodicill of 1751 – was this the Magna Carta of the Sámi?'

## The Lappekodicill gets weaker and the borders close

An important development took place in the early 1800s when Sweden lost her status as a great power. In the Finnish War (1808–9) with Russia, Sweden lost Finland which then became an autonomous grand duchy of the Russian Empire in 1809.

In the forest and fell regions of Lapland, the raising of cattle and the growing of hay, together with the last phases of Finnish agricultural settlement, combined to produce new conflicts between the farmers and the reindeer-herding Sámi. Since the early 1800s, there are records of claims for damages caused to hay fields by reindeer, especially in the Finnish and Norwegian parts of Lapland (Wiklund & Qvigstad 1908). By the 1880s, the development of reindeer husbandry in Finland had begun to differ from that of Sweden and Norway. In Finland, it was possible for a farmer to own reindeer. In this way, the Siida in Finland were colonized by an agrarian culture, which gradually replaced the reindeer-herding culture based on the system of the Siida. One of the first perceivable consequences of this was the foundation of reindeer-herding fence companies in Finland from the 1840s onwards. Officially, these companies were established to promote reindeer herding. But their principal task in practice was to protect the interests of the cattle farmers against the interests of the reindeer herders.

The Lappekodicill was unable to solve the problems of the border districts. Nomadic Sámi migrating with their reindeer herds caused many complaints from the agrarian population who demanded that these problems be eliminated. Hearings were arranged as they were 100 years before between

1742 and 1745. Reindeer-herding Sámi were interviewed again and again concerning their needs, rights, and land use, even up to the early 1900s. Investigations of the Sámi system of reindeer herding have been recorded in the reports of numerous committees. Such documentation amounts to thousands of pages of material from Norway, Sweden, and Finland. The reindeer-herding Sámi were compelled to make themselves familiar with all sorts of statutes, orders, restrictions, penalties, and agreements in a more exact way than the farmers. The Sámi were moving and migrating through lands controlled by Norway and Sweden, and had to master many languages. As a result, they became experts in the various agreements on how to move across the northern borders. So the idea of nomads living ourside civilization often presented by outsiders is a myth without any foundation in reality. In this sort of research, the Sámi are often misrepresented as being romantic, unrealistic, and exotic, irregular, and inconsistent.

As confirmed by the Lappekodicill, the right of the Sámi to move freely across the Norwegian–Finnish border was considered important by the government of Norway, and the Norwegian government wanted to preserve ths right. Also, the Russian Empire took a positive attitude toward the legitimate claims of the Sámi. In Finland (then under Russian rule), there were increasing demands by farmers and local authorities to keep the big reindeer herds from the border areas because the movement of these herds disturbed the peaceful life of the permanent agrarian population. Consultations between Norway and Russia failed to yield adequate results, and the border between Norway and Finland was closed between 1852 and 1854. This action has effectively prevented reindeer herders from herding their reindeer across the Norwegian–Finnish border from 1852 to the present (Tikkanen 1966).

Closing the border and prohibiting free entry to winter pasture in Finland produced dramatic consequences. As an example of this, 30 families with their reindeer migrated officially from Kautokeino in Norway to Karesuando in Sweden (Arell 1977) where they tried to continue using winter pastures in Finland. This too became impossible in 1889 when the border between Sweden and Finland was closed. This border is still closed to reindeer herders migrating across the Swedish–Finnish border with their herds.

Even today, the Lappekodicill has legal consequences for Norway and Sweden, because agreement on reindeer pasturage between these two countries has its origin in this document (Pohjoiskalottikomitea 1981). Even today some of the Swedish reindeer Sámi can cross the Norwegian border with their reindeer herds and use the summer pasturage in Norway. In the same way, some of the Norwegian Sámi reindeer herders can use the winter pastures in Sweden.

## Chaos in the border regions and the Sámi move East

The drawing and closing of national borders in Lapland created many difficulties for the reindeer-herding Sámi. For example, ten reindeer-herding

Sámi families migrated from Norway to the former district of Sompio in Finnish Lapland during 1870–90 (see also Linkola 1967).

Originally these ten families lived in five Sámi villages or Siidas in Norway. Most of the families lived at Kautokeino (O). One family lived at Rounala (M). One family which was living at Suonttavaara (N) at the time of the migration to Sompio had previously moved to Suonttavaara from Tingevaara (K), presumably because of marriage or because they had purchased a new home there. One family is supposed to have been living at Peldojärvi (T). In the Siida, they had a well-functioning administration of their own with all communication being carried out in the Sámi language. All of these families settled down principally in the Siidas of Sodankylä (X) and Sompio (Y) in Finland. (The letters in brackets refer to locations marked in Fig. 9.1.)

The family names of those who migrated were: Hetta (Fig. 9.2), Bongo (Ponku), Turi (Tuuri), Baer, Eira, Sara, Qvaenangen, Beldovuobme (Peltovuoma), Nicodemus (Nikodemus) and Magga (Fig. 9.3). All these families were nomadic. For the Sámi, this meant living deep in the inland forests of Lapland in winter and moving with their reindeer to the coast and islands of the Arctic Ocean for the summer (Fig. 9.4). The distance between these summer and winter pastures could be very great. The autumn and the time of reindeer calving in late spring was spent in the fell area. Inside the geographical area covered by the Siida, those areas used by each family were precisely defined and known. The migration routes were ancient and permanent. Accurate information on the locations and borders of these areas used in the 1800s has been found out quite recently. Different committee reports and other written documents (i.e. tax rolls, landownership lists, parish archives, and the archives of reindeer herding associations) have formed the most important sources of information. Interviews made in Finland and Norway during the progress of this research (since 1977) contributed substantially in solving this jigsaw puzzle. The personnel and collections of the University of Tromsø were invaluable in conducting this research. Especially significant were recent studies in legal history (Korppijaakko 1985a, b, Hyvärinen 1985).

Most of the summer pastures of these ten Sámi families in the 1800s were located in the areas of Skjervøy and Lyngen in Tromsø County in Norway. This means that the summer pastures were in the islands and peninsulas of the fjords of Kvaenangsfjord, Reisafjord, Lyngen, Ullsfjord, and Balsfjord (Fig. 9.4). It is documented as early as 1742–5 in the report of Schnitler that the Sámi migrating in summer to Nordreisa stayed in winter at Kautokeino, accompanied there by some of the Enontekiö Sámi (Schnitler 1962). Some of the Sámi migrated for the summer to the Lyngen fjord, and others migrated to the fjords of Ullsfjord and Balsfjord (Schnitler 1929).

Portions of inherited land located in the Siidas and belonging to two Sámi families have been identified (Korppijaakko 1986, pers. comm.). Up to 1760, the Nicodemus family lived in their old hereditary lands called Orbus in the Siida of Rounala (Rounala. Marked M. in Fig. 9.1). At the end of the 1700s and the beginning of the 1800s, they were living on their lands called Wuotakavuoma in the Siida of Suonttavaara.

**Figure 9.2** Turf hut of Isak Johannesen Hetta in present day Vuotso, formerly Muotkataival in Sompio. The photograph was taken in 1902. The people from left to right are Isak Hetta (born in Kautokeino in 1861 and son of Jon Johannesen Hetta), Inkeri Hetta, Maria Gunilla Hetta (née Bongo), Jon Mathis Hetta, Elsa Hetta, Uula Hetta (born in Kautokeino in 1859 and another son of Jon Johannesen Hetta), Lars Nikodemus (born in Enontekiö in 1826), Brita Maria Karppinen, and Niila Uulanpoika Hetta. (From the archives of the Finnish National Board of Antiquities and Historial Monuments.)

**Figure 9.3** Guttorm Magga (born in Kautokeino 1843) sitting in his reindeer sledge. This photograph was taken in Sompio by K. Granit, a member of the Finnish Polar Expedition during the expedition's visit to Sompio in 1883–6. (Reproduced by permission of the National Museum of Finland.)

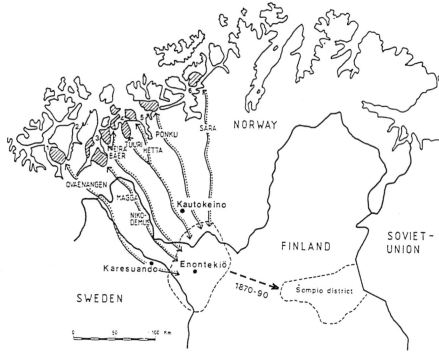

**Figure 9.4** The migration routes of some nomadic Sámi families in Norway before their migration to the district of Sompio in Finnish Lapland.
*Key*: 1 – Balsfjord    2 – Ullsfjord    3 – Lyngen    4 – Reisafjord
           5 – Kvaenangsfjord    6 – Altafjord

Porovuoma was the property of the Magga family (in the Siida of Rounala. Marked M in Fig. 9.1) in the 1860s. The family obtained the land and moved there either through marriage or through purchase. These Maggas are called Orponen. The name Orponen may refer to the Orbus family, the hereditary lands owned by this family, or to Nils Magga (born 1843) who was an orphan ('orpo' is the Sámi word for 'orphan').

The rest of the Sámi families which migrated to Sompio in Finland (Hetta, Bongo, Turi, Baer, Eira, Qvaenangen) originated in the Kautokeino District of Norway (marked O in Fig. 9.1).

Detailed kinship studies have been made concerning the migrant families (Aikio 1983). Utilizing historical souces, we have reconstructed the areas where these families lived before the first border closing in 1852. We have not found any comparable reconstruction of the history of the reindeer Sámi in the literature. Vorren (1962) described the nomadic reindeer Sámi during the post-World War II period in Finnmark, the northernmost province of Norway, but he did so without identifying persons or families.

When conflicts with the farmers became more frequent, some of the reindeer-herding Sámi considered that the position of collective landownership as organized by the Sámi village system or Siida was weaker than that of individual landownership as practised by the farmers. Some of the Sámi tried to strengthen their position by buying land. This was the solution assumed by the Nikodemus family, among others. This family purchased land first in Iddonjarga on the west side of Lyngenfjord. Gradually the border district became overcrowded, and after the closure of the Norwegian–Finnish border it became impossible to use the winter pastures in Finland.

These Sámi did not move out at random. Oral Sámi tradition tells that in 1866 in the hut of Tommus-Aslak at the base of the Halti Fell in the former Siida of Rounala (marked M in Fig. 9.1), a conference was held and a decision was made to send an expedition of three men eastwards to scout out the pastures there (SKNA). At the present time, the location of this hut is on the Norwegian–Finnish border in a place which even today is considered to be uninhabited by ordinary Finns. According to another local Sámi oral tradition, strange western Sámi were said to have been sleeping on their sleds, wrapped in furs in the freezing cold, at Savukoski in the eastern part of present-day Finnish Lapland.

Migration to Sompio partially took place via Sweden, because the border between Sweden and Finland was closed only in 1889. Some Sámi thought that if they officially moved to Sweden then they could continue to use the winter pastures in Finland.

The nomadic reindeer-herding Sámi were wealthy. Once in Sompio, they quickly became familiar with the vast areas of forest and fells in Sompio. They also soon started to herd the reindeer of farmers living in Kittilä and Sodankylä when the farmers requested this. In the beginning, the reindeer that were accustomed to the coast ran away and returned home. Part of them vanished. In one sense, living in the border area was very free, but this free type of life ended when the reindeer herders had to assume the citizenship of either Norway, Sweden, or Finland. The reindeer Sámi who migrated to Sompio finally made up their minds to become citizens of Finland in 1914 after having been in Finland for decades, some of them over 40 years.

One of the Sámi who applied all his personal skills and talents to herd reindeer under entirely new circumstances was Matti Ponku. He, like other reindeer-herding Sámi, mastered and used vast territories. The Sámi moved through the whole of Lapland from the Norwegian coasts on the Arctic Ocean to the inland coniferous forests of Finland and Sweden (Figs. 9.1 and 9.4). If one follows the tracks of Matti Ponku, who migrated to Sompio (Fig. 9.5), we can see that he, his extended family, and their reindeer herds (more than 3000 reindeer) lived in about 15 different places in Sompio at different times between 1870 and 1900. In addition to this, he made a fast and efficient visit to Inari and Polmak Lake in Utsjoki to see if he could find a new migratory path via Lake Polmak to Varangerfjord in northern Norway (Fig. 9.5). The extent of the area was about 200 x 150 km (30,000 km²), and the migration distance with the reindeer in one direction to the coast of the Arctic Ocean was 300 to 500 km (see Fig. 9.4, migration route number 5 of Bongo in 1800s before migration to Sompio).

**Figure 9.5** Migration routes of Matti Ponku (born Mathis Bongo in Kautokeino in 1843) and his extended family, in Finland between 1870 and 1900.

The reindeer Sámi migrated eastwards to Sompio, then occupied by descendants of the forest Sámis. The migrating Sámis brought large reindeer herds with them to the almost empty fells. The migrating Sámis adapted themselves quickly to the new reindeer-herding system, originating partially from the agrarian culture. Nevertheless, they were able to carry on herding reindeer in an almost nomadic way.

The Finnish Civil War (1918) and World War II brought disruption and economic losses to the descendants of the immigrant reindeer-herding Sámi who moved to Sompio. During these times, thousands of their reindeer were requisitioned to feed the military forces and the civilian population. The end of the 1950s marked the beginning of remarkable environmental changes to Finnish Lapland as Finland's economic expansion became more rapid. For example, whole forests in the Sompio area were cut down for timber. In the 1960s, the largest man-made lakes in western Europe were created in Sompio to produce hydroelectric power. The fell areas of Sompio formerly used for reindeer herding are one of the most popular recreation areas in Finland. One of these was converted into a national park in the 1980s (P. Aikio 1978, 1983).

All these changes have brought new problems of adaptation (to the descendants of the reindeer-herding Sámi who migrated to Sompio over 100 years ago. Formerly wealthy nomads have become remarkably poorer.

## Conclusions and recommendations

In the first phase of defining national borders in Lapland, an attempt was made to preserve the rights of migrating Sámi. But this objective failed as shown by the border closures in 1852–4 and 1889. The use of the upper Finnmark plain (Finnmarksvidda) and the areas of Enontekiö and Karesuando as a part of the Sámi reindeer-herding system was effectively prevented. This reason, among others, caused many Sámi families to move out of the region.

As modern technology and large environmental changes encroached massively upon areas occupied by the Sámi community, the people became helpless, inefficient, and unable to defend and protect themselves and their interests against the machinery of modern society. Thus the people felt like outsiders, even in their own culture and community. This phenomenon is related to the concept of 'stranger' as defined by sociologists.

The fate of the reindeer Sámi presented in this chapter shows clearly how these Sámi, after their migration to Sompio, lost all the legal rights recognized by Norway and Sweden. In their new home in the district of Sompio in Finland, they became exposed to outside influences and exploitation against which they had to, and still must, constantly defend themselves. These pressures have included the unsettled times during World Wars I and II, Finnish colonization, the highly mechanized character of the modern forest industry, the largest man-made lakes in western Europe, and finally the giving up of large mountain areas to be incorporated into a huge national park. In the 1900s, this Sámi group shifted their language from Sámi to Finnish (M. Aikio 1984) and lost almost all of their remaining cultural traditions. Only reindeer herding has so far preserved or maintained some of the characteristics of traditional Sámi culture.

The Sámi's traditional rights became the object of a very intensive study at the end of the 1970s and in the 1980s in Finland, Sweden, and Norway. At the present time, there is sufficient information to conclude that the Sámi were entitled to control their areas north of the Lapland Boundary, and these rights were still in force in the 1770s. This was a legal right recognized by Sweden and Norway according to the legal system in force in both these countries.

What we need now is the political will to realize Sámi cultural autonomy. This could be done, for example, according to those principles which are at present in force in Åland's associate status with Finland.

The situation of the Nordic Sámi people is a part of the destiny of the indigenous peoples of the world. We can find the same denial and exploitation of the people's rights and culture among the North American Indians and among the indigenous peoples of Central and South America, Australia, Tasmania, etc. Often the only difference in the exploitation of indigenous people is the difference in degree. In the case of the Sámi, a process of acculturation and assimilation has gone further than that which occurred among other indigenous peoples.

At the international level, the indigenous peoples of the world, including the Sámi, wish to co-operate with the various bodies and organizations of the United Nations. Quite recently within organizations of the United Nations, there have been many positive developments regarding the rights of indigenous peoples. At the present time, the ILO is working on a partial revision of the Indigenous Tribal Populations Convention 1957 (no. 107). This document was not ratified by the Nordic countries at that time. The Finnish Sámi parliament has also released a statement on this proposed revision. In 1981, a meeting of Norwegian archaeologists dealt with this Convention. They agreed that the northernmost province of Norway (Finnmark) and parts of other provinces definitely must be considered as a Sámi cultural region. This was based on archaeological finds and other historical material dating from the time of the Norwegian colonization of Finnmark which began in the Middle Ages. Thus, the Sámi in Norway must be considered as an indigenous people as stated in the ILO convention number 107 (Naess 1985).

Especially when studying the life of tribal or indigenous people, the interpretation of research results is often made according to the conqueror's ethnocentric view. The Swedish archaeologist Zachrisson (1987) has shown that Viking settlements in the Province of Härjedalen in the south of Sweden (south of latitude 62°) thought to indicate the progress of Viking conquests were in fact old Sámi settlements. Almost everything that is written about reindeer herding has been written from the viewpoint of an outsider (but see M. & P. Aikio 1983, 1985, P. Aikio 1988, S. Aikio 1977).

Those representing the indigenous peoples have indicated that the time has now come for their own people to research, study, describe, and interpret their own history, traditions, and culture. The statement was made at the South American Indian Council (CISA) that the life of tribal and indigenous peoples can be studied only by their own members. Also, some of the Sámi students studying archaeology at the University of Tromsø have demanded that in northern Norway there should be no further archaeological excavations before the Sámi archaeologists themselves can take over and perform this invaluable work. The Sámi with their insights into their own culture can help in the more accurate interpretation of archaeological results. New theories are needed about Sámi life and culture, and these are best formulated by the Sámi themselves because Sámi archaeologists and historians are the ones with the most direct and tangible link with Sámi ethnic identity. The time for this change seems to be ripe.

## Acknowledgements

This research was supported by the Finnish Academy, the University of Lapland, and the Nordic Sámi Institute. The authors wish to thank them for their valuable help and assistance.

The authors also wish to thank Timo Hirvelä for drawing the figures, and Nick Gardner and Erkki Pääkkönen for their help in preparing the English version.

## References

Aikio, M. 1984. The position and use of the Sámi language: historical, contemporary and future perspectives. *Journal of Multilingual and Multicultural Development* **5**, 277–91.

Aikio, M. & P. Aikio 1983. Sompion seudun saamelaiset suvut. Käsikirjoitus (Sámi families of the Sompio district). (Manuscript.)

Aikio, M. & P. Aikio 1985. Sámi and ethnicity problems in Finland. *Ethnicity in Canada. International Examples and Perspectives. Marburger Geographische Schriften*, 121–33. Marburg: Lahn.

Aikio, P. 1978. The breakdown of a Lappish ecosystem in northern Finland. *Consequences of economic change in circumpolar regions* (occasional publication) **14**, 91–104.

Aikio, P. 1983. National parks and Lappish reindeer husbandry. *Production Pastorale et Société. Bulletin de l'equipe et anthropologie des sociétés pastorales* **12**, 71–8.

Aikio, P. 1989. The changing role of reindeer in the life of the Sámi. In *The walking larder*, J. Clutton-Brock (ed.), ch. 16. London: Unwin Hyman.

Aikio, S. 1977. Reunahuomautuksia saamelaisten taloushistoriaan (Notes on the economic history of the Sámi). *Suomen antropologi* **2**, 91–4.

Arell, N. 1977. Rennomadismen i Torne Lappmark ⁓ markanvändning under kolonisationsepoken i fr.a. Enontekis socken (Reindeer pastoralism in Tornio Lapland. The use of land during the time of colonization in the parish of Enontekiö). *Kungl. Skytteanska samfundets handlingar* **17**. Umeå.

Bengtsson, B. 1987. *Statsmakten och äganderätten* (The state and the right of ownership). Bjärnum: Studieförbundet Näringsliv och samhälle Förlag.

Carpelan, C. 1985. Saamelaisten esihistoriaa ja saamelaisarkeologiaa (Sámi prehistory and Sámi archaeology). In *Lapin esihistoria*, Matti Huurre (ed.) (Lappi 4), 36–7. Hämeenlinna: Karisto.

Carpelan, C. 1987. Juikenttä – Keskiajan ja uuden ajan alun metsäsaamelainen yhteisö arkeologisen aineiston valossa (Juikenttä – the forest Sámi community in the middle ages and at the beginning of modern times in the light of archaeological findings). *Saamelaiset – sovinnolliset sopeutujat. Lapin Maakuntamuseon julkaisuja* **5**, 62–70. Oulu.

Hultblad, F. 1968. Övergång från nomadism till agrar bosättning i Jokkmokks socken (Transition from nomadism to agrarian settlement in the parish of Jokkmokk, Sweden). *Nordiska Museet: Acta Lapponica* **14**. Lund.

Huurre, M. 1979. *9000 vuotta Suomen esihistoriaa* (9000 years of Finnish prehistory). Helsinki: Otava.

Hyvärinen, H. 1985. The land and water rights of the Sámi in Finland. *Nordisk tidskrift for international ret. Acta Scandinavica juris gentium* **59**, 33–42.

Julku, K. 1968. Kemin pitäjän ja Kemin Lapin raja (The boundary between the parish of Kemi and Kemi Lapland). *Oulun yliopisto. Historian laitos. Eripainossarja* 2. Kemi.

Korppijaakko, K. 1985a. Maaton saamelainen (The landless Sámi). *Tiede* 2, 4–8. Helsinki.

Korppijaakko, K. 1985b. Saamelaiset ja maanomistusoikeus 1 (The Sámi and landownership 1). *Diedut* 3. Kautokeino: Sami Instituhtta.

Linkola, M. 1967. Sompion porolappalaiset (The reindeer Lapps in Sompio). *Entinen Kemijoki* 251–63. Helsinki.

Naess, J. R. (ed.) 1985. Arkeologi og urbefolkning (Archaeology and the indigenous peoples). In *Arkeologi og etnisitet. Norsk arkeologmöte. Ams-Varia* 15, 109–13. Stavanger.

Pohjoiskalottikomitean J. 1981. *Porotalous pohjoiskalotilla* (Reindeer husbandry in the north Calotte). Tromsö.

Rivas Riva S. 1987. Racismo lucha de clases y dominacion sociocultural. (Manuscript.)

Schnitler, P. 1929, 1962. Major Peter Schnitlers grenseeksaminasjons protokoller 1742–1745 (The minutes of the border inquiries by Major Peter Schnitler). (Utgitt av Kjeldeskriftfondet.) I og II. Oslo.

Tanner, V. 1929 Skoltlapparna (The Skolt Lapps). *Fennia* 49, 1–518.

Tikkanen, H. 1966. Lapin pohjoisrajan kysymyksiä 1800-luvulla (Issues on the northern boundary of Lapland during the 1800s). *Lapin Tutkimusseuran vuosikirja* VII. Kemi.

Vorren, Ö. 1962. Finnmark samenes nomadisme I–II (The reindeer nomadism of the Finnmark Sámi I–II). *Tromsö museums skrifter* 9. Oslo.

Wiklund, K.B. & J. Qvigstad 1913. Dokument angånde flytlapparna. Renbeteskomissionen af 1913 (Documents relating to nomadic Lapps. Commission on Reindeer Pasturage. 1913).

Zachrisson, I. 1987. Samer i syd (The Sámi in the south). *Populär arkeologi* 1, 4–9. Lund.

# 10   *A proper place for the dead: a critical review of the 'reburial' issue*

JANE HUBERT

## Background

The issue that is now widely referred to as the 'reburial' issue has grasped archaeologists in some areas of the world firmly by the throat – and it shows no sign of letting go. Many of these archaeologists have faced the situation and are now seeking a solution. Others (e.g. Chippindale 1987) who are well aware of the issue, and even involved to some extent, do not want to have it discussed, least of all with the people it most concerns – those who maintain that their past relatives make up the human remains involved. In some areas of the world many archaeologists may not yet be aware of the issue at all.

The issue, in brief, concerns human remains that are excavated, studied, displayed to the public or stored in museums, laboratories, university departments and elsewhere. In North America and Australia, and increasingly, in other parts of the world, indigenous groups are protesting against the excavation of their burial sites and the use of their ancestors' remains for scientific study or display. In many instances they demand that the human remains be given back for redisposition, usually by reburial. Archaeologists and physical anthropologists, on the other hand, are concerned that a vital source of information about the past will no longer be available for study. Human remains provide unique data on such things as patterns of disease in past populations, diet, adaptation to the environment, and biological changes, as well as on cultural practices, data which cannot be obtained from any other source. Some scientists see the scientific value as completely overriding the cultural beliefs of the living populations.

Others see both sides of the argument and would like to find a compromise between the two, which are – when taken to their extremes – incompatible. There is some middle ground, however. Not all those who are asking for the return of human remains are demanding everything back. Some only claim those remains that are known to be the forebears of their own particular group (e.g. Moore, ch. 15, this volume); others only those who are named individuals. Whether it is all or only a part of the material that is being demanded, the intention is to rebury the remains, with due ceremony, or dispose of them in a manner appropriate to the customs of the cultural group from which they came. As a first step, some groups are requesting that their skeletal material currently on display in museums should be taken off display.

Archaeologists and physical anthropologists are divided in their response to the demands of the people who lay claim to the remains of their ancestors. Even those who are the most violently opposed to any ban on excavation of burial sites would, presumably, draw the line somewhere, if the threat were to the graves of their own relatives. This being so, they should be able, logically, to understand the emotions of others who draw the line at a different point.

What is quite clear is that within many cultures a wide range of conflicting views and beliefs exist about what should or should not be done with bodies and bones. There may be a consensus of views about the bodies of close kin, and most people would perhaps fight to protect the graves of their own parents, or sibling or child. Others might extend this further back to grandparents and other relatives within 'living memory'. Recently, in England, there has been opposition to the projected destruction of whole cemeteries to make way for new building projects. Headlines such as 'Sacrilege to dig up graves' (*Bucks Herald*, 11 Feb. 1988) appear at regular intervals in local newspapers around the country.

Why do English people object to the destruction of the physical remains of their dead? Why should it matter to a person that their parents' bones are disturbed or even dug up, drilled or destroyed for the sake of research, especially in the context of a society that encourages people to donate their eyes or kidneys to someone else after their death, or even their whole body for dissection by medical students? In some contexts, and insofar as we demand that they be treated with respect, it seems that we do believe that the bones of our relatives in some way *are* our relatives, that in some indefinable way they still contain an essence of the living person. Yet the fact that cremation is widespread in England suggests that many people do not think that the soul or individual identity of a person remains in the body after death. It seems that there are may different beliefs about the dead within a culture, not only among those of different religions, but also among those within the same religion. In fact, one individual may have conflicting and inconsistent beliefs, which may remain unresolved. The beliefs of an American Indian, or Papua New Guinean who says 'I see people, I do not see bones', may not, in reality, be far removed from some of the beliefs held by many of those American and European individuals who fight to retain control over human remains, which, in their role as scientists, they prefer to call 'specimens'.

## Variety in Judaeo-Christian attitudes

In 20th-century Britain there is growing concern about the archaeological excavation of ancient skeletons and the display of human remains, and a number of well-publicized cases where excavation of burial sites has caused public concern. Current public reaction to the practice of developing cemeteries for other purposes because of the premium on land has been one of distress and outrage.

Even in the case of long-disused burial grounds, there is opposition to the disturbance of the dead. In some instances reburial ceremonies have taken place as a 'new' phenomenon. Philip Rahtz documents an example of the Jewish community in Britain opposing the bulldozing of a 12th-century Jewish cemetery (Rahtz 1985). The York Archaeological Trust sought support for excavation of the site, rather than destruction by bulldozers which were moving in to make way for a Sainsbury's car park. The Chief Rabbi refused to countenance the idea of a Jewish cemetery being disturbed, but supported the idea of a small excavation to see if there were in fact any bones, provided no bones were removed from the site. Many burials were found, but since they were all oriented north-south and had coffin-nails, the Chief Rabbi's Court of Beth Din disclaimed the cemetery. Under the Disused Burial Grounds Amendment Act of 1981, Sainsbury's were legally obliged to remove all the skeletons, and undertook to rebury them in nearby 'safe' ground. Over 500 graves were unearthed, and systematic research was begun on the skeletons by human biologists at York University. Rahtz (1985, p.44) continues:

> The Chief Rabbi may have had second thoughts . . . for he immediately complained to the Home Office. They, duly sensitive to the interest of religious minorities in Britain, ordered . . . immediate reburial. Sainsbury's were asked to dig a hole for reburial and the University to give up the bones.

The bones were eventually reburied, each skeleton in a separate heat-sealed polythene bag, with a plastic identity disc, on the same day, as Rahtz points out, that lightning destroyed the south transept of York Minster!

In Chichester, in the early 1970s, a medieval burial site on consecrated ground was excavated before an industrial development ploughed up the land. Local Church authorities were totally against the skeletons being removed and examined, and within two weeks of the excavation they were ordered to be reburied.

The opposite view was taken by the Church authorities about a deserted medieval village in Yorkshire, in which skeletons from medieval times up until the present century have been released for examination and research purposes, on condition that they are returned for reburial. So far they remain unburied.

Recently, symbolic 'token' burials have taken place in England. A skeleton of one of many sailors found on the Mary Rose (the ship recovered after centuries at the bottom of the sea) was reburied with great pomp and ceremony. This was apparently done in part to pacify those who saw the sunken ship as a 'war grave' which should not have been disturbed.

In another case a few of the many bones unearthed in recent excavations in Winchester have been reburied in a symbolic ceremony, and in February 1988 bodies thought to be Christians of Roman origin, dating from c. AD 300, were buried with full Christian ceremony in a Norfolk churchyard, watched by an audience of schoolchildren. A coin dug up with the bodies was incorporated into a carved headstone by a local stonemason.

Rahtz (1988, p. 33) has drawn attention to the existence of firms such as

'Necropolis', whose business is 'to clear cemeteries as fast as possible and with as little public awareness as can be managed' presumably by-passing the archaeologists and thus avoiding the high costs involved in 'expert archaeological supervision with full recording'.

Cultural beliefs and activities are not static and unchanging. It is clear that in burial rites, as in all other cultural activity, change is a constant dynamic force. Our own practices in England have changed, as elsewhere, on numerous occasions; for example, from including burial goods to including none, from burial to cremation, from burial inside the church to outside, from graveyard to cemetery. In the case of living American Indians (and also Australian Aborigines, e.g. Truganini, see below) it is currently the fear of scientists that is influencing a change towards cremation. When such traditions change, for whatever reason, the 'charter' of belief and myth also changes to accommodate and explain the change of practice. It is such changes that archaeologists and physical anthropologists often claim in other cultures to be mere political manipulation of the evidence.

In many cases changes in custom and situation require rethought and time before appropriate reactions can be determined by religious leaders. In England, much time is taken to decide on the rules that should govern new practices, and to develop an ideology which will encompass them. The Anglican Church took many decades to come up with an acceptable 'justification' of cremation, which had become a widespread practice. In another context the comparatively recent acceptance by the Church of burial rites for pets has meant that church officials have had to develop appropriate ceremonies.

Archaeologists and museum curators, on the other hand, often expect immediate answers. But why should American Indians, if it has never happened before, know what to do with a large amount of unprovenanced skeletons? Or know, without due consideration, whether an ancestor's soul can be at rest if his skeleton is incomplete, as, for example, in Groote Eylandt (see below), where Aborigines took a long time to decide how to deal with the return of a skeleton whose skull had been 'mislaid' by the missionary who had originally stolen the remains.

Practices regarding the dead have changed dramatically over time. In Britain as elsewhere, there has often been a chasm between the emotions and beliefs held by the majority of the population about their own dead, and the lack of emotions and apparently different beliefs held by scientists about the dead of *others*. It is perhaps not surprising that archaeologists, until it was brought to their attention in recent years, did not take seriously the accusations of grave-robbing directed against them. Among British scientists, respect for the dead in their own churchyards is a comparatively modern phenomenon, let alone respect for the dead of societies whose living populations are unfamiliar to them.

In a study of grave-robbing in England, Richardson (1987) describes the grotesque behaviour of anatomists and surgeons who, from the 17th century until the enactment of the 1832 Anatomy Act, dug up the bodies of the poor –

whose graves were the easiest to get at – for dissection in the medical schools of Britain. In the early 19th century:

> Corpses were bought and sold, they were touted, priced, haggled over, negotiated for, discussed in terms of supply and demand, delivered, imported, exported, transported. Human bodies were compressed into boxes, packed in sawdust, packed in hay, trussed up in sacks, roped up like hams, sewn in canvas, packed in cases, casks, barrels, crates and hampers; salted, pickled or injected with preservative. They were carried in carts and waggons, in barrows and steam-boats; manhandled, damaged in transit, and hidden under loads of vegetables. They were stored in cellars and on quays. Human bodies were dismembered and sold in pieces, or measured and sold by the inch.
>
> (Richardson 1987, p.72)

This practice was in no way condoned or approved of by the rest of the population. Richardson describes the grief and anguish which resulted from the discovery that a member of the family had been illegally exhumed and carted away to be cut up on the slab. The revulsion of the public to this practice grew stronger, and this revulsion was not, at least by the 1830s, restricted only to cases in which the identity of the body was known. In 1832, for example, it was discovered that an anatomy school in Aberdeen was reburying mangled bodies and pieces of chopped-up bodies in the grounds of the school. Angry rioters burnt the building to the ground, and carried off the corpses.

> Burial of remains without funeral or rite in the earth of the school's backyard constituted a cavalier disregard of publicly recognised norms.
>
> (Richardson 1987, p.92)

By this time even some anatomists and surgeons were beginning to feel uneasy about the practice of body-snatching. The Select Committee on Anatomy produced a *Report* in 1828 (Richardson 1987, p.121) whose guidelines, in parts, show an uncanny resemblance to more contemporary documents on the treatment of human remains. The *Report* (1828) states that if it is important:

> to the feelings of the community that the remains of friends and relations should rest undisturbed, that object can only be effected by giving up for dissection [others], in order to preserve the remainder from disturbance. Exhumation is condemned as seizing its objects indiscriminately [and] in consequence, exciting apprehension in the minds of the whole community . . . bodies ought to be selected . . who have either no known relations whose feelings would be outraged, or such only as, by not claiming the body, would evince indifference on the subject of dissection.
>
> (Richardson 1987, p. 122)

It followed from the *Report*, in practice, that bodies that were 'unclaimed' within a certain time after death could be 'given up, under proper regulations, to the anatomist' (*Report* 1828). The 1832 Anatomy Act, which resulted from this *Report*, is still in force to this day.

Given such a recent history of disregard for our own dead, our lack of regard for the dead of others is not, perhaps, so surprising. Only 150 or so years ago the bodies of people whose relatives or friends were too poor to bury them in deep and secure graves were unceremoniously dug up and sold by the thousands. In the 100 years following the Anatomy Act of 1832 over 50,000 bodies of the poor who had died in institutions ended up on the dissection table, often against the wishes of their kin, who were themselves too poor to give them a proper burial, and thus were forced to leave them unclaimed. In this context it is not so difficult to understand how archaeologists and others have felt little compunction in digging up and dismembering the bodies of distant American Indian, Australian Aboriginal or Sámi strangers. In Britain there is no consistent pattern of beliefs and attitudes towards the treatment of human remains. McGuire (Ch. 11, this volume) describes similarly contradictory attitudes regarding human remains in a white American town. In other European countries there are equally conflicting values existing within relatively homogeneous cultures.

In Hallstatt, Austria, the Swedish osteologist Sjøvold (1987) found attitudes to skeletal remains somewhat contradictory. Between 1973 and 1980 he made a number of visits to Hallstatt to solve some 'anthropological questions by means of a very unique collection of decorated and named skulls' (Sjøvold 1987, p.5). The practice of decorating skulls in this way was apparently common in the Eastern Alps during the 18th and 19th century, but at the turn of the last century 'many priests seem to have considered the practice . . . detestable, and most collections were reburied during that time and even during this century, often in connection with some kind of funeral service' (Sjøvold 1987, p.6). When Sjøvold began his work at Hallstatt he expected the descendants in the village to show animosity to the idea of a foreigner studying the skulls of their past relatives, but found that his question about this was 'in some way being considered as completely irrelevant'. Equally, tourists were encouraged to view the skulls. The villagers themselves hardly ever visited the bone house, although they frequently visited the grave in the churchyard, and tended the graves meticulously, showing apparent reverence for these, even though many of the bodies in them were presumably without their skulls. The practice of decorating skulls, which had died out in the 1960s, has apparently been resumed with the hiring, in 1980, of a new grave-digger who is also 'an artist'.

## Grave-'robbing'

Accusations that archaeologists are grave-robbers continue to be made, for burials are still disturbed and desecrated, though archaeologists throughout the world are becoming more aware of the responsibility they have towards the people whose sacred places, including burial sites, yield such rich archaeological material (see also Zimmerman, ch. 16, this volume).

Grave-robbing is not confined to archaeologists and people who come from other cultures. There is ample evidence that whenever there are grave goods people have tried to rob them, and this also happened in prehistoric Europe and ancient Egyptian times. There is evidence to suggest that those fortune hunters who plundered and desecrated were from the same culture, even, perhaps from the same society. The same seems to have been true of some North American Indian societies (Mathur 1972, Zimmerman, ch. 16, this volume). Mathur writes that the Iroquois, in the 18th century, had been so corrupted by the coming of the Europeans that they also 'looted the graves for the wampum which had become hard to obtain' (Mathur 1972, p.89). Archaeologists and museum curators can, and do to some extent, turn around the accusations of grave-robbing, claiming that their controlled and careful excavation and curation of human remains and grave goods is far preferable to the haphazard plundering of treasure-hunters. The tombs of Egypt have been looted and destroyed over the centuries, and no amount of protection has kept their contents safe. Archaeologists are also often involved in 'rescue' excavations, retrieving remains and grave goods before sites are destroyed by natural or man-made invasions. Even their critics consider this essential, but the conflict then arises in regard to the redisposition of the human remains.

## The reburial issue in the USA

Many American Indians (of different groups) are clear in their demands regarding the human remains of their ancestors. They intend to retrieve all Indian human remains from the museums, laboratories, and university departments throughout the world, to rebury them and thus to bring peace to the ancestors. Jan Hammil (now Jan Hammil-Bear Shield), a Mescalero Apache Indian, and Director of the American Indians Against Desecration (AIAD), and Robert Cruz, a Tohono O'odham Indian of the International Indian Treaty Council, have presented the viewpoint of AIAD elsewhere in this volume (ch. 14). AIAD has already had some considerable success. Many remains, albeit only a minute proportion of all those that exist in collections all over the world, have already been reburied with due ceremony. AIAD also opposes excavation of all burial sites, and where this is necessary in the face of redevelopment of the land, insists on the return of the skeletal remains to the Indian communities concerned. Cecil Antone, a Pima Indian from Phoenix, Arizona, representing the Sacaton community, visited museums in England, where he saw the remains of his ancestors lying on a shelf:

The other day I saw one of my tribe in a museum here in your country. I said to myself, why is my ancestor here, what is he doing here? They don't belong here, this is foreign to them, they belong at home. His spirit is wandering out there, wandering out there in a limbo state, because he is not familiar with the country. He remembers when he was small, his life, the happy times he had, and the land – his land. I thought about it at night, when I heard about the list of all the tribes that are in this country – it's over half the Indian nation in our country. Every tribe is in this country, just about . . . this person from my tribe – he was probably sold three or four different times. How can a civilisation, mankind, sell human beings? These people were once human beings – how can you sell them? It hurts, it hurts real bad . . .

He suggests that archaeology is:

a profession that has been established by the dominant society in our area . . . They understand the past – but we *know* the past.

He condemns archaeologists for exploiting the American Indians for the advancement of scientific theory:

For some time the American Indian and his ancestors have been exploited by archaeologists in order to provide the scientific world with a new theory or idea of evolution. It has been an issue which the archaeologists have maintained is the justification for the storage and study of Indian human remains. The rationale is that new techniques are being developed to further improve their studies to a degree that will be useful in one way or another. Is every bone viewed as scientific even if it has been excavated within 50 years? The answer is probably 'yes'. As an American Indian I feel that the study of our ancestors is unjust and degrading. Religious beliefs and opinions are sidestepped. No living man on earth has the power to infringe on an individual who has been laid to rest, or even keep his or her bones stored in a box for eternity.

However, Antone does not condemn all archaeological research:

I see some good in archaeology, it has brought some history to our people, but there is one facet of archaeology that our Indian people . . . do not agree with . . . the Indian people believe that when a person is laid to rest he should not be bothered at all. He has done his work in this world and he is going to another world to go back to the mother earth where we all came from . . . if he is disturbed he is out there, wandering, his spirit is not fully with the mother earth . . .

He also cites an instance in which archaeologists working with Colorado River Indians on a cave site on BLM land were instrumental in the preservation and even renewing of oral history:

Some of the earliest traditional songs relating to that site were somewhat lost, by the Mojave people, but when the BLM and the contracting archaeologists did their work there with the tribe . . . they came across earlier songs they had got in the museum. They taped them and presented them to the elders and the elders started remembering. It started coming back to them. They started singing, and somehow, the tribe got involved in trying to recoup those old songs that had been lost. If it had not been for archaeology, those songs would have been lost. The elders would not have picked up some of those songs if they had not gotten about them from the project. What happened was, the songs were sung and then they were translated into English, what this cave meant to the Mojave people.

Without archaeology, he says, these songs would have been lost.

Robert Cruz also condemns those archaeologists who excavate Indian remains:

I am angry that they disturb [the graves] and express to us their own values when they don't consult with Indian people about what they will do, and I am angry at the lies they create to divide our people, the Indian people. I am angry at the exploitation and the degradation that they bring on to Indian people by disturbing and desecrating sacred Indian burials and ceremonial sites, and stealing, robbing us of our traditional culture. I am angry at them because they have hurt so many people, they've caused so much pain and so much suffering, and it's like they are working hand in hand with the devil.

His concern is not only for the spirits of the ancestors, who must live in a limbo, unable to rest until they are returned to the earth, but also for the effect the digging up of the ancestors has on the natural world:

[We must] take care of the mother earth, take care of the spiritual world, and no digging up of ancestral graves and sacred sites and bulldozing cemeteries and digging up the liver of mother earth, the veins, the rivers of mother earth . . . the natural world is what we would like to preserve for our future generations, we would like them to see what we see today, where they can enjoy seeing their brothers, their clan relatives, the eagles, the crows, the buzzards, the rattlesnakes and those animals, those human beings – the sonora fruit cactus – the various cacti and trees who through the burials have grown up into trees and into cactus, and they are with us too in that form, and we want our relations to be with us in whatever form they are.

He blames many of the misfortunes that have befallen the Indians on the disturbance of the ancestors:

We want to get rid of the sicknesses, we want to get rid of the unhappy land . . . that is the result of digging up and leaving empty the homes of

the ancestors. From the empty homes, that is where the sickness comes
. . . the unhappiness; that is how our children are killed, that is how we
lose them, because we have disturbed and desecrated those areas where
we had our ancestors' homes. Those are their homes, and we should
allow them to stay where they were left . . .

In February 1987, at the Arizona Inter Tribal Council in Phoenix, Robert Cruz
told the meeting that after a large ceremonial reburial of skeletal remains near
Sells in Arizona:

The ancestors came back, and said that they were very happy to be released from their prisons – the museums were their prisons.

This idea that museums are prisons for the ancestors led Robert Cruz into trying to discover what it was like to be imprisoned in this way. He began to visit
Death Row in an American gaol, talking to inmates in order to discover how
the ancestors must feel when they are condemned to the prisons of museum
boxes and shelves.

Ernest Turner, a member of the Athabascan Tribe from Alaska, was distressed to see skulls on display in the Smithsonian Institution, in Washington,
D.C.:

It is not respectful to the people . . . I was horrified, I had no idea that
they had that in the museum . . . I was shocked that that was happening.

On the other hand, he also relates (ch. 13, this volume) how he informed the
Aleut community that their dead ancestors were on display, and received a non-
committal response. This is indicative of the range of current attitudes even
among the native peoples of North America.

The views of American archaeologists towards display and reburial also vary,
and range from total support of AIAD to total opposition to reburial of any
human material in the possession of museums or university departments. The
position taken by the American Committee for Preservation of Archaeological
Collections (ACPAC) is one of the most extreme. In their *Newsletter* (November
1986) they exhort:

Archaeologists, your profession is on the line. Now is the time to dig
deep and help ACPAC with its expenses for legal fees. Next year or next
month will be too late; we have to act immediately to fight this issue.
This one will be resolved in court, not by the press. We will be able to
cross-examine Indians on their tribal affinities, religion, and connection
to the archaeological remains they seek to destroy. We will be able to
challenge anti-science laws based on race and religion. We can make a
strong case, but it takes money. Send some!

Cecil Antone also criticizes any legislation which is based on the proof of affinity
with human remains, but for quite opposite reasons:

If the legislation  . . says that reburial can happen *if* you claim affinity to the person being excavated, my perception of affinity is totally different, I guess. Even the archaeologists that know about the Southwest cannot define the differentiation between O'odham and us, the Pimas, that we are descendants of the Hohokam. We don't need education or scientific values to determine that – we already know. It is obsolete, in my perspective, yet still they want us to go through this legislation process, claiming affinity, or kinship, to our people.

The Society for American Archaeology, the Society of Professional Archaeologists and many other regional, professional and 'interested' groups have debated the issue and come up with their own guidelines and decisions. The arguments put forward by many archaeologists in North America and elsewhere for the preservation of at least some skeletal remains for present and future research are, from an archaeological or physical anthropological point of view, overwhelming. On the other hand, the arguments presented by indigenous populations whose ancestors are the skeletal remains in questions, are equally overwhelming.

Is there a way out of the dilemma faced by scientists who respect the wishes of the indigenous peoples (who request the return of their ancestors), but still wish to contine to be able to obtain the kinds of data that can only be obtained from human skeletal remains? Many of the States in the USA have set up consultative bodies with local Indian communities to discuss ways that research can continue, with reburial as the eventual outcome and several have introduced legislation (see also ch. 16). There are many different problems, and different strategies must be worked out for each. In some cases the collections already exist in museums or departments, in other cases human remains are currently being unearthed by road, bridge or building projects; some human remains in collections are provenanced, others are not; some are clearly 'ancient', other comparatively more recent; some have been obtained dishonourably, other by relatively honourable means, and so on.

Indian pressure has recently succeeded in obtaining promises to remove many public displays of Indian remains. Among those who have made these promises is Dr Robert McC. Adams, Secretary of the Smithsonian Institution in Washington. In correspondence with the Smithsonian, Jan Hammil-Bear Shield, for the AIAD, has written (pers. comm., 6 February, 1987):

> We request that the Smithsonian remove the display of Indian bodies . . .
> We suggest you consider that any empty room would be of greater educational value, combined with a notice stating the following:
>
> > The remains of the American Indians previously on exhibit have been removed from public display by the Smithsonian in co-operation and out of respect for traditional religious beliefs, practices, and customs of the American Indian. Current efforts to replace the exhibit include a co-ordinated effort with American Indians to develop a future display which would better meet the objectives of the Smithsonian.

In England, the Pitt Rivers Museum in Oxford has already removed all Indian remains from display, and has produced a list of Indian material held there, as a basis for discussion with representatives of AIAD. Within the context of ambiguous legislation regarding the treatment of human remains (see also Moore, ch. 15, this volume), Tom King, one of the small band of American archaeologists who has supported the Indians' claims to their skeletal remains, and Director of the Office of Cultural Resource Preservation of the Advisory Council on Historical Preservation, has produced draft guidelines (King n.d.) for the consideration of traditional cultural values in historic preservation. This was sent out as a discussion draft mainly to Indian organizations and Federal agencies, and comments from both groups were largely favourable. In summary, the draft stated that human remains should be treated with due respect for the wishes of the dead individuals that they represent, and thus left undisturbed whenever possible. Human remains may have deep emotional significance for their genetic and cultural descendants, and are often the object of religious veneration. Thus any activity that may infringe on their constitutionally protected free exercise of religion must be 'planned with great care'. On the other hand, King recognizes the fact that human remains often have substantial scientific value in archaeological research, in physical, social and cultural anthropology, in genetics and in medical research. Because it is not possible to predict future research questions, or future research methods, King is worried that scientists tend to seek to retain human remains in laboratory settings 'in perpetuity'.

Conflict is therefore virtually inevitable. King proposes that the proper treatment of human remains can be achieved by consultation, or justification of any scientific study, and by adequate funding for prompt work and for reburial of remains in a dignified manner 'consistent with the cultural traditions of the deceased and their genetic or cultural descendants'. The draft lays down specific guidelines to scientists. Briefly these are:

1. that human remains should not be disinterred unless this is necessary because of the danger of destruction as the result of land disturbance, erosion, vandalism or similar phenomena,

2. that even in cases where scientists do not need to disinter for research purposes, all remains should be recovered if threatened, and

3. disinterred remains should be reburied after consultation with descendants and their spiritual leaders. Before reburial any justified scientific study should be carried out, with a definite and reasonable schedule drawn up for study and reinterment.

The draft document leaves much room for manoeuvre. On the one hand, it states that wide-scale autopsy-type examinations should not be carried out if there is no need for them (whatever that might mean), if genetic or cultural descendants feel strongly that they should not. On the other hand, it says that there may be instances where the interests of science may override the wishes of the dead, and of their descendants. In some cases a compromise may be reached whereby remains are reinterred in such a way that they can be disinterred later if necessary. The precise arrangements for study and reinterment should, King suggests, be worked out 'through consultation between project sponsors, American Indian communities, or other genetic and/or cultural descendants, and anthropologists or others having research interests in human remains' (King n.d.).

In its April 1987 *Newsletter,* the Society of Professional Archaeologists (SOPA) puts forward a very similar set of guidelines (Niquette 1987). Both sets of guidelines will go some way towards easing the current situation, by recognizing the necessity for consultation with American Indian representatives of, as SOPA suggests: 'those tribes and groups that occupy or previously occupied the lands in which the deceased lay' or have 'biological or cultural relations with the deceased'. However, the onus would still be on the Indians concerned to prove these conditions, and consultation does not necessarily lead to agreement, not least because, unless there is a pan-Indian attitude to reburial, there could be an inherent tendency to dispute between the current occupiers of the land, and any previous occupants. Much less acceptable to Indian groups, though, is the statement in the SOPA guidelines, that 'as a rule' those human remains and associated artefacts that have demonstrated 'extreme significance in contemporary or predictable future research' may be 'retained for analysis in perpetuity'. This applies to all human material over 50 years old. Such a recommendation leaves little room for 'consultation', and to some extent makes a mockery of the rest of the recommendations since, in the last analysis, it denies the fundamental right of the Indian people to rebury certain remains – even some people who might have been buried within living memory. It is to be hoped that the overriding interests of the scientist in this clause could be counteracted by the final clause, which stages, again 'as a rule', that if human remains and associated artefacts are of extreme 'cultural or religious significance' then they should be 'reinterred without analysis'. The SOPA guidelines, which have been distributed mainly to archaeologists, that is, a rather different audience from King's, have generally received a somewhat negative reaction.

Thus the conflict remains, though the influence that Indians now wield in the treatment and disposition of the remains of their ancestors is increasing. This would not be true, however, if the Society for American Archaeology (SAA)'s (1986) approach, as laid out in its *Statement Concerning the Treatment of Human Remains* in May 1986, were adopted:

> Archaeologists are committed to understanding and communicating the richness of the cultural heritage of humanity, and they acknowledge and respect the diversity of beliefs about, and interests in, the past and its material remains.
>
> It is the ethical responsibility of archaeologists 'to advocate and to aid in the conservation of archaeological data', as specified in the Bylaws of the Society for American Archaeology. Mortuary evidence is an integral part of the archaeological record of past culture and behaviour in that it informs directly upon social structure and organization and, less directly, upon aspects of religion and ideology. Human remains, as an integral part of the mortuary record, provide unique information about demography, diet, disease, and genetic relationships among human groups. Research in

archaeology, bioarchaeology, biological anthropology, and medicine depends upon responsible scholars having collections of human remains available both for replicative research and research that addresses new questions or employs new analytical techniques.

There is great diversity in cultural religious values concerning the treatment of human remains. Individuals and cultural groups have legitimate concerns derived from cultural and religious beliefs about the treatment and disposition of remains of their ancestors or members that may conflict with legitimate scientific interests in those remains. The concerns of different cultures, as presented by their designated representatives and leaders, must be recognized and respected.

The Society for American Archaeology recognizes both scientific and traditional interests in human remains. Human skeletal materials must at all times be treated with dignity and respect. Commercial exploitation of ancient human remains is abhorrent. Whatever their ultimate disposition, all [sic] human remains should receive appropriate scientific study, should be responsibly and carefully conserved, and should be accessible only for legitimate scientific or educational purposes.

The Society for American Archaeology opposes universal or indiscriminate reburial of human remains, either from ongoing excavations or from extant collections. Conflicting claims concerning the proper treatment and disposition of particular human remains must be resolved on a case-by-case basis through consideration of the scientific importance of the material, the cultural religious values of the interested individuals or groups, and the strength of their relationship to the remains in question.

The scientific importance of particular human remains should be determined by their potential to aid in present and future research, and this depends on professional judgements concerning the degree of their physical and contextual integrity. The weight accorded any claim made by an individual or group concerning particular human remains should depend upon the strength of their demonstrated biological or cultural affinity with the remains in question. If remains can be identified as those of a known individual from whom specific biological descendants can be traced, the disposition of those remains, including possible reburial, should be determined by the closest living relatives.

The Society for American Archaeology encourages close and effective communications between scholars engaged in the study of human remains and the communities that may have biological or cultural affinities to those remains. Because vandalism and looting threaten the record of the human past, including human remains, the protection of this record necessitates co-operation between archaeologists and others who share that goal.

Because controversies involving the treatment of human remains cannot properly be resolved nation-wide in a uniform way, the Society opposes any Federal legislation that seeks to impose a uniform standard for determining the disposition of all human remains.

Recognizing the diversity of potential legal interests in the material record of the human past, archaeologists have a professional responsibility to seek to ensure that laws governing that record are consistent with the objecives, principles, and formal statements of the Society for American Archaeology.

What makes this SAA document all the more remarkable is that it was issued just a few days after the American Indians Against Desecration had addressed some 1000 archaeologists at the SAA Plenary Session on the reburial of Indian remains. In that address, AIAD expressed its frustration in its dealings with professional archaeologists by describing how much easier it had been to discuss the issues, and find an acceptable compromise, with the US Air Force and with the US Forest Service, than it had been, and still was, with archaeologists.

The unsympathetic stance taken by the SAA has already been opposed by some American archaeologists, notably Tom King and Larry Zimmerman (see *World Archaeological Bulletin* No.2, 1988, and Zimmerman, chs 4 & 16, this volume).

The SAA statement specifically opposes any Federal legislation that seeks to impose a uniform standard for determining the disposition of all human remains. However, in January 1987, Melcher (1987), in introducing his bill to the Senate, stated:

Mr President, most of us know where our ancestors are buried, where their remains reside, where we have placed them ‘with some respect and dignity. But there are a great number of native Americans and perhaps native Hawaiians who do not know where their ancestors' remains are placed.

Mr President, there are scores of museums in the United States and abroad. There are several universities, Mr President, that have the remains of native Americans in skeletal form on display or just their bones collected in boxes without the consent of the families or the tribes. In addition to that, there are numerous artefacts of sacred nature to tribes of native Americans that are in museums without the consent of the tribes. There are religious artefacts of a sacred nature to various tribes. To correct that, Mr President, I am introducing this bill, S. 187, which is the same bill that I introduced on the last day of the last Congress. I introduced it at that time in order to provide an opportunity for its consideration by various museums, various groups of people, various tribes and clans, and families of native Americans and native Hawaiians.

The response we have had to the bill during the past 2 or 3 months since adjournment has been very much on the positive side. The bill will set up a system of repatriation, and that means just as it sounds, the return of the remains of these people taken from their native grounds and returned now with some dignity to the tribes or the clans or the families of native Americans and native Hawaiians, where they properly can be given respect and be cared for by the people.

In addition, the same will be true of the sacred offerings. The bill sets up a system for figuring out whose bones are stored in the Smithsonian. Right now there are scores of boxes, literally hundreds of boxes of native Americans' bones stored in the Smithsonian in its attics and nooks and crannies. The religious objects and the remains of these native Americans will be identified. Then a system is set up within the bill to return them and the respect will be paid.

I think the bill is absolutely essential. I think it is a shame on our country, on our people as whole, that we have not corrected this problem. I believe respect is due, dignity is due and now is the time to do it. That is the purpose of the introduction of this bill.

The Melcher Bill drew immediate response from Jane Buikstra, Chair of the Committee to Promote Scientific Study of Human Remains, in a memo to professional colleagues, in which she says that her committee believes the Bill to be a 'serious threat to physical anthropology'. She writes:

In addition to this Bill, Senator Inouye (Hawaii) has drafted proposed legislation that has two provisions: (1) the Smithsonian would have five years to survey its collections and to return all tribally affiliated remains to the tribes and (2) the remainder of the North American collection would then be buried in the mall with a suitable monument erected.

(Buikstra 1987, p.2)

The memo urges archaeologists to write to Senators, Representatives, and members of the Senate Select Committee on Indian Affairs. It offers a sample letter, which suggests that the Bill 'provides for rights to native peoples that others in this country do not enjoy' – a strange statement to be made in the context of a system that, when white and Indian bodies are unearthed, arranges for immediate reburial of the white bodies in consecrated ground, and sends the Indian bodies to the museum to be labelled, shelved and used for research purposes. In fact the Melcher Bill, and Inouye's proposed legislation, now appear to be moribund.

The kind of discriminatory practice (see McGuire, ch.11, this volume) regularly carried out when Indian and non-Indian burials are excavated is forgotten by those who dismiss the Indians' request for the return of their ancestors as a purely political gesture, as opposed to being a cultural or religious statement, but the conflict *is*, fundamentally, one of beliefs. It is not unusual for differences in cultural beliefs to develop into political issues, especially when the cultural groups concerned are the oppressors and the oppressed, the colonial majority and the indigenous minority.

In the United States some Indian groups which had previously not been aware of the dispersal of their ancestral remains all over the world, or, more important, had not conceived the implications of this to their religious beliefs, are now requesting the return of their ancestors. Because this is a comparatively recent phenomenon some archaeologists protest that the current concern with the spirits of the dead is not a real or valid one, and is merely an attempt not to get left behind by the political 'bandwagon' of the moment.

In February 1987 I visited Arizona, and discussed the reburial issue with Tohono O'odham, Pima, Navaho, and Hopi communities, and attended a meeting of the Arizona Inter Tribal Council in Phoenix. From these discussions it was quite clear that the reburial issue is very much alive, not only among politicized Indian groups, but also among those living in scattered villages and on reservations. The strength of the belief in the need for the ancestors to be in the earth was undeniable, and existed quite apart from the overall reburial issue, which was, in some cases, quite new to them.

Maria Garcia Dominges, a Tohono O'odham elder, living just across the border in Mexico, said:

Archaeologists must stop digging our ancestors up. Give back what you have taken; you have not had permission from us. To the whole world I say: stop digging things up, for it shows no respect for the dead. Bones turn to dust, and that is what should happen.

At a meeting with Elders in Old Oraibi on the Second Mesa the message was also clear. They want not only all their remains to be returned, but also their cultural objects. They asked for a list to be sent to them of all Hopi remains and objects held in English museums.

Larry Anderson, on behalf of the Chairman of the Navaho Nation, gave a message specifically to be published:

We would welcome statements on the preservation of artefacts and regarding human remains and their return to the reservations for reburials. We would be very interested in the appointment of Navaho Council members for checking any directive of action to be taken by the World Archaeological Congress for Tribal Councils, for Elders' Councils and other Indian Councils. There should be no display of human skeletal material in museums.

At the Arizona Inter Tribal Council meeting in Pheonix, attended by representatives of all the tribal groups in the State, there was long discussion about the reburial issue, and much talk about 'angry spirits' and the intransigence of archaeologists and museum curators. There was very great concern for the unburied ancestors, and yet another reason was given as to why the bones had to be returned:

Bones should become dust. Mother earth lacks these bodies; if they are not returned there will be earthquakes and mother earth will take all these people.

Robert Cruz described the big reburial the Tohono O'odham had held in the mountains near Sells. This was the first reburial ceremony they had held, and none of them really knew what would happen or what they should do, even the medicine woman who was in charge of it. Cruz said that they began to sing as they buried the bodies, and found that the long forgotten words came to them as they sang. The actual ceremony had drawn hundreds of people, young and old, and since then, the young men had taken it upon themselves to take care of the site, to protect it from strangers and from harm: 'every day the young men run there to see that no one takes [the ancestors] away'. Although the reburial was the first among the Tohono O'odham it was an occasion of immense spiritual significance.

More skeletal material has been reburied in other Indian communities. In at least one case the museum curators and archaeologists who offered to return quantities of material to an Indian community were surprised and angry that the Indians did not take them at once, and interpreted this as evidence that the Indians do not really want their bones back. In fact the community concerned needed time to decide what to do with the bones until they could be reburied, and had to wait until the medicine woman said that it was the right time to take them back. Problems are arising because the whole situation is a new one, both to those who are trying to concede to the Indians' requests, and to the Indians themselves.

Also cited as evidence against the strength of the Indians' beliefs is the fact that some Indians do take part in excavations, even of their own burial grounds. Edmo (1972) reports that young Bannock and Shoshone Indians from the reservation at Fort Hall have been trained, under the direction of skilled archaeologists, to excavate their own sites:

> At the project's outset, there was some justifiable complaint that the activity was contrary to Indian religion and tradition. Had it been yet another exploitation of Indians in the name of anthropology, the project would have collapsed there and then. Instead, under Indian direction [Edmo's] the project became a means of acquainting Indians with the universal skills of exploration into prehistory.
>
> (Edmo 1972, p.14)

In other areas, Indians have worked on excavations with archaeologists, and a few are now trained archaeologists themselves, who must face the almost inevitable dilemma that is inherent in their dual role (see also Bielawski, ch.18, this volume). Cecil Antone points out (and there is evidence that other Indian groups support him) that American Indians and archaeologists in fact:

> have the same concern for cultural preservation and the need for stricter legislation to guard against vandalism, looting, and desecration of archaeological sites. It is basically a matter of understanding and working

together. If this does not occur the battle will continue until the American Indians are satisfied.

Archaeologists and American Indians, at least in some areas, may have begun to work together, but on other fronts the battle continues unabated. In April 1988 American Indians living in northern California lost their case in the Supreme Court to prevent the US Forest Service from building a road through the forest at Chimney Rock, a sacred area where some 5000 Indians go to communicate with the "great Creator" and to carry out rituals essential to the welfare of their people. According to a newspaper report (*Independent* 21.4.88.):

> Now the Supreme Court has ruled . . . that the Indians have no right under the Constitution's freedom of religion clause in the First Amendment to prevent the US Forest Service building a road through Chimney Rock and their sacred grounds. Justice Sandra Day O'Connor wrote for the majority of the nine judges that the Constitution provided no protection against 'the incidental effects of government programmes', even if those programmes gravely disrupt religious practices. 'Government simply could not operate if it were required to satisfy every citizen's religious needs and desires.'

## The reburial issue in Australia

In Australia, the concern for the treatment of Aboriginal skeletal remains has come into the public eye chiefly through the spate of books and films about Tasmania, especially about Truganini, the so-called 'last Tasmanian'. Archaeologists in Australia, however, have been confronting the problem for many years. The Australian Aborigines have actively opposed the excavation of sacred sites, including burial sites, and the display and storage of Aboriginal skeletal remains in museums and university departments in Australia and elsewhere, and any research on their human remains. As in America, there remains the conflict between the interest of those scientists who consider Aboriginal skeletal remains to be of great scientific significance, and the interests of the indigenous population, whose relatives and ancestors constitute these skeletal remains. For the Aborigines, the significance of the skeletal remains of their ancestors is complex. Traditionally, as with the American Indians and Europeans, the dead are disposed of in a variety of different ways and with a wide range of complexity of ritual and ceremony. That these dead should be left undisturbed is as important as it is for those Aborigines who are buried in Christian cemeteries, as many are. In addition, these remains are often significant to Aborigines because they have become symbolic of European oppression and callous practices in the past, as they have with American Indians.

There are huge collections of Aboriginal material in museums, some acquired through archeological work, others by less acceptable means. Many of the 'last Tasmanians' buried in a Christian cemetery in Tasmania underwent horrific treatment after they were dug up, before becoming the 'Crowther Collection', now returned to the Aboriginal community for disposal (see Richardson, ch.12, this volume).

The history of Truganini's remains, possibly the most famous bones in the world, is of particular interest. In 1974, Australian scientists on the Specialist Advisory Committee for Prehistory and Human Biology of the Australian Institute of Aboriginal Studies (AIAS) agreed that the Director of the Tasmanian Museum should be informed that the Institute recommended that Truganini's remains should be disposed of immediately in accordance with her own wishes or those of her descendants (a public acknowledgement that she had not been the 'last of the Tasmanians'). Any suggestion that her remains should be housed in a mausoleum especially designed to enable future research was rejected. It is important to note that this historic recommendation reversed the previous stance of only a few years earlier, and in many cases it was the same scientists who had now altered their opinions. The AIAS considered this to be of such importance that it requested the Minister for Aboriginal Affairs to report the issue to the Prime Minister. Nevertheless the Institute's decision had the following explanatory qualification:

> It was felt that the case of Truganini, a known  historical person, is an exceptional one and that the moral issue involved overrides any other consideration.
>
> (Ucko 1975, p.7)

In the light of this advice, as well as Federal-State political pressure, the Tasmanian State government agreed to cooperate with representatives of the Tasmanian Aboriginal Information Centre in burying her in a final and secure grave. Given the history of the treatment of Truganini's corpse, such an arrangement was not enough. It is reported that Truganini herself had lived in fear of her body being exploited after death by those who would wish to study or sell it; she is said to have favoured cremation to avoid such abuses. Only one day after her death in May 1876 the Secretary of the Royal Society of Tasmania requested her body as a valuable scientific specimen. This request was refused and Truganini was buried privately a few days later. Two years later she was sent for study to Melbourne, then to England, and in 1904 back again to Melbourne. She was on public display in the Tasmanian Museum until 1947 when she was placed in the museum vaults, available only to scientists.

In 1974, after the pressure from AIAS scientists and, more important, the Aboriginal community, whose existence had been recognized in Tasmania only since 1972, the Tasmanian cabinet agreed that Truganini should be cremated. Museum objections were overruled, and the skeleton was taken into Crown custody. Truganini was cremated on 30 April 1976 and her ashes scattered in the D'Entresateaux Channel the next day.

As recently as 1987 Ida West, a Tasmanian Aborigine wrote:

One night while watching television I saw a Legal Aid person for my people talking to someone about what Europeans did to Aborigines, cutting off their heads and so on. He pulled out a drawer filled with Aboriginal heads all shapes and sizes, and the sight of the skulls started to turn my stomach. The second drawer was full also. By the third drawer I felt faint. The Legal Aid person said, 'Would you like to have your grandfather's head in there?'

(West 1987, pp.1–2)

In 1984, in response to growing protest from Aborigines, and corresponding unease among many archaeologists and anthropologists, the Government of the State of Victoria amended their Archaeological and Aboriginal Relics Preservation Act (1972). Meehan, expressing the fears of the scientific community, wrote:

At one stage it seemed likely that once all Aboriginal skeletal remains had been transferred to the Museum of Victoria, which was deemed to be the only institution entitled to house them, they would be handed over to the Victorian Aboriginal community for reburial thus bringing to a halt all research into the biological history of the Australian Aboriginal population based on Victorian material. It also seemed that this transfer and subsequent reburial would happen very quickly. A few months after the Victorian Government had passed the amendments to their 1972 Act, the Tasmanian Government had announced that it too was preparing to transfer all Aboriginal remains held in the Tasmanian Museum and Art Gallery and the Queen Victoria Museum at Launceston to the Tasmanian Aboriginal community to dispose of as they saw fit. It was understood that the Tasmanian remains would probably be cremated.

(Meehan 1984, p.122)

The Australian Archaeological Association (AAA) responded to this situation by forming a committee to produce a working document outlining the nature and extent of the scientific importance of all Aboriginal skeletal remains. The resulting document continued to stress the vital importance to research of Aboriginal skeletal remains, and although supporting the reburial of the remains of known individuals, reiterated the AAA's position that no other skeletal remains should be destroyed by burial or cremation. This stance was very much in line with the 1984 resolution of the Society for American Archaeology, and of the Canadian Association for Physical Anthropology in 1982. The AAA document stressed the importance of consultation with Aboriginal communities, of training programmes for Aborigines in museum curatorship and the setting up of Aboriginal Keeping Places, where Aborigines could keep and care for their own skeletal remains, with, again, the training and employment of Aborigines to work in them.

The Australian strategy appears to be to encourage Aborigines to become part of the system, to offer them 'control' over their own skeletal remains, but only – at least in the case of 'unknown' remains – in so far as they are able to accept the overall control of a system that does not allow for the return of these remains to Aboriginal communities for reburial. In Kakadu Park, for example, Aborigines were drawn into the system by being employed as wardens and site recorders. This strategy has also been used by uranium companies, who have employed Aborigines in an attempt to deflect and defuse Aboriginal opposition to mining of their land. In 1986, in spite of the events of recent years, the skeletal sub-committee of the Australian Archaeological Association reported on the continuing lack of communication between relevant groups, and it then set up a programme of consultation and liaison with those Aboriginal communities who had a direct interest in the Murray Black collection, which contains over 1800 individuals. Steven Webb, a physical anthropologist with a distinguished record of research in this field, was appointed to carry out the task.

Webb made his own difficult situation clear in his final report on his year of liaison:

> With widespread Aboriginal support for reburial of all Aboriginal skeletal remains held in museums, there was fear among the scientific community that this would mean the irretrievable loss of unique scientific data. This loss would not only affect the present generation but those, both black and white, in the future. The emphasis of the consultation, therefore, was to try and explain to people at the community level the value of preserving such remains. Their immediate scientific value had to be emphasised together with the long term benefits of such study for the local Aboriginal community and all Aboriginal people. My policy was to recognise the right of the Aboriginal people to have a say in what happened to such remains and to actively help them formulate ways in which they could achieve custodianship of them and gain recognition of their rights in this regard. As a biological anthropologist this was difficult to do, because it meant accepting destruction of the remains by reburial if Aboriginal people wished it. Moreover, I assured people that if they did not want me to study their skeletal remains I could not do so even if the weight of the law was behind me. This was a difficult decision to make also, but one which I felt was necessary if any common ground for discussion was to be reached.
>
> (Webb 1987a, pp.5–6)

Elsewhere he wrote:

> After listening to why people did not want research to continue, I could find no scientific argument to balance or equate with their moral one. It is difficult to argue against the rights of any group of people to choose what should and should not happen to their skeletal remains.
>
> (Webb 1987b, p.293)

However, he also wrote:

> Talks during repeated visits over many months have convinced me that
> many Aboriginal people do not necessarily want to see the skeletal
> collections destroyed by reburial. Individually they see why research is
> deemed important, and many agree that it is valuable to them.
>
> (Webb 1987b, p.295)

And he concluded that:

> it might be appropriate for skeletal biologists who use recent skeletal
> populations to reappraise their working philosophy and temper their
> overwhelming enthusiasm for the search for their particular kind of
> knowledge, with the feelings and aspirations of all peoples who feel their
> ancestral skeletal remains should be protected from scientific scrutiny.
>
> (Webb 1987b, p.296)

The AIAS has faced the existence of Aboriginal opposition to the excavation
of burial sites, and to research on Aboriginal skeletal material for longer than
most organizations and departments in Australia. For example, the excavation
of the Broadbeach Aboriginal burial ground in Queensland was carried out at a
time when there was no legislation to protect Aboriginal 'relics' (1965 to 1968).
According to Haglund, the archaeologist in charge of the excavation, 'the
existence of an Aboriginal burial group here was not known to local Aborigines
. . . The bones of Aborigines along with the soil around them were spread over
gardens on the Gold coast to fertilise the soil' (Haglund 1976a, p.xi). However,
the report of the excavation was not published for many years because: 'It
seemed that a book like this might be offensive to members of the local
Aboriginal community'. It was eventually published, not by the AIAS but by
the University of Queensland Press (Haglund 1976a). In her thesis, also on this
excavation, Haglund wrote:

> one  . .. aspect must be mentioned: the reaction of the Aborigines to this
> activity. When archaeological work was small scale and intermittent it
> was hardly noticed by them. What we may call a sudden flowering, is to
> some of them a sudden lush growth of alien weeds.
>
> (Haglund 1976b, p.9)

It is particularly important to note that the human remains excavated at the
Broadbeach burial ground, which Haglund specifically points out was unknown
to local Aborigines, have now been successfully claimed back by the
Kombumerri people of the Gold Coast:

> As a result of recent negotiations between the Kombumerri people and
> the University of Queensland, ownership of the Broadbeach skeletal
> remains previously held by the university, was returned to the
> Kombumerri people.

The Kombumerri claim to the material is based on a demonstration of descent from the population who buried their dead at Broadbeach between ca. AD 700 and AD 1860. Furthermore, they argued that two decades should have been sufficient for 'science' to get the material recorded and analysed in detail. Since AAA's policy is that Aboriginal groups who can demonstrate descent from such skeletal material can reasonably claim ownership over those skeletons, little effort was made by AAA to argue against the transfer of ownership. The collection is currently housed in the Anatomy Department of Queensland University and will remain there until the Kombumerri rebury their ancestors in land being purchased at present from the local Council. Given the international importance of the collection to science, it was suggested repeatedly to the Kombumerri that reinterment might not be in their own best long term interests. However, they remain firm in their decision to bury the collection.

(Hall 1986, pp. 142–3)

The apparent contradiction in this statement, i.e. that the Australian Archaeological Association (AAA) did not argue against transfer of ownership, but did suggest 'repeatedly' that reinterment might not be in the Kombumerri's best interest, may in fact be an attempt to reach a satisfactory compromise between Aborigines and archaeologists. If Aborigines' ownership of human remains is accepted, then discussion and co-operation can follow regarding the future of the material.

As early as 1976 the AIAS had taken the initiative in returning a skeleton to an Aboriginal community (Ucko 1977). The skeleton (minus the skull, which could not be traced), was that of an Aborigine from Groote Eylandt, Peter Maminyamanja, who had died in 1931 and whose skeleton had been removed by missionaries and found in a Melbourne garage. The skeleton was returned by the AIAS to relatives in Groote Eylandt (see above). Mortuary rituals were carried out and the skeleton was placed for final disposal in a rock shelter on Winchelsea Island.

Ten years later the AIAS has now produced a draft Policy Statement on Aboriginal Human Remains (AIAS 1987). This acknowledges that Aboriginal skeletal material is 'a significant and important part of the Aboriginal heritage', and that this significance dictates that the Aboriginal community must play an active role in decisions concerning this material 'whether in situ or in collections'. Because of past 'unethical or insensitive treatment of Aboriginal skeletal remains . . . and past lack of consultation' the situation is seen as one of 'great sensitivity'. The draft Policy Statement recognizes the extreme importance of Aboriginal skeletal remains as a source of information in a wide range of different fields of research, and also that the management of this material is a matter of relevance to Australian society as a whole'. It stresses the 'multi-faceted significance of the material: Aboriginal, scientific and/or public' and asserts that:

Management of skeletal material will rest on the determination of its significance, through the process of assessment. Most of the material will have more than one value, and proper management will rely on balancing these values.

(AIAS 1987)

The Draft Policy Statement advocates that Aborigines should be involved in management decisions regarding newly discovered material, material in museums and about the future management and disposition of material. It also advocates the setting up of Keeping Places under Aboriginal custodianship while still 'allowing for and encouraging appropriate research by black and white scholars'. With regard to *in situ* material it states:

> *In situ* material should not be removed or disturbed except where there is no other practical option, or where there is a compelling research reason for doing so, and where this research is carried out with the agreement of, or at the request of the Aboriginal community. Mechanisms should be developed to prevent accidental or unnecessary disturbance or removal . . .

The document also lays down guidelines for procedures and consultations.

Archaeologists in Australia can only hope that Aboriginal communities will see the 'compelling' nature of archaeological research, and indeed some communities have requested research to be done, and some Aborigines are now actively involved in archaeology. As Mulvaney writes:

> Aboriginal people are sensitive to archaeological investigations involving human remains. Archaeologists, however, can derive vital clues to ancient ritual life and cognitive systems and so increase Aboriginal knowledge concerning their spiritual life and increase general community respect for Aboriginal society. Material proof of the continuity of spiritual values and ritual practices could become invaluable 'deeds' to land title. For the increasing number of Aboriginal children being educated in the general Australian community, and lacking direct contact with traditional communities, such evidence provides invaluable documentation of their cultural heritage.

(Mulvaney 1986, p.54)

Haglund, however, writes:

> It has been suggested that the study of prehistory is for the sake of the Aborigines to give them a past to be proud of. Traditional Aborigines do not need this . . . they have . . . knowledge as shaped by tradition.

(Haglund 1976b, p.55)

There are, however, specific circumstances in which Aborigines can, and do, quote the archaeological evidence in relation to their prior rights to land, that is in advancing Land Rights cases in the white courts, or in confrontations with Ministers. Aborigines know that the land is theirs, and that their own existence and the existence of the land are inextricably bound together in the Dreamtime. The fact that their bones are found in the earth dating back some 40,000 years may be irrelevant to them, but they realize that it is important evidence to those people whose concept of history is based on a linear system of chronology (see also *Archaeological Review from Cambridge,* Spring 1987, Layton 1989). It is also of no relevance to Aborigines who identify their past with the creation of the land, that scientists claim that some of the early fossil humans found in Australia may not be the same sub-species as Aborigines. As Haglund says:

> Some archaeologists have seized on the physical differences in early skeletal remains and suggest that the Aborigines should take a different attitude to their study. But to most Aborigines this would be meaningless sophistry. The land has been here since the Dreamtime. Human bones are the remains of their ancestors, the landscape itself the remains of ancestral beings and creators.
>
> (Haglund 1976b, p.55)

This is in fact another fundamental issue in the current debate regarding claims to human remains, i.e. fossil versus non-fossil remains. The former are, according to our scientific lights, often not members of the group we call *Homo sapiens sapiens.* Many archaeologists and physical anthropologists who might come to terms with the dilemma as to who should have the final say regarding the appropriate disposition of 'recent' human remains, do not consider that any living population can legitimately lay claim to fossil remains. It is, perhaps, significant that Webb (1987b) generally refers to recent skeletal remains, although he did state that: 'Aboriginal people want recognition that they are the living descendants of any Aboriginal skeletal remains' (1987b, p.295).

## The future

As Aborigines find some use for archaeologists, and come to terms with what appear to be conflicting perceptions, so, perhaps, will archaeologists acknowledge the significance of Aboriginal religious beliefs. There have already been instances in which American Indians have allowed some scientific tests to be made on skeletal material before reburial. In Australia, the concept of Keeping Places presumably includes the possibility of human remains being available for research, with the agreement of the Aborigines concerned. Among the Inuit, according to Bielawski (ch. 18, this volume), this may be difficult since the Inuit start with the idea that archaeologists primarily come in order to take objects or remains to make money from them. However, Bielawski also writes, with reference to archaeological approaches to Inuit culture:

In partnership with those of a cultural tradition totally different from western science, archaeologists may explore new possibilities for finding truth. These may lie somewhere between archaeology and Inuit perceptions of the past.

However, this does not provide a solution to the practical problem of what is to be done when there is a clash between those who seek scientific data and those whose ancestors will be disturbed if the data is to be forthcoming.

In Scandinavia there is a growing awareness, on both sides, of the conflict of interest between scientists and the indigenous population. In Sweden, for example, a document produced in 1983 by the Riksantikvarieämbetet and the Statens Historiska Museer stresses the *scientific* importance of human remains. It does refer to one occasion in Northern Sweden in which local Sámi pressure led to some human remains being reburied without being fully studied, but apart from that there is very little reference to the Sámi population whose past relatives presumably make up much of the skeletal material being excavated by archaeologists. The document says that whereas in the past there may have been religious reasons for not disturbing the dead, in connection with beliefs in the resurrection of the body, nowadays these are of little relevance. The authors conclude that apart from very recent burials, scientists should have access to human remains and that reburials should not be considered. If, however, remains do have to be reburied, it is suggested that this should be done in such a way that it is possible to dig them up again at some later date (Riksantikvarieämbetet 1983). The fact that there has been no revision of these guidelines since 1983 suggests that, in Sweden at least, the Sámi people have not yet succeeded in gaining control of their own past, and that archaeologists, physical anthropologists, and osteologists are still laying prior claim to the human remains of the Sámi people. It is ironic, perhaps, that when it was discovered that the skull of the 18th-century Swedish scientist, Emanuel Swedenborg, had been stolen from his sarcophagus in Uppsala Cathedral and replaced by another, there was an outcry, and in 1978, when the genuine skull turned up at an auction house in England, the Royal Academy of Science in Sweden claimed it in order to reentomb it in its 'rightful place' with the rest of Swedenborg's remains in his sarcophagus at Uppsala.

Bahn (1984, 1986) suggests that the conflicts are intensifying in various parts of the world, and not only in relation to relatively recent human remains:

The question of whether archaeologists should be allowed to excavate and study the dead refuses to go away - if anything, it is growing in intensity as already vociferous opponents increase their muscle and achieve some success in preventing excavation or in retrieving material from the hands of scholars.

This summer saw developments in several different areas. In Israel, for example, an important archaeological site at Tel Haror in the Negev Desert was vandalised in August, most probably by members of Atra

Kadisha, an ultra-orthodox group dedicated to preserving the sanctity of Jewish cemeteries. The site, which dates to the 8th century, is believed by the local Bedouin to be the tomb of a pupil of Mohammed, and the archaeologists in charge of the dig claim that the graves encountered so far have been positively identified as Turkish and Bedouin, dating only to the First World War. Nevertheless, ultra-orthodox Jews that think the graves are 'likely to be Jewish' warn that future excavation will cause a huge public outcry.

(Bahn 1986, p.58)

The conflict between 'scientific' and cultural values is epitomized in situations where it is the archaeologists themselves who are the ones who hold cultural or religious beliefs that are incompatible with certain archaeological practices.

One archaeologist who found himself in a particularly difficult situation is Jo Mangi, from Papua New Guinea (and see ch. 17, this volume):

I am an archaeologist by training, I am also a Kondika by birth and by initiation . . . I wear two hats . . . I am an archaeologist and an indigenous native. As an archaeologist . . . a scientist who is concerned with learning about the past I would argue that we can learn a lot from examining and exhuming from burials. We can learn about aspects such as general burial practices, mortuary goods, social structure, population composition, technology and presence of diseases. As an archaeologist I acknowledge the potential for enlarging our knowledge of the past by studying burials. Also as an archaeologist I would like to put forward a proposal for research for some student in [England]: 'Indicators of social hierarchies from burials' – not from burial goods but from something that can be found on individuals: tooth fillings . . . Let me ask anyone here in [England] if they can tell me what the reception of the local population would be. Now, let us use our imagination – something that archaeologists are renowned for . . .

He stressed that our knowledge of the past is not objective fact, but interpretation:

Archaeologists say that the past belongs to all people . . . this is the area of dilemma. If I, as an archaeologist, in my background, am supposed to be a custodian of the past as so many archaeologists have claimed, one must also understand that I have to interpret the past, and I interpret the past *as I see it* . . . it has become self-evident that we achaeologists of the world *do not see eye to eye*.

Mangi suggests that much useful work can be done without removing skeletal material from burial sites:

I see no reason why . . . humans – as I call them, you may call them scientific samples – should be kept in cardboard boxes. Let us be very honest – I went through the list of what we can learn about (human remains) on site, the context of [them] – that is half of it done.

As a subject of research, rather than as an archaeologist he says, with some bitterness:

There was a journal called *Archaeology and Physical Anthropology in Oceania* which was started . . . in the 1960s. That journal came to an end because they could not sort out my race – Melanesian – they could not sort it out, not with physical anthropology, nor with biological anthropology, and now someone is going to tell me that you are going to keep me in cardboard boxes so that when the time is ripe and technology is developed, you are going to place me into something – I'm sorry . . . it is human beings . . . my mother and my people . . .

His dilemma is acute, for he also believes that archaeological evidence is crucial for the future of Papua New Guinea as a nation.

Bongasu Tanla Kishani, linguist and philosopher from the Cameroon (see also ch.8, this volume), expressed much the same conflict as Jo Mangi. With regard to the excavation of burial and other sacred sites he said:

You still need to educate the people because it is an area where culture is still very lively, very strong, and the people are attached to their sacred places. If someone comes to dig, unless you have educated the people they may tend not to accept [it].

When asked how he felt about it himself he said:

If there was a means of getting information by just getting a small tool and putting it into the earth and getting that information I would be for the idea of letting it remain intact – that is my personal reaction.

African archaeologists have, up until now, seldom had to face the 'reburial issue', though many believe it to be inevitable in the near future, and are asking for guidelines to follow (see Hubert 1988, p. 36). In Zimbabwe problems have already arisen; it is reported that an official of the Museum Service ordered the immediate cessation of the excavation of a burial site, on the grounds that it was disturbing the Shona spirits (pers. comm., P. Sinclair). In other contexts in Africa there remains a conflict between the desire by African nationals to take over archaeology and incorporate it into contemporary life, and the wish to challenge it, at least in part, as a practice hostile to traditional beliefs and practices.

An archaeologist from the Philippines, Florante Henson, paints a bleak picture of the relationship between archaeologists and minority groups in his country:

> Archaeological sites should be the domain of the National Government, and whatever ethnic group may live in an area I think they should give [their sites] to the National Government for what we might call patrimony . . . in principle we have the power to override disagreement . . .

He adds that although the government has the right in principle to the sites, an effort is made to reach a compromise with the local people.

Henson would only have qualms about excavating burials that the descendants do not want disturbed if they really are known kin:

> If these people really are their ancestors – parents, grandparents or great-grandparents – then I would have some qualms about it, but if they cannot prove that – I mean, their original legends are not reliable sources.

In some cases, he says:

> some small groups . . . hunters and gatherers . . . sometimes part-time horticulturalists, sometimes living in caves . . . are co-operating with the National Museum, and in fact they point to the burials of their ancestors and even help in the excavation of . . . the graves of their grandmothers.

Archaeological sites are protected by law but:

> [the law] is very hard to implement, because even the people, the police and the army are violating the law [by] excavating.

Only the Muslim separatist groups have so far avoided having their burial sites excavated by archaeologists because 'we do not want to antagonise the Muslims'. Other minorities or ethnic groups are less fortunate.

The reburial issue is sometimes considered to be merely a political one, but it has immense cultural and ritual significance in many cultures. Archaeologists will not help themselves by hiding their heads in the sand, or by trying to belittle the passion of those whom some see as 'the opposition'. In an attempt to preserve their rights to dig up, or retain the human remains of others, some archaeologists stress the diversity of past practices of Indians, or Aborigines, with regard to the disposition of the dead. They claim that some cultures did not place much importance on the remains themselves, and they try to legislate so that the onus of biological proof is placed on the living cultural and genetic descendants (despite the fact that they were often forcibly dispersed by the dominant group). Such archaeologists are failing to come to grips with existing realities. It may indeed by true that some of the current American Indian and Aboriginal concerns about leaving the skeleton undisturbed in the earth do not derive only from traditional beliefs and practices, anymore than does the contemporary British concern with graveyards and floral displays on graves. But the emotions that are produced by the desecration of current beliefs are no less genuine for this reason. Archaeologists and anthropologists should have given up long ago the idea that cultures, and cultural traditions, are static and unchanging.

Similarly, they should not assume that ways of treating the dead which in their own culture would be considered disrespectful would necessarily be considered so in other cultures. The forms that respect for the dead take may be quite different in different cultures. The ancestors may be revered but their bones may not be left undisturbed. In Madagascar, for example, the Merina occasionally dance with their dead:

> The Merina do not consider tombs as important because they contain specific people but because they contain undifferentiated, and often ground-up together, people; this is produced, quite literally, as a result of the dancing with corpses . . . in the *famadihana* [funeral ceremonies].
>
> (Bloch 1981, p.141)

Dancing with the dead, whether skeleton or cadaver, is also reported among the Western Iroquois (Mathur 1972). She quotes 18th-century sources regarding the Feast of the Dead, in which the dead were dug up and reburied in secondary burial pits, being washed, reclothed, and remourned before (in some cases) being carried lovingly many miles to a new location. Mathur suggests that the great love shown by the Iroquois for their dead kin 'must be contrasted with the treatment of these same remains by non-Indians' (Mathur 1972, p.94).

## Conclusion

In most parts of the world where opposition to the desecration of burials is strengthening as, for example, amongst the Maori of New Zealand (O'Regan 1989), as well as the demands for the return of human remains for reburial, the basis for these are the *current* cultural beliefs of the living populations. These beliefs may be rooted in ancient tradition, or be of comparatively recent origin. Similarly, cultural practices are continually changing and may develop with or without concomitant changes in beliefs, merely expressing old beliefs in new ways.

Although it is not possible to totally disentangle them, there are two distinct bases for opposition to the disturbance of the dead. The first, which most of the foregoing discussion has been about, are the beliefs, attitudes and emotions of living descendants regarding their ancestors. The second are the wishes and intentions of the dead themselves.

Obviously, in the first instance, the descendants believe themselves to be acting in the best interests of the ancestors, as, for example, those American Indians who want to rescue the souls of the dead from limbo and lay them to rest. However, this is only voiced in terms of their own current religious beliefs.

There are some people, however, who take a more extreme position regarding the disturbance of the dead. They take the view not that it is their own beliefs that are being ignored, but the beliefs of the dead themselves, and that it is the wishes of those who are buried that must prevail. For them there is no real hope of compromise. For example, in ancient Egypt it is quite clear what people intended for their bodies after death. Despite the enormous complexity of ancient Egyptian beliefs and practices, which themselves varied and changed over time, there are certain aspects of direct relevance to this issue. Budge stated:

> the physical body of a man was called KHAT, a word which indicated something in which decay is inherent; it was this which was buried in the tomb after mummification, and its preservation from destruction of every kind was the object of all amulets, magical ceremonies, prayers, and formulae, from the earliest to the latest times.
>
> (Budge 1899, p. 163)

It was part of ancient Egyptian belief that human beings contained various essences, and that these survived after physical death, and were active in various ways. The physical body was intended 'never to leave the tomb', never to 'rise' – but despite this, and despite the fact that it was known that, after death and mummification, bodies often rotted, or were plundered and destroyed, nevertheless 'the Egyptians never ceased to take every possible precaution to preserve the body intact', and thus to preserve the relationship between body and spirit.

For those who believe that it is the wishes of the deceased which should be paramount in considering the legitimacy of archaeological activity, there is a clear message to be learnt from Frankfort's summary of ancient Egyptian belief:

> A man's body rested in the tomb, and the Egyptians could not abstract the survival of man's immortal parts from the continued existence of his body . . . So, while they admitted that man suffered physical death and nevertheless survived, they could not imagine such a survival without a physical substratum. Man without a body seemed incomplete and ineffectual. He required his body in perpetuity . . . hence the development of mummification and the elaborate measures against tomb robbers . . .
>
> (Frankfort 1948, pp.92–3)

There is little doubt what the attitude of the ancient Egyptians would have been to the dispersal of their bodies in the museums of the world. There is clear evidence not only that they wished their bodies to remain undisturbed, but also that they should be buried in their own country, in their own tombs. The Story of Sinuhe (c.1960 BC) describes Sinuhe's overwhelming desire to return from Asia to his own country to die and to be buried in his pyramid on the banks of the Nile. Even the King exhorts him to return:

> You shall not die abroad! Nor shall Asiatics inter you. Think of your corpse – come back!

In spite of this it is almost inconceivable that museums will ever return or rebury the ancient Egyptian mummies that they have, let alone the funerary equipment which delights and informs the public who visit the museums of the world. Not totally inconceivable, perhaps, because attitudes and beliefs do change over time, but it is highly unlikely that any living group will ever successfully lay claim to what have become some of the most famous museum pieces in the world.

If the demand for the return of human remains for redisposition is not to be based on the last intentions or wishes of the dead themselves, where then is the battle line to be drawn? Should it be drawn at all? To what extent should the religious beliefs of a cultural group be picked over and dissected so that outsiders can find some acceptable reason, or justification, for the way that group behaves?

Some scientists and social scientists claim that the quest for knowledge is of paramount importance, and that truth belongs in the public domain. Yet our society does set limits when it comes to our own individual privacy. Only recently, in England, legislation was brought in which limits intrusion into our private lives by outsiders whose quest for knowledge and truth, in other spheres, may go unchallenged. There *are* areas of life that are considered sacrosanct, and which are not infringed by those who accept the validity of the boundary lines. With regard to cultures such as those of the American Indians or Australian Aborigines, perhaps the belief in the continuing presence of the ancestors, and in the necessity for their spirits to be at rest (see also Zimmerman 1987), could also be designated a domain free from the threat of invasion. Only when archaeologists no longer dispute that indigenous peoples have prior rights to the remains of their ancestors, will they be in a moral position to negotiate about the possibility of access to the material for future research. Both archaeologists and indigenous peoples would then be in a position to recognize their genuine common interest in the preservation and protection of the evidence of the past.

## Acknowledgements

I would like to thank Kathy Emmott, Kate Saull, and Ann Wise of the Archaeology and Education team of the Department of Archaeology, University of Southampton, for their help with interviews during the Congress. I am also grateful to Peter Stone for his comments on an earlier draft, to Brian Molyneaux for his comments on this draft, and to Peter Ucko for his advice and comments at all stages.

Part of this chapter was published under the title, 'The Disposition of the Dead' in the *World Archaeological Bulletin*, No.2, 1988, pp. 12–39.

**Note**

1   Unattributed quotations in the text are either from interviews taped during the week of the World Archaeological Congress in Southampton in September 1986, from an evening meeting held by the American Indian and Papua New Guinean participants, or from meetings held in Arizona in February 1987.

**References**

ACAP 1986 *Newsletter*. California: American Committee for Preservation of Archaeological Collections.

AIAS 1987. Aboriginal human remains: policy statement. In *The Aboriginal community liaison program carried out in the Murray Valley and Tasmania*, S. Webb, Appendix 7. Canberra: Australian National University.

*Archaeological Review from Cambridge* 1987. Time and archaeology. **6** (1).

Bahn, P. 1984. Do not disturb? Archaeology and the rights of the dead. *Oxford Journal of Archaeology* **3**(1), 127–39.

Bahn, P. 1986. Skeletons in the cupboard. *New Scientist*, 13 November, 58.

Bielawski, E. 1989. Dual perceptions of the past: archaeology and Inuit culture. In *Conflict in the archaeology of living traditions*, R. Layton (ed.), ch. 18. London: Unwin Hyman.

Bloch, M. 1981. Tombs and states. In *Mortality and immortality: the anthropology and archaeology of death*, S. C. Humphreys & H. King (eds), 137–47. London: Academic Press.

Budge, E. A. Wallis 1899. *Egyptian religion: Egyptian ideas of the future life*. London: Routledge & Kegan Paul. (Reprinted 1980.)

Buikstra, J. 1987. *Memo to AAPA membership*. Chicago.

Chippindale, C. 1987. Editorial. *Antiquity* **61** (232), 163–8.

Edmo, J. 1972. The Bannock-Shoshone project. In *The American Indian reader: anthropology*, J. Henry (ed.), 170–4. San Francisco: Indian Historian Press.

Frankfort, H. 1948. *Ancient Egyptian religion: an interpretation*. New York: Harper Torchbooks.

Haglund, L. 1976a. *The Broadbeach Aboriginal burial ground: an archaeological analysis*. Queensland: University of Queensland Press.

Haglund, L. 1976b. *Disposal of the dead among Australian Aborigines: archaeological data and interpretation*. Sweden: Institute of Archaeology at the University of Stockholm.

Hall, J. 1986. President's report. *Australian Archaeology* **22** (June), 140–5.

Hammil, J. & R. Cruz 1989. Statement of American Indians against desecration before the World Archaeological Congress. In *Conflict in the archaeology of living traditions*, R. Layton (ed.), ch. 14. London: Unwin Hyman.

Hubert, J. 1988. The desposition of the dead. *World Archaeological Bulletin* **2**, 12–39.

King, T. n.d. *Guidelines for consideration of traditional cultural values in historic preservation review*. Washington.

Kishani, B. T. 1989. The role of language in African perceptions of the past: an appraisal of African language policies and practices. In *Conflict in the archaeology of living traditions*, R. Layton (ed.), ch. 8. London: Unwin Hyman.

Layton, R. 1989. Introduction. In *Who needs the past?*, R. Layton (ed.). London: Unwin Hyman.

McGuire, R. H. 1989. The sanctity of the grave: White concepts and American Indian burials. In *Conflict in the archaeology of living traditions*, R. Layton (ed.), ch. 11. London: Unwin Hyman.

Mangi, J. 1989. The role of archaeology in nation building. In *Conflict in the archaeology of living traditions*, R. Layton (ed.), ch. 17. London: Unwin Hyman.

Mathur, M. F. 1972. Death, burial and mourning among the Western Iroquios. In *The American Indian reader: anthropology*, J. Henry (ed.), 87–95. San Francisco: Indian Historian Press.

Meehan, B. 1984. Aboriginal skeletal remains. *Australian Archaeology* **19** (December), 122–3.

Melcher, Senator 1987. A bill to provide for the protection of Native American rights for the remains of their dead and sacred artifacts and for the creation of Native American cultural museums: to the Select Committee on Indian Affairs. *Congressional Record*. Washington DC: Senate.

Moore, S. 1989. Federal Indian burial policy: historical anachronism or contemporary reality? In *Conflict in the archaeology of living traditions*, R. Layton (ed.), ch. 15. Unwin Hyman.

Mulvaney, J. 1986. Wentworth lecture. *Australian Aboriginal Studies* **2**, 48–56.

Niquette, C. M. 1987. A proposed SOPA policy on treatment of human remains. *Society of Professional Archaeologists, Newsletter* **11**(4), 1–2.

O'Regan, S. 1989. The Maori control of the Maori heritage. In *The politics of the past*. P. Gathercole & D. Lowenthal (eds), ch. 7. London: Unwin Hyman.

Rahtz, P. 1985. *Invitation to archaeology*. Oxford: Basil Blackwell.

Rahtz, P. 1988. The president's piece: archaeology and the dead. *British Archaeological News* **3**(4), 33.

Richardson, L. 1989. The acquisition, storage and handling of Aboriginal skeletal remains in museums: an indigenous perspective. In *Conflict in the archaeology of living traditions*, R. Layton (ed.), ch. 12. London: Unwin Hyman.

Richardson, R. 1987. *Death, dissection, and the destitute*. London: Routledge & Kegan Paul.

Riksantikvarieämbetet och Statens Historiska Museer 1983. *Omhändertagande, Förvaring och Återbegravning av Forntida och Medeltida Skelettmaterlal*. Stockholm.

Sjøvold, T. 1987. Decorated skulls from Hallstatt, Austria: the development of a research project. In *Theoretical approaches to artefacts, settlement and society*, G. Burenhult, A. Carlsson, A. Hyenstrand & T. Sjøvold (eds), 5–22. Oxford: BAR International Series 366.

Society for American Archaeology 1986. Statement concerning the treatment of human relations. *Bulletin* **4**(3), 7–8.

Turner, E. 1989. The souls of my dead brothers. In *Conflict in the archaeology of living traditions*, R. Layton (ed.), ch. 13. London: Unwin Hyman.

Ucko, P. J. 1975. Review of AIAS activities, 1974. *AIAS Newsletter* **3**, 6–17.

Ucko, P. J. 1977. Review of AIAS activities, 1976. *AIAS Newsletter* **7**, 6–24.

Webb, S. 1987. *The Aboriginal community liaison program carried out in the Murray Valley and Tasmania*. Canberra: Australian National University.

Webb, S. 1987b. Reburying Australian skeletons. *Antiquity* **61**(232), 292–6.

West, I. 1987. *Pride against prejudice: reminiscences of a Tasmanian Aborigine*. Canberra: Australian Institute of Aboriginal Studies.

Zimmerman, L. J. 1987. The impact of the concepts of time and past on the concept of archaeology: some lessons from the reburial issue. *Archaeological Review from Cambridge* **6**(1), 42–50.

Zimmerman, L. J. 1989a. Made radical by my own: an archaeologist learns to accept reburial. In *Conflict in the archaeology of living traditions*, R. Layton (ed.), ch. 4. London: Unwin Hyman.

Zimmerman, L. J. 1989b. Human bones as symbols of power: aboriginal American belief systems toward bones and grave-robbing archaeologists. In *Conflict in the archaeology of living traditions*, R. Layton (ed.), ch. 16. London: Unwin Hyman.

# 11  *The sanctity of the grave: White concepts and American Indian burials*

RANDALL H. McGUIRE

For the past four years I have been conducting research on mortuary customs, death rituals, forms of memorialization, and beliefs about death in Binghamton, New York. As an archaeologist, my focus on these studies has been on the material aspects of death in upstate New York, particularly gravestones and cemeteries. During the same time period, I have also been involved in a more traditional archaeological, mortuary study – the analysis of grave lots associated with over 250 Hohokam cremations from the site of La Ciudad in Phoenix, Arizona. This second pursuit has directly embroiled me in the controversies surrounding the disturbance, the disposition, and the interpretation of Indian burials.

My research on Binghamton mortuary customs has proceeded in a fashion very different from my research on the Hohokam. My students and I have gone into the cemeteries of Binghamton, not with spades, trowels, and screens, but with pencils, clipboards, and cameras. In the cemeteries we took extreme care not to disturb graves or monuments in any way. At La Ciudad we used standard archaeological techniques of excavation to expose, record, and collect the cremations. Whereas our study in Binghamton left no marks on the graves, the excavation of the La Ciudad cremations left no trace of the cremations.

It could be argued that the differences in method between the two projects solely result from the nature of the data in each case. If I had not excavated at La Ciudad I could not have studied Hohokam burials, because there was no surface evidence of their existence and we have no written records to describe them. Furthermore, the burials at La Ciudad lay in the path of a motorway interchange and would have been destroyed if they had not been excavated.

I do, however, have questions about the cemeteries in Binghamton that can only be answered through excavation. The cemeteries, expecially those dating to the 19th century, contain many unmarked graves. Contrary to our initial expectation, no cemeteries of this age had complete detailed records identifying the individuals buried in the cemetery. Nor do we know if the patterns of the changing investment that we see in the memorials is the same for the caskets in the ground. This information is not obtainable from funeral home records, because such records rarely survive from the 19th century. If we had broken ground in a Binghamton cemetery we would have been quickly ejected from the cemetery and faced the probability of criminal prosecution.

The citizens of Binghamton have received my study with interest and approval. I have given talks on the gravestone project to public school teachers, students, churches, and civic groups, and have become a regular on the breakfast and lunch club circuit.

The O'odham (Pima) Indians of southern Arizona have had a much more negative reaction to my research at La Ciudad. O'odhams working on the excavation crew alternated between being excited and fascinated by the exposure to their ancestors' homes and irrigation works to stony silence, visible discomfort, and emotional distress when burials were excavated. The Inter-tribal Council of Arizona protested our excavations and laid out a series of demands, including one that the burials – both bones and artefacts – be returned to the O'odham when our work was complete, that Indian observers be present on our site during the excavation and that our final reports be submitted to the O'odham as well as to a panel of archaeologists for review.

When I talk to the people of Binghamton about cemeteries and burials they uniformly support the sanctity of the grave. Repeatedly they state that once in the ground a burial is to be undisturbed and a burial plot maintained in perpetuity. They are unaware of how frequently graves are moved or disturbed. Often when I mention some instance of a white grave being disturbed, a cemetery being abandoned or destroyed, they react in surprise that such activities are, in fact, legal.

Paradoxically, these same people do not object to the excavation and display of ancient burials, even when they are European in origin. They also accept without question the routine excavation and curation of Indian graves which they equate with the ancient graves regardless of the age of the Indian burials. Such inconsistencies led me to ask why ancient graves should not be accorded the sanctity of the grave, and more importantly why should Indian graves so automatically be classified as ancient?

To answer this question, we need to know how the sanctity of the grave is respected in practice and why some graves are violated and others are not. Two cases where Binghamton cemeteries were removed to allow for economic development suggest that the sanctity of the grave has been differentially respected depending on class and race. An understanding of why popular opinion accepts these deviations from the commonly held norm requires a historical consideration of how the modern American ideologies regarding both graves and Indian people developed.

## Cemetery removal in Broome County

Cemetery abandonments are far more common in Broome County, New York than most of its citizens realize. All of the churches established in the first half of the 19th century had graveyards adjacent or near to them. All but three such churchyard cemeteries were removed to accommodate church expansion or economic development. Many early historic cemeteries lacked or lost permanent markers and these have been disturbed by construction projects, especially road building. Some unmarked cemeteries, such as the Broome

County poor farm cemetery and the Binghamton Psychiatric Center cemetery, included hundreds of individuals. Finally construction activities and farming occasionally destroy scattered, small, family cemeteries.

## The Christ Episcopal Church graveyard

The Christ Episcopal Church, in downtown Binghamton was one of the first churches in the county, and one of the last to remove its graveyard (Miller 1985). The congregation started burying people in the churchyard in 1824. Burials occurred regularly from 1824 to 1869, during which time at least 305 individuals were interred in the churchyard (Christ Church 1818–59, 1859–69, 1869–84). The occupants of the Christ Church yard included several prominent founders of Binghamton.

The church began moving graves from the cemetery as early as 1853 when the vestry paid $29.50 for the removal of bodies to clear space for a new church building (Christ Church 1816–75, June 28, 1853). By the late 19th century the Christ Church cemetery was an anachronism and in the way of the church's activities. Descendants removed many graves to family plots in the newer secular cemeteries in Broome County. The church's location in downtown Binghamton eventually made the land far too valuable to be used as a graveyard. The church slowly dismantled the cemetery, in at least two episodes of removal between 1854 and 1915, including the sale of a portion of the cemetery to the YMCA in 1904 (Binghamton Press 1930c). By 1915 only a remnant of 24 to 30 marked graves dating from 1820 to 1879 remained, and the church initiated efforts to remove these graves (Westcott 1915, Brownlow 1930).

In 1929 the vestry proposed to earn money for the church by renting the cemetery area to a car dealer for use as a parking lot (Christ Church 1914–32, p. 234). In 1930 the church notified the families of individuals in the marked graves about the removal of the cemetery and family members claimed all but four of the graves.

In a series of letters the descendants expressed their concerns (Christ Church 1929). The families raised two issues: would the graves be moved to another appropriate place, and who would pay for it? As long as the graves were moved to an appropriate place and the church paid for it there, no one objected to the removal.

A series of letters dating between 1915 and 1930 from Lewis Morris to church officials suggest that the care followed by the church in the 1930 removal was inspired by Mr Morris' constant attention to the yard. In 1915 he wrote to protest against the removal of all but two of the headstones from the graves, and demanded that the church restore the markers to the graves (Morris 1915). He interpreted the movement of the stones as an attempt by the church to convert the cemetery to a new use without proper reburial of the bodies. Several years later he argued that the bodies could not be ignored if the church built a new rectory, because a Mrs Coerr living in Binghamton had relatives in the cemetery. 'Any desecration of their graves would break her heart' (Morris

1919). Mr Morris also had seven relatives buried in the yard and wrote to the rector, 'I have confidence in you and am trusting you to have the work [reburial] done thoroughly, carefully, and with reverence' (Morris 1925). In 1930 Mr Morris faithfully observed the 11-day process of removal and reburial (Binghamton Press 1930a, c).

The removal of the cemetery attracted a lot of public attention, because the burials included prominent citizens and also because the church was downtown, in the public eye (Binghamton Press 1930a, b, c). Hundreds of people observed the process from the pavement adjacent to the yard (Binghamton Press 1930a).

Only marked graves were moved and no effort was made to locate unmarked graves. The laws of New York, at that time, required removal and reburial of only the marked graves (Schreiner 1929). James Brownlow, then clerk of the vestry, told the local paper, 'All that I am concerned with is the removal of bodies in graves plainly marked' (Binghamton Press 1930b).

## The Broome County poor farm cemetery and the Comfort site

In 1962 construction crews building Interstate 81, north of Binghamton, encountered a large unmarked cemetery which had been associated with the 19th-century Broome County poor farm. The Comfort site, an 18th-century Indian village, and an earlier prehistoric Owasco Phase component was at the same location. Construction activities disturbed both prehistoric and historic Indian graves in the site. The 18th-century village contained Indians from several different tribes, and from 1753 to 1778 Nanticokes occupied the area later disturbed by motorway construction (Elliot 1977, p. 100). There were three episodes of grave removal: 1962–1963, 1969, and 1971–72 corresponding to phases of road construction and construction of a comfort station on the location. No archaeological report has ever been published on this project and my information comes from interviews with individuals involved in the project and the existing field notes (SUNY 1971).

The state contracted with a local undertaker for the removal and immediate reburial of the poor-farm graves. In the case of these indigent unmarked graves the sanctity of the grave was respected in a most cursory manner. With no descendants to insist on correct procedures, a rural location, and barricades to hide the bodies from public view, the cemetery was removed quickly with a minimum of fuss and concern.

When the archaeological laboratory of the State University of New York at Binghamton raised objection to the destruction of archaeological materials in 1971 they were allowed to come in and excavate the Indian graves and other parts of the prehistoric site. The archaeologist in the field decided what was an Indian grave and what was an indigent White grave. The department of transportation would then call the undertaker to get the White graves. The decision seemed to be based primarily on whether there were goods with the graves of obvious Indian origin, the presence or absence of a casket, and the position of the body. The archaeologists excavated at least nine Indian graves, eight prehistoric and one (burial 7) in a coffin and clearly historic (SUNY

1971). Other historic Indian burials were probably removed by the undertaker because they were mistaken for Whites (Elliot pers. comm.). The graves dug up by the archaeologist were put in boxes and curated; they have never been studied.

The treatment of both indigent and Indian graves contrasts markedly with that of Christ's Church, where extreme care was taken to remove the marked graves of middle class and prominent individuals. Even in the case of the Christ Church graveyard it seems that some pressure from a descendant was required to guarantee that the sanctity of the burials was respected. The respect for the sanctity of the grave would appear to be a relatively weak or ambiguous concept in the modern United States which is likely to be set aside for economic or other considerations unless forcefully defended.

These cases suggest several conclusions regarding the nature of contemporary American beliefs about graves. The movement of graves does not appear to be problematic as long as the burials are handled with respect and reinterred in an appropriate place. Marked graves are far more likely to be respected, left alone, or reburied than unmarked graves. Graves are regarded as being primarily of concern to the family of the deceased and of far less importance to the community, church, or state. The justification for respecting graves is based more on a consideration for the feelings of descendants than concern for the spiritual wellbeing or sacredness of the dead. Historic Indian burials have been classified apart from White graves and treated as archaeological (that is ancient) specimens.

Rosen (1980) in a review of US federal and state laws regarding burials found that these laws are structured by the same set of beliefs regarding graves as are evident in the Broome County cases. Rosen argues that because Indian graves are not marked, often perceived as abandoned, seldom in recognized cemeteries, and often difficult to connect to specific descendants, they rarely receive protection under existing laws to protect the sanctity of the grave (see also Hopkins 1973, Talmage 1982, Echo-Hawk 1986).

These same factors work to produce a class bias in the treatment of graves. The graves of the poor were (and are) often unmarked, interred in unkempt (abandoned) cemeteries, and often difficult to connect to specific descendants. In the Broome County cases they were accorded reburial, but not with the same respect or care as middle class individuals.

Relations of power structure the treatment of graves in the United States. These relations are obscured to the general public and to the archaeological community by historically constructed ideologies regarding death and Indians. Beliefs about death define what the concept of the sanctity of the grave entails, and the White notion of the Indian determines how that concept will be applied to Indian graves.

## White attitudes towards burials and Indian people

From the Middle Ages until the present, Western culture has embodied a belief in the sanctity of the grave. At no time has this sanctity been extended to all individuals nor has it entailed prohibitions against moving remains. Through time, however, the reasons for sanctity, the proper treatment of graves, how far into the past sanctity is extended, the sanctions against violation of sanctity, and who is responsible for (concerned with) sanctity has changed greatly (Stannard 1975).

White American attitudes towards Indian people have always originated from a definition of the Indian as an alien (Berkhofer 1978, p. xv, Trigger 1980). Defining Indians as alien placed them outside the usual rights and privileges of society, and lumping them as a singular group denied them an identity except in relationship to Whites.

Whites have attempted to characterize the 'otherness' of Indians in terms of an opposition between the noble savage and the savage savage. Two more basic ideas about American Indians, however, mediate this seemingly incompatible dichotomy. Both of these views see the Indian as a primitive. In Western thought, primitive is a temporal concept that creates otherness by relegating people to an ancient time, regardless of their true historical context (Fabian 1983, p. 18). The coeval existence of the primitive Indian and American civilization has been historically reconciled in the United States by the notion that the Indian was vanishing or had vanished. Regardless of the Indians' character (noble or savage), the assumption of their inevitable demise, either as a race or as cultural groups, became the guiding principle justifying how they were treated (Dippie 1982, pp. xi–xii). The conceptualization of Indians as vanishing (or vanished) primitive others, has combined with changing White attitudes towards burials to justify the denial of sanctity for Indian graves in different ways through time.

## Medieval Christians

The concept of the sanctity of the graves is a very ancient concept in Western thought (Ariès 1974). Early Christians believed that entrance to heaven required a person's body be undisturbed on the Day of Judgment. Only martyred saints were guaranteed entrance to heaven, so medieval Christians sought burial *ad sancto,* that is, burial near the saints. As the saints' graves were often associated with churches, the custom was generalized to burial in the church or churchyard cemetery.

Throughout the medieval period the bodies of the dead were committed to the hands of the church (Ariès 1974, 1985). The rich and the powerful were often laid in ornate sarcophagi which we still see today in the cathedrals of southern England. Most people ended up in the cemetery, but not a cemetery we would recognize. There was no plan to the placement of graves; there were few markers and graves were intruded, one into the other. The gravediggers threw the disturbed bone up on the ground and collected it and stored it in massive charnel houses along either side of the cemetery. In the charnel houses they sorted the bone by type, stacks of skulls, stacks of rib bones, and stacks of leg bones, etc. In some parts of Germany and Italy the remains were artistically displayed with scenes, such as the nativity, constructed from the skeletons and bones (Ariès 1985).

The disturbance and moving of bones within the church grounds extended to all forms of burial. The sarcophagi of the élite were often reused and the skull of the old body left in the box with the new body (Ariès 1985). We might assume that this constant movement of bone violated the sanctity of the grave, but it did not. The medieval Europeans believed that once the bodies had been committed to the church, it did not matter what the church did with them as long as they were kept on the grounds of the church.

Not everyone automatically received the sanctity of the churchyard (Ariès 1985). Only those who had led virtuous lives and were good Christians were entitled to a church burial. Indeed legal procedures existed whereby people's remains could be removed from the cemetery. Such expulsion meant, in the belief of the time, that these individuals would be prevented from entering heaven on the day of judgement. The bones of saved Christians were accorded sanctity, but the bones of sinners and non-Christians were denied sanctity.

In England during the 17th and early 18th century the appearance of individually marked graves located outside the church signalled a radical departure from the medieval pattern (Ariès 1985). Graves were marked so that they would not be accidentally or intentionally violated. Some of the rich forsook the inside of the church for burial in the churchyard. Even within the church the dead began to demand their remains not be violated, as evident in William Shakespeare's 1616 epitaph:

Good frend for Jesus sake forebare to digg the dust enclosed heare.
Blesed be ye man ye spares thes stones and curst be he y moves my bones.

In this time period, sanctity of the grave came to require that the integrity and identity of individual remains be maintained, and markers became important to fulfil these functions.

## Colonial America

Initially the Puritans in America did not use gravestones but, by the middle of the 17th century, they had imported this innovative pattern to New England (Tashjian & Tashjian 1974). Puritan gravestones were an innovative burial practice, different and less conservative than contemporary practices in England or the southern colonies (Ariès 1985), not quaint medieval survivals.

Colonial Americans excluded Indians from the sanctified inviolate grave on the medieval principle. Indians were infidels, they were heathens and therefore they were denied Christian burial and the sanctity of the grave. Europeans could debate the nobility of the Indian, but in the American colonies the Indian others were 'doleful creatures who were the veriest ruines of mankind, which were found on the earth' (Pearce 1965, p. 29). Christian Indians, in theory, gave up their Indianness and were to be treated like Whites, but in reality they were treated little differently to their heathen brethren (Dippie 1982). In the colonial period a definite dichotomy was established between Indian graves and the graves of Whites.

## The new republic

The cemeteries of Broome County appear at the end of the 18th century and vary little from their New England counterparts. Throughout the first half of the 19th century cemeteries were community graveyards, the property of churches or towns. Individuals gained access to the cemetery by virtue of their membership in the town or the church. The graves themselves remained the property of the community and did not pass to private ownership. The community granted families use-rights to the cemetery and the graves clustered in family groupings. Responsibility and concern for the sanctity of the grave was vested in these community groups such as the Christ Church.

The Broome County cemetery of the early 19th century arranged the dead to create the ideal community which the community of the living could never truly obtain. The boundary fence around it separated member from non-member in death, and redefined this relationship to the living. Within the cemetery distinctions existed between husband and wife, adult and child; but not between the familiar units that comprised the community. The inequalities and relations of power within the communities were obscured in death, denying their efficacy among the living by declaring them transitory and fleeing manifestations of this life to be left behind in a better life that waited.

The cemetery expressed the certainty of death and the hope of redemption (Saum 1975). The epitaphs speak of escaping of the troubles of this world to the glories of the next. They also implied that the deceased waited on the 'other side' to be reunited with family and loved one. The willow tree, so prominently displayed on many headstones, was a symbol of death and mourning, but a beautiful and inviting symbol.

The cemetery became a memorial landscape to preserve the memory of individuals as members of a community. Sanctity required not only the preservation of the grave, but also the creation of a landscape suitable for use by the living for contemplation and remembrance. The emphasis on sanctity was subtly shifted from a concern for the spiritual welfare of the dead to a respect for the emotional needs of the living.

In the early 19th century the movement of the frontier west of the Appalachians, and the removal, destruction, or concentration of east coast Indians for the first time created a situation where most White Americans would have little or no first-hand contact with Indians in their lifetime. The American Indian had vanished from the practical experience of most Whites, and the myth of the vanishing Indian appeared to be confirmed in their day-to-day existence (Dippie 1982, pp.12–18). Scholars reinforced the popular conception with a litany of lost tribes and declining numbers (Heckewelder 1876, p.93, Emerson & Forbes 1914, p.23).

Debates concerning the nobility of the Indian moved to American soil and then (as now) the nobility of the savage seemed directly proportional to the distance separating the commentator from day-to-day contact with Indian people. The noble savage, however, could only exist in the untamed wilderness of the west, and as the advance of American civilization transformed the wilderness the primitive had inevitably to perish (Berkhofer 1978, p.89, Dippie 1982, p.28). The Indians who survived the advance of civilization and lived in small concentrations in the east or on the fringe of the frontier were a reality that denied the noble image. Their drunkenness, beggary, and savagery was explained as degradation resulting from their contact with civilization. They were fallen noble savages, unworthy of their heritage (Dippie 1982, pp.25–8).

The romantic sentimentality for graves provided a vehicle for lamenting the passing of the noble Indian. Numerous poets used the setting of the 'old Indian burying ground' to pen requiems for the vanishing race (Freneau 1907, pp.369–70, Bryant 1826, p.17). Once 'abandoned', the Indian burial ground, like the nation itself, became the property of the Whites to be put to beneficial use by the poet or the scholar.

The 18th-century theory of environmentalism held that differences in the natural and social environment produced the diversity of the human species. According to this theory the primitive state of the Indian resulted from the environment of the Western Hemisphere, raising the possibility that the new American republic might ultimately sink to the same state (Gerbi 1973, Berkhofer 1978, pp.42–3, Dippie 1982, pp. 32–4).

Thomas Jefferson (1964) accepted the environmental theory, but attempted to refute the idea that the North American environment created an inferior flora, fauna, and humanity. To help establish this point Jefferson excavated an Indian burial mound, being the first to disturb Indian graves for the sake of scholarly inquiry. According to Jefferson (1964, pp.91–2) the Indians were a noble and powerful race that had vanished from the east coast due to the vices of civilization, not deficiencies in the environment. White Americans with the benefit of the virtues of civilization could only build a great nation.

Jefferson and other romantic American nationalists of the early 19th century identified the Indian as the first 'American' to establish a distinctive national identity for the new republic, much as Europeans of the same period resurrected Celts, Goths, Magyars, and Anglo-Saxons to legitimate their own nationality (Dippie 1982, pp.16–17). Those who were troubled by a savage ancestry promulgated the 'myth of the mound builders', that a civilized, often white, race had built the great earthen monuments of the midwest only to be overrun by red savages (Dippie 1982, pp. 17–18). Both of these notions appropriated the Indian past to legitimate the White Nation. The mound-builder theory did not withstand empirical scrutiny in the late 19th century, but the identification of Indians as the first Americans is a fundamental part of the modern concept of an American national heritage.

The scholarly and political debates of the late 18th and early 19th century linked Indians and the environment of North America as the font of an American nation and a proper arena of scholarly inquiry. The establishement, in 1794, of the first museum of national history, Peale's Museum in

Philadelphia, institutionalized Indians as a subject of natural history (Goetzmann & Goetzmann 1986 p.15, Sellers 1980). While Schoolcraft (1851–57) and Heckewelder (1876) sought to record the vanishing memory culture of the eastern Indians, adventurers like George Catlin (1841) and Prince Maximilian travelled west to try and preserve the primitive culture of the plains Indians before it vanished (Dippie 1982, pp.25–9, Goetzmann & Goetzmann 1986, pp.15–35, 44–57).

By the middle of the century the Indian had become an essential part of the American heritage, and because the Indian was vanishing it was up to the White intellectuals to preserve what they could of Indian culture. The Indian was transformed in the popular imagination of the east from a savage threat to life and limb to a curiosity and subject of scholarly investigation.

## The American Victorian

The expansion of capitalism and industrialization in mid-19th-century America brought with it an alteration of the ideology in which the cemetery participated. The new ideology stressed self-achievement and matured in the latter part of the century as a doctrine of Social Darwinism.

Starting in the third decade of the 19th century the form of the American cemetery shifted to take on a new configuration. The start of the rural cemetery movement in Boston marks the appearance of this shift (French 1975, Darnall 1983). The rural cemetery movement was a reaction to, and explicit rejection of, the old community cemetery. The advocates of the movement condemned the early cemeteries as filthy, unhealthy, and unattractive. They argued that a more sanitary and attractive way must be found to dispose of the dead. They sought to relocate the cemetery in rural areas removed from human habitations, in park-like settings where people could come, picnic, walk, contemplate and absorb the moral lessons woven into the landscape of the cemetery. To accomplish this goal they formed associations which established and managed the cemeteries. Individuals and families became members of the association by purchasing plots in the cemetery.

The rural cemetery movement transferred the care of the dead, and responsibility for the dead, from the community, the church, the town, or some other community group, to the individual family. In the mid-19th century the dead became principally a family concern and ceased to be a primary concern for the community. Throughout the remainder of the 19th century and into the 20th, most churches and towns in Binghamton attempted to divest themselves of their old cemeteries, either by removing them or turning them over to associations.

In the mid to late 19th century, Victorian Americans dealt with the pain and shock of death by maintaining a relationship with the dead (Douglas 1975, Fallows 1885, Farrell 1980, Jackson 1977, Pike & Armstrong 1980). This was accomplished though a wide variety of practices and in material culture. The cemetery was a bridge that connected the living and the dead, and the family plot an extension of the house. As long as the connection between the cemetery plot and the family home was maintained, then death had not triumphed, death had been denied.

Markers had been important in the first part of the century as memorials, in the second half of the century they gained significance, because they identified the family and reinforced their social position and status (McGuire 1988). The poor of the 19th century could not afford the elaborate monuments and large plots required to maintain this ongoing relationship with the dead; just as their lives violated social conventions, so too did their deaths. With a weakened sense of community responsibility for the dead, the poor's inability to maintain the proper forms of memorialization became a justification for disregarding the sanctity of their graves, just as their failure to maintain the proper forms of dress, housing, family, and decorum in life had justified their exploitation.

By the 1870s all of the Indians of the United States had been concentrated in small areas or forced into the more undesirable corners of the west. This reduction of the Indian population to reservations opened up the west for White settlement, and it removed Indian people from the day-to-day experience of most Whites in the west, as well as the east. The Indians on reservations, contrary to earlier predictions, did not vanish as a race but lived on as 'fallen noble savages'. The notion of the vanishing Indians was preserved, because the salvation of the Indians as people required that they be lifted from their debased condition and since they could not return to nature they must assimilate and discard their Indianness (Dippie 1982, pp.162–4). The policy makers of the late 19th century did not envision a romantic death for the Indian, but a less dramatic cultural extinction as Indians joined the melting pot of American society by shedding their primitiveness.

In the scientific world the movement of Indian policy towards assimilation was supported by a dominant theory of cultural evolution. In 1879 John Wesley Powell established the Bureau of American Ethnology and instituted research based on evolutionary principles. His goals were much like Indian scholars of a generation before, to preserve the vanishing culture of the American Indian and to advise the government on Indian policy (Dippie 1982, pp.167–9, Berkhofer 1978, p.54).

Powell, along with many of the other late 19th-century ethnologists, including McGee, Morgan, Grinnell, and McClintock, saw their study of the Indian as part of a larger interest in natural history (Dippie 1982, pp.223–8). The scholarly treatment of Indians as objects of natural history, their remains to be collected like fossils and botanical specimens, was firmly institutionalized and taken for granted in the Department of Interior, and in the great natural history museums such as the National Museum at the Smithsonian, the Peabody, the Chicago Field Museum and the American Museum of Natural History, all established in the mid to late 1800s (Willey & Sabloff 1980, pp.41–5).

During the later half of the 19th century archaeology established itself as an academic discipline (Willey & Sabloff 1980, p.34). From the beginning in the United States, it was treated as a subfield of anthropology, a part of the greater study of the disappearing American Indian, and institutionalized in the museums of natural history and the federal government. The major debate throughout the 19th century concerned the mound-builder controversy, which was finally resolved in favour of the Indians by a former entomologist, Cyrus Thomas (1894). Thomas' conclusions rehabilitated the Indian as a noble savage capable of great achievements.

Cultural evolution guided both 19th-century archaeology and cultural anthropology. As Trigger (1980) has discussed, archaeologists consistently refused to recognize Indian progress along the unilineal evolutionary ladder. The Indians were generally regarded as the prime examples of a single stage of evolution, barbarism. Furthermore, they were commonly thought to have been in North America for a relatively short time, so that the mounds in the east and the standing-wall ruins of the south-west were all dated to a relatively short time span not long before European contact and conquest.

By the end of the 19th century the poets had abandoned the Indian burial grounds, leaving them to the archaeologist, and the pre-eminent right of archaeologists to these remains was unquestioned. Indian people, like the poor, had little power to protect the sanctity of their graves and the nature of their burials did not accord them sanctity in the popular mind. The burials were rarely marked, often abandoned, and seldom traceable to particular families. They violated the conventions of the time, and this failure to maintain correct forms made them all the more unquestionably objects of natural history, the remains of a lost primitive race.

## The modern age

The glorification of death did not survive the first half of the 20th century. From the time of World War I until the 1930s the Victorian customs were attacked as morbid and wasteful (Becker 1973). The competing ideology has been called the pornography of death (Gorer 1955). It attempts to deal with death by denying it and removing it from the living (Ariès 1974).

The shift in belief was facilitated by a declining death rate, especially among children, and the increased use of hospitals to house the dying. These changes removed the reality of death from normal experience, and have been accompanied by ritual denials of death. The deceased is usually embalmed to a life-like state, and laid to rest in a slumber room at the mortuary. Following the funeral there are prolonged periods of mourning and the wearing of black and everyday activities are discouraged as morbid and deleterious to the recovery from grief (Huntington & Metcalf 1979, Warner 1959).

In the mid-20th century, the cemetery also becomes unobtrusive (Dethlefsen 1977). The memorial park cemetery provides the final expression of a denial of death. The one Broome County memorial park, established in the 1930s, resembles a golf course, except its steep terrain. Those who pass it are not confronted with the dead at all through their monuments, but instead observe a verdant well-kept lawn with scattered vases of flowers.

Modern Binghamtonians express this denial of death, and it accounts in large part for the ambiguous feelings towards burials and the usually weak concern for protection of the sanctity of the grave seen in the examples of cemetery removal. All people support the sanctity of the grave, but have little knowledge of the processes involved in burial or the maintenance of cemeteries. Despite the near universal belief in sanctity, only a small minority of people consider the disturbance of graves to be a major issue. Many individuals see the caring and visitation of family graves as a guilt-provoking chore, and express a desire for cremation with a scattering of the ashes so that their children will be spared the responsibility. The sancity of the grave is regarded as being primarily a concern of the family and the cemetery, and only secondarily as a community matter.

The most common justification given for maintaining the sanctity of the grave is respect for the feelings of the dead individual's family. These justifications exclude burials of persons that the informant does not identify as individuals, and burials that cannot be linked to living descendants. That is, they exclude the dead of an ancient and vanished race.

Throughout the first third of the 20th century both the public and scholarly community accepted the idea that the demise of the American Indian was inevitable and imminent (Dippie 1982, p.273). Franz Boas shifted American anthropology away from an evolutionary perspective, but like several generations of researchers before him he and his students took to the field to salvage and save what they could of vanishing Indian culture (Berkhofer 1978, pp.61–9). Concurrently archaeology shifted its emphasis to chronological reconstructions and tracing cultural boundaries (Willey & Sabloff 1980, p.83). This shift also entailed a decreasing interest in Indian ethnology on the part of most archaeologists, removing all but a few from an awareness of Indian concerns and interests in the past (Trigger 1980, p.667).

The turn of the century brought a general awareness that the natural wonders of the United States were in danger of destruction, and a nationwide conservationist movement developed. This movement linked the preservation of Indian culture with the preservation of natural features (Dippie 1982, pp.222–36). In 1906 the federal Antiquities Act was passed to protect archaeological remains on federal land from pothunters, and to provide for the establishment of national monuments to preserve archaeological sites and properties with natural features of exceptional interest. Subsequent laws passed in the 1930s, 1960s, and 1970s continued this precedent of defining prehistoric Indian graves as archaeological resources and restricting their excavation to archaeologists. The major piece of US environmental legislation, the National Environmental Policy Act of 1969, identified archaeological sites as environmental resources.

In the 1930s scholarly opinion in the US began to reject the notion that Indians would vanish either as cultural groups or as a race (Dippie 1982, pp.273–5). The thrust of anthropological research on Indians shifted first to cultural change, then in the 1960s to a glorification of the survival of Indian tribes and groups. These shifts had little effect on archaeology, expecially because the emphasis on scientific research and the discovery of universal laws of cultural change starting in the early 1960s only served to increase the alienation of archaeologists from Indian interests in their own past (Trigger 1980, p.672). American archaeologists were honestly shocked and confused in the early 1970s when Indian activists interfered with archaeological excavations and seized collections.

The general public has been slow to discard the notion of the vanishing Indian. Very few Americans have regular contact with Indian people, and the vast majority derive what awareness they have of Indian people from the media and their public school educations. During the early 1970s Indians became somewhat of a *cause célèbre* in the media, and several major magazines pronounced that the Indian was no longer vanishing (Dippie 1982, p.xi). Despite this flash of attention the popular media and many public school texts generally stereotype Indians as a foreign and vanishing race different and removed from the rest of us (Hirschfelder 1982, Stedman 1982, Hoxie 1985).

One of the major goals of the Indian rights movement continues to be raising the awareness of the general public to the continued existence of Indian people. Reburial is an important political issue in Indian rights, in part because by asserting their rights to protect the sanctity of their ancestors Indian people assert that they have not vanished, and that their beliefs and feelings are entitled to the same respect as other Americans.

All Indian people do not hold the exact same beliefs regarding the sanctity of burials, but consistent themes characterize the objections raised to the scientific study of Indian burials (Medicine 1973, Hamil & Zimmerman 1983, Talbot 1984, Haudenosaunee 1986, NCAI 1986, McW. Quick 1985). The Indian arguments tend to base sanctity on the sacred nature of the burials and a concern for the spiritual wellbeing of the deceased. The concept of ancestry they apply to the dead is a communal one that requires respect for the sanctity of the grave even in the absence of direct familial relations. Indian people differ on how large a community they envision. Some are only concerned with the burials of their own tribe, and others extend the community to all Indian dead. The degree or intensity of concern certainly varies among Indian people, but the sanctity of the grave is clearly of greater religious, emotional, and political interest to Indian people than Whites. Despite the variability that does exist among Indians on this issue it is very difficult to find Indian people that approve of the disturbance, study, and curation of Indian burials.

## Conclusions

The people of modern Binghamton accept the differential treatment of White and Indian burials because they equate the Indian with the past, and view all Indian remains as ancient. The differential treatment of Indian graves is therefore justified, because the White population assumes that no Indian familial descendants exist that would be interested in or hurt by the disturbance.

There are several important difference between the generally held White concept of the sanctity of the grave, and the concept currently being expressed by Indian activists. For Whites, burials should be left undisturbed primarily out of respect for surviving family members. This is a secular concern, unlike the Indians' arguments which base sanctity on the sacred nature of the burials. The idea of communal ancestral relations being expressed by the Indians is foreign to the American public, who are primarily interested only with their direct blood relatives, and see the cemetery and burials as a major concern only to direct blood relatives.

The White emphasis on blood relations manifests itself in the views of most archaeologists. The policy statement of the Society for American Archaeology on reburial gives non-scientific interests in burials clear priority over scientific concerns only when 'specific biological descendants can be traced', in which case disposition of the remains 'should be determined by the closest living relatives' (SAA 1986). The distinction between historical and ancient burials which follows from the emphasis on blood relations appears in most arguments for the scientific investigation and curation of burials (Buikstra 1981, p.27, Early Man 1981, p.1, Turner 1986, p.1). The notion of the primitive, vanishing Indian, however, produced cases such as the Comfort site where Indian remains were treated as ancient regardless of their actual age.

The near universal expression of respect for the dead on the part of Whites suggests that most people in Broome County would be sympathetic to the desires of Indian people for the reburial of their ancestors, despite the difference in the reasons given by Indians and Whites for the sanctity of the grave. The passing of reburial laws in a number of states including Iowa, California, and Massachusetts suggests that such sympathies are widely held in the United States (Anderson 1985, Zimmerman 1985). The different rationales for the sanctity of the grave do not become points of contention between the general public and Indian people, because of Whites' ambiguous feelings about the dead, and because the Indian position grants sanctity in all cases the Whites normally would.

The different rationales do become points of contention between archaeologists and Indian people, because the Indians' broader concept of sanctity restricts or denies the archaeologists access to Indian burials. The practice of archaeology and physical anthropology developed in conformity with the White concept of sanctity. Archeologists and physical anthropologists tend to take the White beliefs as given and natural. These beliefs are not given and natural, but historically and culturally created in contexts of power relations and exploitation. We find ourselves embroiled in a controversy with Indian people today because of this history.

## Note

A very abbreviated version of this chapter was published under the title, White American attitudes concerning burials, in *World Archaeological Bulletin* 2, 1988, pp. 40–5.

# References

Anderson, D. 1985. Reburial: Is it reasonable? *Archaeology* **38**(5), 57–8.

Ariès, P. 1974. *Western attitudes towards death from the Middle Ages to the present*. Baltimore: Johns Hopkins University Press.

Ariès, P. 1985. *Images of man and death*. Cambridge, Mass.: Harvard University Press.

Becker, E. 1973. *The denial of death*. New York: Free Press.

Berkhofer, R.F. Jr. 1978. *The White man's Indian*. New York: Alfred A. Knopf.

*Binghamton Press* 23 April, 1930a. Sleep of centuries is broken.

*Binghamton Press* 26 April, 1930b. Sailor's body removed.

*Binghamton Press* 6 May, 1930c. Stuarts body long removed, search ended.

Brownlow, J.G. 1930. Typed list of bodies removed from Christ Churchyard between 25 April and 8 May, 1930. Christ Church archives, old churchyard cemetery 1929–1931 file, 407.8 179, Binghamton.

Bryant, W.C. 1826. *Miscellaneous Poems Selected From the United States Literary Gazette*. Boston.

Buikstra, J.E. 1981. A specialist in ancient cemetery studies looks at the reburial issue. *Early Man*. Autumn, 26–7.

Catlin, George 1841. *North American Indians, being letters and notes on their manners, customs, written during eight years of travel amongst the wildest tribes of Indians in America*. Edinburgh: John Grant.

Christ Church 1816–75. Vestry notes, book 1. 406.2.1 A-70, Binghamton.

Christ Church 1818–59. Parish register book 1. 404.1.1 A-123, Binghamton.

Christ Church 1859–69. Parish register book 2. 404.1.2 A-124, Binghamton.

Christ Church 1869–84. Parish register book 3. 404.1.3 A-125, Binghamton.

Christ Church 1914–32. Vestry minutes book 5. 406.2.5 A-66, Binghamton.

Christ Church 1929. Old churchyard cemetery file. 407.8 A-179, Binghamton.

Darnall, M.J. 1983. The American cemetery as picturesque landscape: Bellefontaine Cemetery, St Louis. *Winterthur Portfolio* **18**, 249–70.

Dethlefsen, E.J. 1977. The cemetery and culture change: Archaeological focus and ethnographic perspective. In *The archaeology of US*, R.A. Gould & M.B. Schiffer (eds), 137–60. New York: Academic Press.

Dippie, B.W. 1982. *The vanishing American: White attitudes and U.S. Indian policy*. Middletown: Wesleyan University Press.

Douglas, A. 1975. Heaven our home: consolation literature in the northern United States, 1830–1880. In *Death in America*, D.E. Stannard (ed.), 49–68. Philadelphia: University of Pennsylvania Press.

Early Man, 1981. Notes & discoveries. *Early Man*. Winter, (1).

Echo-Hawk, W.R. 1986. Museum rights vs Indian rights: guidelines for assessing competing legal interests in native cultural resources. *New York University review of law* **14**, 437–53.

Elliot, D. 1977. Otsiningo, an example of an eighteenth century settlement pattern. In *Current perspectives in northeastern archaeology: essays in honor of William A. Ritchie*, R.E. Funk & C.F. Hayes III (eds), *Research and transactions of the New York State Archaeological Association* **17**, 93–105.

Emerson, E.W. & W.E. Forbes (eds) 1914. *Journals of Ralph Waldo Emerson*. Boston: Houghton Mifflin.

Fabian, Johannes 1983. *Time and the other*. Columbia University Press: New York.

Fallows, D.D. 1885. *The home beyond, or views of heaven and its relation to earth*. Chicago: Fairbanks and Palmer Publishing.

Farrell, J. 1980. *Inventing the American way of death, 1830–1920.* Philadelphia: Temple University Press.

French, S. 1975. The cemetery as cultural institution: The establishment of Mount Auburn and the 'rural cemetery movement'. In *Death in America*, D.E. Stannard (ed.), 69–91. Philadelphia: University of Pennsylvania Press.

Freneau, P. 1907 [original 1787]. The Indian burial ground. In *The poems of Philip Freneau, poet of the American revolution*, vol. 2, F.L. Pattee (ed.), 369–70. Princeton: Princeton University Press.

Gerbi, A. 1973. *The dispute of the New World: the history of a polemic, 1750–1900.* Pittsburgh: University of Pittsburgh Press.

Goetzmann, W.H. & W.N. Goetzmann 1986. *The west of the imagination.* New York: W.W. Norton.

Gorer, G. 1955. The pornography of death. *Encounter* **5**, 49–52.

Haudenosaunee 1986. Communiqué issued by the Haudenosaunee Grand Council of Chiefs, Northeastern Anthropological Association Meetings, Buffalo, New York, March 20–23.

Hammil, J. & L.J. Zimmerman (eds) 1983. *Reburial of human skeletal remains: Perspectives from Lakota spiritual men and elders.* Indianapolis: American Indians Against Desecration.

Heckewelder, John 1876 [original 1818]. *History, manners, and customs of the Indian nations who once inhabited Pennsylvania and the neighboring states.* Philadelphia.

Hirschfelder, A.B. (ed.) 1982. *American Indian stereotypes in the world of children: A reader and bibliography.* Metuchen: The Scarecrow Press.

Hopkins, K.R. 1973. Finders keepers. *Museum news* March, 4–5.

Hoxie, F.E. 1985. The Indians versus the textbooks: is there a way out? *Perspectives* **23**.

Huntington, R. & P. Metcalf 1979. *Celebrations of death: The anthropology of mortuary ritual.* Cambridge: Cambridge University Press.

Jackson, C.O. 1977. *Passing – The vision of death in America.* Westport: Greenwood Press.

Jefferson, T. 1964 [original 1785]. *Notes on the state of Virginia.* New York: Torchbooks.

Medicine, B. 1973. Finders keepers. *Museum News*. March, 5–7.

McGuire, R.H. 1988. Dialogues with the dead: ideology and the cemetery. In *The recovery of meaning in historical archaeology*, M.P. Leone & P.B. Potter jr. (eds), Washington D.C.: Smithsonian Institution Press.

McW. Quick, P. (ed.) 1985. *Proceedings: Conference on reburial.* Washington D.C.: Society for American Archaeology.

Miller, S. 1985. *Christ Church: A church and its community.* Binghamton: Christ Church.

Morris, L.H. 7 Sept. 1915. Letter to Mr Wescott. Christ Church archives, Old churchyard cemetery 1929–31 file, 407.8 179, Binghamton.

Morris, L.H. 16 June 1919. Letter to Mr Dewees. Christ Church archives, Old churchyard cemetery 1929–31 file, 407.8 179, Binghamton.

Morris, L.H. 28 July 1925. Letter to Mr Dewees. Christ Church archives, Old churchyard cemetery 1929–31 file, 407.8 179, Binghamton.

NCAI 1986. National Congress of American Indian resolution P-86-57-CC, Phoenix, Arizona.

Pearce, R.H. 1965. *Savagism and civilization: a study of the Indian and the American mind.* Baltimore: Johns Hopkins University Press.

Pike, M.V. & J. Gray Armstrong 1980. *A time to mourn: expressions of grief in nineteenth century America.* Stony Brook: The Museum of Stony Brook.

Rosen, L. 1980. The excavation of American Indian burial sites: A problem in law and professional responsibility. *American Anthropologist* **82**, 5–27.

SAA 1986. Statement concerning the treatment of human remains. *Bulletin of the Society for American Archaeology* **4**(3), 7–8.

Saum, L.O. 1975. Death in the popular mind of pre-Civil War America. In *Death in America*, D.E. Stannard (ed.), 30–48. Philadelphia: University of Pennsylvania Press.

Schoolcraft, H.R. 1857. *Information respecting the history, condition, and prospects of the Indian tribes of the United States*. Philadelphia.

Schreiner, E. 1929. Letter to Anna M. Parks, Registrar of vital statistics, Binghamton. Christ Church archives, Old churchyard cemetery 1929–31 file, 407.8 179, Binghamton.

Sellers, Charles Coleman 1980. *Mr. Peale's Museum*. New York: W.W. Norton.

Stannard, D.E. (ed.) 1975. *Death in America*. Philadelphia: University of Pennsylvania Press.

Stedman, R.W. 1982. *Shadows of the Indian*. Norman: University of Oklahoma Press.

Stilgoe, J.R. 1982. *Common landscapes of America 1580–1845*. New Haven: Yale University Press.

SUNY 1971. Field notes from the Comfort Site. Ms on file, Department of Anthropology.

Talbot, S. 1984. Desecration and American Indian religious freedom. *Akwesasne Notes*. **16**(4), 20–1.

Talmage, V.A. 1982. The violation of the sepulture: is it legal to excavate human burials? *Archaeology* **35**(6), 44–9.

Tashjian, D. & A. Tashjian 1974. *Memorials for children of change*. Middletown: Wesleyan University Press.

Thomas, C. 1894. Report on the mound excavations of the Bureau of Ethnology. *Bureau of American Ethnology twelfth annual report*. 3–730.

Trigger, B.G. 1980. Archaeology and the image of the American Indian. *American Antiquity* **45**, 662–76.

Turner, C.G. III 1986. What is lost with skeletal reburial? I. Adaptation. *Quarterly Review of Archaeology* **7**, 1–2.

Warner, W. Lloyd 1959. *The living and the dead*. New Haven: Yale University Press.

Westcott, F. 1915. Form letter to descendants of individuals buried in the churchyard. Christ Church archives, Old churchyard cemetery 1929–31 file, 407.8 179, Binghamton.

Willey, G.R. & J.A. Sabloff 1980. *A history of American archaeology*. London: Thames & Hudson.

Zimmerman, L.J. 1985. A perspective on the reburial issue from South Dakota. In *Proceedings: conference on reburial issues*, P. McW. Quick (ed.), document 2, Washington, D.C.: Society for American Archaeology.

# 12  The acquisition, storage and handling of Aboriginal skeletal remains in museums: an indigenous perspective

LORI RICHARDSON

In its beginnings, colonization is but an enterprise of personal, one-sided and selfish interest, something that the stronger imposes on the weaker. Such are the facts of history.

(Albert Sarrault)

I will show that museums had an important ideological role to play in the process of colonialism and imperialism. The collection and handling of the essence of the museum, the objects themselves, needs to be understood with an emphasis on both synchronic and diachronic perspectives. The synchronic perspective is crucial to explain contemporary beliefs and scholarships which led to the acquisition of the material. On the other hand, an understanding of the diachronic perspective is imperative in understanding the consequences of the acquisition and subsequent research in a colonial and post-colonial context.

The aim of this short chapter is to state my opinion concerning the acquisition, storage and handling of Aboriginal skeletal remains in Australia and overseas. I will attempt to do this by discussing the difficulties facing Aboriginal people in regaining control of this material. Furthermore, I will explore possible ways to remedy this situation.

My views are largely moulded by my socialization as an Aboriginal person in Australia in the post-colonial era. They especially relate to the period after 1967, the year that the indigenous people of Australia were first included on the national census. Consequently, for the first time, Aboriginal people were considered citizens of their own country.

When Darwinian ideas were dominant in Europe, much scholarship was aimed at discovering answers to some of the questions raised, regarding the evolution of *Homo sapien sapiens*, by focusing on Australia. The discovery of Neanderthal man and the new interest in the morphology of the indigenous people of Tasmania led to an assumption that the two were related. The Tasmanian Aboriginal was seen as a survivor of the Neanderthal prototype. This fired the curiosity of scholars and medical practitioners, not only in Europe, but also in the newly colonized Australian mainland. The competition to acquire the largest numbers of skulls and other skeletal remains, between the different museums in Australia and overseas, was unprecedented. For instance, the Murray Black collection, housed in the National Museum of Australia, Canberra, and the Museum of Victoria, Melbourne, comprises some 1800 individuals. However, such was the intellect of Black, that he stored the cranial and post-cranial remains separately. The post-cranial remains were stored according to bone-type. For example, the scapulae were all stored together, the femora were all stored together, etc. Thus, in this collection, no skeletons were kept complete.

It is indisputable that the way Aboriginal people were treated was inhuman and the way their skeletal remains had been collected was barbaric. It is only just, therefore, that members of communities whose ancestors' skeletons are hoarded and displayed across the world are now requesting that the remains be returned. Such institutions relied on acts of grave-robbing and body-snatching to establish and maintain their collections.

For example, the body of William Lanney, the last Tasmanian Aboriginal male of unmixed genetic descent, was barbarically decapitated and mutilated less than 24 hours after his death. His head was cut off and stolen by a member of the Royal College of Surgeons, and never recovered. His hands, feet, nose, and ears were also stolen, and a tobacco pouch was made from a portion of his skin (Ryan 1982, pp. 216–17). Numerous requests for the return of Lanney's head have been submitted by the Tasmanian Aboriginal Centre to the University of Edinburgh's Anatomy Department; however, no signs of repatriation are imminent.

There are numerous cases of Aboriginal bodies and skeletal remains being transported overseas. For example, prior to World War II, Tasmanian remains in Europe numbered approximately 82 skulls or crania, including three heads, as well as five skeletons. Of these three skeletons and approximately 35 skulls or crania were destroyed in the war (Macintosh & Barker 1965, p. 11).

In 1907, Hermann Klaatsch hermetically sealed an Aboriginal corpse in a tank of preserving fluid, before shipping it to the Breslau University, Germany, for later dissection (Basedow 1929, p. 42). The skeleton may still be there.

Lemaistre, in about 1872, stole a Torres Strait Island mummy, shipping it back to Europe, where it later became the 'property' of the Royal College of Surgeons. It is noted that other heads of mummies from the same area may be seen in the Museum of the College, and in the British Museum. The British Museum is also said to retain a microcephalic head from the Torres Strait, however, the 'skin is now nearly all stripped off it, so that its characters can be well seen' (Flower 1879, p. 393).

Such was the desire of overseas institutions to acquire Aboriginal skeletal remains that a collector from the Godefroy Museum, Hamburg (c. 1863–73), tried to induce a squatter to shoot an Aboriginal, so that the skeleton could be sent back to the Museum (Roth 1908, p. 81).

The list of Aboriginal skeletal remains stored in overseas institutions is long. The examples listed above give some insight into the irreverent and inhumane manner with which whites regarded blacks.

According to Mansell (1985, p. 27), institutions such as the British Museum (Natural History), University of Oxford, Royal College of Surgeons (England), Royal College of Surgeons (Ireland), Royal Scottish Museum, University of Edinburgh (Anatomy Department), Musée de l'Homme (Paris), Ethnografiska Museet of Stockholm, Natural History Museum (Brussels), Natural History Museum (Vienna), and the Natural History Museum (Chicago), are all believed to house Aboriginal skeletal remains. The failure of these institutions to return these remains condones the actions of the past.

Even though Aboriginal people are aware of the callous manner in which skeletal collections were acquired, some communities are still prepared to compromise and accept the purpose of the retention of this material. Findings about dietary, medical, and cultural practices can be obtained through scientific research. This can be beneficial for Aboriginal people, especially for future generations. However, it is essential that all research being carried out on Aboriginal skeletal remains be under the control of Aboriginal people.

One way in which this can be done is for Aboriginal communities to create their own museums, or keeping places. In these structures, Aboriginal people are the custodians of their own tribal material, on their own tribal land. In this way, Aboriginal people can monitor the types of research being carried out, and pass on any knowledge gained to the community. For too long, white academics have been accumulating and circulating research data amongst themselves, while the 'subjects' of their research have been kept ignorant. This is no longer acceptable. Further, if the community decides to bury or cremate their ancestral remains its decision must be respected. Institutions must release Aboriginal skeletal remains unconditionally.

There is yet another aspect that is of great consequence to the dignity and self-esteem of Aboriginal people. This concerns the handling, display, and organization of such material in museums. If we are to talk about a democratic society, indigenous groups reduced to a minority should at least have a say, or more preferably, be involved in handling the material that is theirs, both spiritually and morally.

In conclusion, one of the only options remaining for Aboriginal people is to lobby for public support. This can only be achieved by conveying knowledge about the past and the nature of present-day demands.

However, Aboriginal people do not have the resources to accomplish this alone. Academics must play a more active role in educating the larger society about the problems facing Aboriginal people. They must not confine themselves to seminar rooms and conference halls. After all, academics have provided the intellectual justification for colonialism and imperialism. For example, Sir John Cleland, a former South Australian State Coroner and Professor of Pathology, reasoning that, with the march of civilization, 'pure-blooded natives' would become extinct, sealed four Aboriginal bodies in a tank of preserving fluid and stored them in the basement of the South Australian Museum for over 60 years. Consequently, he was ensuring that 'specimens' would be available for future generations to study. In 1983, Aboriginal groups learnt of Cleland's 'gift' to the future. They lobbied for the return of the bodies and within two years had gained custodianship and buried the bodies in their respective tribal areas.

For 200 years, Aboriginal people have been struggling to maintain their cultural identity. Until academics and the general public can accept and understand the Aboriginal way of life, the struggle will continue. For only then can there be some hope for the future.

> The problem of what to do with the race, the most interesting at present on earth, and the least deserving to be exterminated by us, and the most wronged at our hands, is not a difficult one to solve, were a solution really desired.

(Smith 1909)

## References

Basedow, H. 1929. *The Australian Aboriginal.* Adelaide: F.W. Preece and Sons.

Flower, W.H. 1879. Illustrations of the mode of preserving the dead. *Journal of the Royal Anthropological Institute.* **3**, 389–95.

Macintosh, N.W.G. & B.C.W. Barker 1965. The osteology of Aboriginal man in Tasmania. *The Oceania Monographs* **12.**

Mansell, M. 1985. Tasmanian Aboriginal bones. *Anthropology Today* **1**, 6, 27.

Roth, H.L. 1908. *Port Mackay, Queensland.* F. King and Sons Ltd.

Ryan, L. 1982. *The Aboriginal Tasmanians.* Brisbane: University of Queensland Press.

Smith, R. 1909. The Australian Aboriginal as a human being. In *Commonwealth Year Book.*

# 13    *The souls of my dead brothers*

ERNEST TURNER

I live at present in the city of Washington, but I am originally from Alaska, from the Athabascan tribe. There are about 40 clans in the west central part of Alaska. I was raised partially by my traditional family in the village and partially by a missionary. There was a great missionary influence throughout Alaska when I was a child. In fact as a child I always thought God was an Episcopal; I didn't realize the difference. But I've gone through many changes since that time and resisted a lot of other changes in my life, in terms of the dominant society and some of the teachings that they try to force on us. There are other influences, especially in the burial [customs] in my village. There's a lot of influence [exerted] by the Russians that came into that part of Alaska. After that the burials, the Indian graves, were in miniature houses much like the Russians use, with picket fences.

My tribe lived in many parts of that country, because of the vastness of the country and the difficulty in getting food. In the summer time we lived in fishing villages and in the winter time we followed the herds of the caribou. There wasn't any burial because if you tried to dig with the tools of that time into the permafrost you would be trying for ever to bury them. They were left on platforms in the trees along the river banks to be taken off. The belief being that we are part of the earth: we came from the earth and will return to the earth in our natural state. The other influences were of the miners that came to that part of the country in the early days. The miners, in a lot of instances, had no affiliation with any churches. In my view when they died they were just taken and buried up on the hillside and that was it, that was the end of any memory of them in any sense.

As a child in the village there used to be some anthropologists that pitched tents outside of the village and some archaeologists that dug around a little bit. At that time I didn't even know that they were related to the human race. They got away with some mysterious things. As a child I was taught not to eat mushrooms because we would die from them. We watched the archaeologists, as children, gathering mushrooms and eating them, and we'd sit and wait for them to die. They seemed to have a different God than we had.

I moved to the city of Seattle back in the 1950s and being in a totally different culture and totally out of my environment it was very difficult to adopt some of the beliefs of what was going on at that time. Much like I feel like a fish out of water over here in Europe. There were many different tribes and bands in the Seattle area. I'd like to share with you some of what Chief Seattle said (the city of Seattle is named after Chief Seattle). In 1854 Chief Seattle addressed Governor Stephens when he surrendered and signed the treaty. I'd like to share with you some of the beliefs that I adopted from the people of this country when I moved to this part of the country.

## Chief Seattle's speech

Addressed to Governor Stevens and the settlers of Seattle in the presence of the assembled Indian tribes, on the occasion of the treaty signing, December 1854.

Yonder sky that has wept tears of compassion upon our fathers for centuries untold, and which to us looks eternal, may change. Today it is fair, tomorrow it may be overcast with clouds.

My words are like the stars that never set. What Seattle says the Great Chief at Washington can rely upon with as much certainty as our paleface brothers can rely upon the return of the seasons.

The son of the White Chief says his father sends us greetings of friendship and goodwill. This is kind of him, for we know he has little need of our friendship in return because his people are many. They are like the grass that covers the vast prairies, while my people are few; they resemble the scattering trees of a storm-swept plain.

The Great – and I presume – good White Chief, sends us word that he wants to buy our lands but is willing to allow us to reserve enough to live on comfortably. This indeed appears generous for the Red Man no longer has rights that he need respect, and the offer may be wise, also, for we are no longer in need of a great country.

There was a time when our people covered the whole land as the waves of a wind-ruffled sea covers its shell-paved floor, but that time has long since passed away with the greatness of tribes now almost forgotten. I will not dwell on nor mourn over our untimely decay, nor reproach my paleface brothers with hastening it, for we, too, may have been somewhat to blame.

Youth is impulsive. When our young men grow angry at some real or imagined wrong, and disfigure their faces with black paint, their hearts also are disfigured and turn black, and then they are often cruel and relentless and know no bounds, and our old men are unable to restrain them.

Thus it has ever been. Thus it was when the White Man first began to push our forefathers westward. But let us hope that the hostilities between the Red Man and his paleface brother may never return. We would have everything to lose and nothing to gain.

It is true that revenge by young braves is considered gain, even at the cost of their own lives, but old men who stay at home in times of war, and mothers who have sons to lose, know better.

Our good father at Washington – for I presume he is now our father as well as yours, since King George has moved his boundaries farther north – our great and good father, I say, sends us word that if we do as he desires he will protect us.

His brave warriors will be to us a bristling wall of strength, and his great ships of war will fill our harbors so that our ancient enemies far to the northward – the Sinsiams, Hydas and Tsimpsians – will no longer frighten our women and old men. Then will he be our father and we his children.

But can that ever be? Your God is not our God! Your God loves your people and hates mine! He folds His strong arms lovingly around the White Man and leads him as a father leads his infant son – but He has forsaken His Red Children, if they are really His. Our God, the Great Spirit, seems, also, to have forsaken us. Your God makes your people wax strong every day – soon they will fill all the land.

My people are ebbing away like a fast receding tide that will never flow again. The White Man's God cannot love His Red Children or He would protect them. We seem to be orphans who can look nowhere for help.

How, then, can we become brothers? How can your God become our God and renew our prosperity and awaken in us dreams of returning greatness?

Your God seems to us to be partial. He came to the White Man. We never saw him, never heard His voice. He gave the White Man laws, but had no word for His Red Children whose teeming millions once filled this vast continent as the stars fill the firmament.

No. We are two distinct races, and must ever remain so, with separate origins and separate destinies. There is little in common between us.

To us the ashes of our ancestors are sacred and their final resting place is hallowed ground, while you wander far from the graves of your ancestors and, seemingly, without regret.

Your religion was written on tablets of stone by the iron finger of an angry God, lest you might forget it. The Red Man could never comprehend nor remember it.

Our religion is the traditions of our ancestors – the dreams of our old men, given to them in the solemn hours of night by the Great Spirit, and the visions of our Sachems, and is written in the hearts of our people.

Your dead cease to love you and the land of their nativity as soon as they pass the portals of the tomb – they wander far away beyond the stars, are soon forgotten and never return.

Our dead never forget this beautiful world that gave them being. They still love its winding rivers, its great mountains and its sequestered vales, and they ever yearn in tenderest affection over the lonely-hearted living, and often return to visit, guide and comfort them.

Day and Night cannot dwell together. The Red Man has ever fled the approach of the White Man, as the changing mist on the mountain side flees before the blazing sun.

However, your proposition seems a just one, and I think that my people will accept it and will retire to the reservation you offer them. Then we will dwell apart in peace, for the words of the Great White Chief seem to be the voice of Nature speaking to my people out of the thick darkness, that is fast gathering around them like a dense fog floating inward from a midnight sea.

It matters little where we pass the remnant of our days. They are not many. The Indian's night promises to be dark. No bright star hovers above his horizon. Sad-voiced winds moan in the distance. Some grim Fate of our race is on the Red Man's trail, and wherever he goes he will still hear the sure approaching footsteps of his fell destroyer and prepare to stolidly meet his doom, as does the wounded doe that hears the approaching footsteps of the hunter.

A few more moons, a few more winters – and not one of all the mighty hosts that once filled this broad land and that now roam in fragmentary bands through these vast solitudes or lived in happy homes, protected by the Great Spirit, will remain to weep over the graves of a people once as powerful and as hopeful as your own!

But why should I repine? Why should I murmur at the fate of my people? Tribes are made up of individuals and are no better than they. Men come and go like the waves of the sea. A tear, a tamanamus, a dirge and they are gone from our longing eyes forever. It is the order of Nature. Even the White Man, whose God walked and talked with him as friend to friend, is not exempt from the common destiny. We may be brothers, after all. We will see.

We will ponder your proposition, and when we decide we will tell you. But should we accept it, I here and now make this the first condition – that we will not be denied the privilege, without molestation, of visiting at will the graves of our ancestors, friends and children.

Every part of this country is sacred to my people. Every hillside, every valley, every plain and grove has been hallowed by some fond memory or some sad experience of my tribe. Even the rocks, which seem to lie dumb as they swelter in the sun along the silent sea shore in solemn grandeur thrill with memories of past events connected with the lives of my people.

The very dust under your feet responds more lovingly to our footsteps than to yours, because it is the ashes of our ancestors, and our bare feet are conscious of the sympathetic touch, for the soil is rich with the life of our kindred.

The noble braves, fond mothers, glad, happy-hearted maidens, and even the little children, who lived and rejoiced here for a brief season, and whose very names are now forgotten, still love these sombre solitudes and their deep fastnesses, which, at eventide, grow shadowy with the presence of dusky spirits.

And when the last Red Man shall have perished from the earth and his memory among the White Men shall have become a myth, these shores will swarm with the invisible dead of my tribe; and when your children's children shall think themselves alone in the fields, the store, the shop, upon the highway, or in the silence of the pathless woods, they will not be alone. In all the earth there is no place dedicated to solitude.

At night, when the streets of your cities and villages will be silent and you think them deserted, they will throng with the returning hosts that once filled and still love this beautiful land.

The White Man will never be alone. Let him be just and deal kindly with my people, for the dead are not powerless.

Dead – did I say? There is no death. Only a change of worlds!

## Implications

This is a speech that Chief Seattle gave when he signed the treaty, when they surrendered. It was addressed to the settlers of Seattle, to the Governor of that area and to some of the assembled Indian tribes. What he said in 1854 still exists today. This is what I believe, and what most members of my tribe that I've talked to believe. I've returned home at least once a year for the Spring spiritual conference where we have many of the elders and many of the young people and many of the traditional Christian churches all come together and begin to talk to each other and learn from each others. There's a changing taking place, as I see it, from the time when I was very young. When I was very young I was told this is the way it is and forever it shall remain so, but I see a lot of changes coming about.

We came from the earth and will return to the earth. We're part of the earth. We are here but a brief moment. But what is time? It is infinity, it goes on forever. What does the study of archaeology provide for native Americans? How do archaeologists interpret the bones and the artefacts that are dug up from my ancestors? What do they tell archaeologists? I venture to say that no archaeologist could interpret with accuracy what I'm trying to convey today, and I'm still living. So at best archaeological interpretation would be glorified guessing as to what it was like. The missionaries in Alaska thought that the totem poles were a pagan god and they ordered them destroyed. They ordered the history of the Indian people to be destroyed. Because the totem poles are not a pagan god, they are history for the people. There are very few of the totem poles that have been preserved, so the history of our ancestors has been destroyed because of a misinterpretation. Archaeologists look at artefacts and they look at bones and, seemingly, the bones talk to them. Seemingly the bones tell them a story. In what Chief Seattle says, the story is passed on from generation to generation and it is told in the heart because, in the spirit, this is the true story. That cannot be misinterpreted, and it goes on forever. I've been very fortunate that I've travelled all over the United States and visited with many Indian tribes. The commonality of that belief exists and is passed on in the heart. It's not passed on in books.

I was not too interested in archaeology or bones until about ten years ago when I visited the Smithsonian Institution and I was horrified to see mummies of the Aleut people. It totally horrified me to see them. Then, a few years later, I got a call to say that there were crates of Aleut bones in an Institution in the Midwest. I got in touch with a lot of the Aleut people and they seemingly didn't care too much about what happened to the bones, but it created an interest in me; about what *does* happen? Where did all these bones come from? How did they get back to the Midwest and why were they put in the Institution and forgotten? How can we get those bones back to Alaska? How can we then rebury them in the rightful burying place? We can't do it by fighting because there are too few of us and we will lose. The only way we can do it is by talking and working together. So what are the benefits for us? What respect do we have for our beliefs and our values? That is why I would like to start a dialogue with archaeologists and gain some respect for our ancestors, get them buried in their rightful burying places back home where they belong, so that they can then exist in peace, their souls can exist in peace.

I came very near to death on a number of occasions because of a life-style that I led. One time in hospital they had to use a jumper cable to get me going again. I got a glimpse of the other side during that time. It was very peaceful. All of my ancestors and all of my relatives that were dead spoke to me in that brief period. The souls of my dead brothers are all waiting for me. They will greet me lovingly and kindly when I get there. But they are disturbed by what has happened. They are disturbed about what is happening to their bones; but also about what is happening to the earth, because we are part of the earth.

# 14 Statement of American Indians Against Desecration before the World Archaeological Congress

JAN HAMMIL AND ROBERT CRUZ

American Indians Against Desecration (AIAD) is a project of the International Indian Treaty Council which was formed on the Standing Rock Reservation of South Dakota in 1974 with delegates representing some 97 Indian tribes and Nations from across North and South America. We hold non-governmental status in the United Nations.

AIAD was formed as a result of the Longest Walk when Indian people walked from California to Washington D.C. in support of Treaty Rights.

As we crossed the country and visited the universities, museums, and laboratories, we found the bodies of our ancestors stored in cardboard boxes, plastic bags, and paper sacks. We found our sacred burial places stripped and desecrated, the bodies and sacred objects buried with our dead on display for the curious and labelled 'collections', 'specimens', and 'objects of antiquities'. AIAD estimates that in the United States, half a million Indian bodies have and continue to be so treated, most as a result of federal projects, using federal monies and stored at federally supported institutions.

Further, we estimate an additional half a million bodies of our ancestors have been shipped to European countries. It is AIAD's objective, goal and intent to ensure that all Indian remains and sacred objects buried therewith are returned to their nations, relatives and allies for appropriate disposition as was occurring prior to their theft and desecration.

Anything less is unacceptable and to ensure our objective's success, we are training our children and grandchildren in locating and securing the return of our ancestors and sacred items. To that extent, we have accepted and are prepared for a very long war against those enemies who seek to destroy Indian religious practices, customs, and traditions.

As traditional Indians from many Indian nations, members of AIAD share basic religious beliefs concerning the sanctity of our graves. We believe in an afterlife. That which is called death, to us, is only a change in life as we continue on a journey to the spirit world and thereby become one with our Mother, the Earth.

Any disruption, delay or halt in that journey is a violation of personal religious beliefs to that individual, to his descendants who incorporate and are responsible for his spirit in their daily lives and religious ceremonies, and to those of the present and the future who will embark on that journey. Therefore, when we find our ancestors' bodies and graves desecrated by the hundreds of thousands, we consider this an intolerable violation of religious freedom which must be addressed and must be resolved. Anything less would be a prostitution of the religious practices, customs, and traditions of our ancestors, our relatives, our allies and, therefore, of ourselves.

As the most studied peoples on the face of the earth, the American Indian is well acquainted with the 'Indian Expert' as found in the anthropological, archaeological, paleopathological, physical anthropological associations. 'Why,' we ask, 'would "Indian Experts" assume that American Indians were any different than the white, black or yellow man in expectations of and belief in the sanctity of our graves?'

We knew archaeologists were aware that the American Indian conducted religious ceremonies for the burial of the dead which were sacred with the ground consecrated and therefore not to be disturbed. Archaeologists knew that neither we nor our ancestors started the journey to the spirit world with the thought or desire that that journey be interrupted by an archaeologist. He was aware that use of preservatives on the bones of our ancestors compounded the original act of desecration, thereby halting the journey into perpetuity, making his actions a permanent religious violation.

We recalled an archaeologist pledging his friendship to Indian people in support of our struggle for survival and religious freedom. We remembered how he was welcomed by the elders as they told the children about the journey to the spirit world and the return to our Mother, the Earth. We tried to understand the nature of an individual who listened and partook in what little we had left to share with the white man while simultaneously orchestrating plans ensuring that, for the American Indian, the journey to the spirit world would end in a cardboard box, plastic bag or paper sack in the basement of his laboratory.

'Why,' we ask, 'would the archaeologist destroy that which he professed to protect? What moral or legal authority did the archaeologist have to change religious customs practised since time immemorial thereby interfering with the relationship and instructions given to Indian people by the Great Mystery; the Creator; God?'

Could it be that the 'Indian Experts' didn't care that their acts were interfering and affecting traditional religious practices or did they justify the genocide of Indian religion by placing a higher priority on their objectives? Just as the US Government justified wholesale slaughter and extermination of hundreds of thousands of Indian people with noble objectives, had the archaeologist concluded that altering and destroying traditional Indian religious practices was justified by the results of their scholarly studies and research – acceptable casualty rates, so to speak?

Was such disregard of God's instructions possible or had archaeologists concluded that the religious beliefs of the American Indian were wrong? There was no journey, no instructions, no Creator, no God? In their personal embrace of atheism, had archaeologists inflicted those beliefs on the American Indian and to hell with the changes on Indian lives?

That which had been the journey to the spirit world would now be a journey to the cardboard boxes with which they, the archaeologists – not God – would control. The God of the archaeologist was science and research, and in further-ance of that God, Indian people would be subservient whether they chose to or not. What had been the Lakota, Cheyenne and Delaware or the Piscataway, Papago and Pueblo, the red man of the red nations of the Western Hemisphere were now the collections, specimens and the objects of antiquity.

To our inquiries, the archaeologist replied, 'don't you realize that we're doing this for you? By destroying your religion,' he said, 'we are preserving your culture. When we dig up Indian specimens,' he added, 'and place those specimens in paper sacks and plastic bags, we treat them with great dignity and respect'.

The death of Raymond Yellow Thunder in Gordon, Nebraska marked the beginning of the end of the 'Indian Experts'. During a meeting and dance spon-sored by the local Veterans of Foreign War, Raymond Yellow Thunder was tortured to death and his mutilated body found in the trunk of an abandoned vehicle. When those responsible were not indicted, Indians throughout South Dakota travelled to Gordon, Nebraska to join with the American Indian Move-ment in vowing that no longer would the American Indian beg the white man for the right to exist. From the flames of Gordon came a renewed pride retrieved from the depths to which it had plunged by perverted logic in the understanding of respect and dignity.

Direction and advice was sought from the elders and spiritual leaders, and the elders and medicine men travelled from throughout the Western hemi-sphere and explained that our ancestors made treaties with the US Government and those treaties gave away no property rights to the graves of our ancestors and they expected those treaties to be honoured. That no archaeologist or anthropologist spoke for Indian people, and that archaeological activities were hurting Indian people; they were violating Indian religious customs and prac-tices and this was totally unacceptable. That Indian people did not need archae-ologists; that for hundreds of thousands of years, Indian people were able to take care of their dead without the assistance of archaeologists and we saw no need for their help now. No archaeologist or physical anthropologist repre-sented Indian interest. No study was wanted or needed on Indian bodies. Any Indian bodies found, Indian people could take care of and the archaeologist could take a flying leap off the highest ledge and the American Indian Move-ment said yes, archaeologists are the enemy of Indian people and the issue would be addressed and would be resolved and the ancestors would be reburied.

Throughout the United States, 'attitude adjustment sessions' were arranged for archaeologists, and the 'Indian Experts' learned new meaning and defi-nitions for 'respect' and 'dignity'. In New York, Iowa, South Dakota and California, reburial laws were developed. Relationships progressed from extreme polarization to tolerance and, finally, to alliances as both sides worked towards better preservation programmes and consideration for traditional practices in cultural management programmes.

On 4 April 1981 in the Black Hills of South Dakota, 800 acres were acquisitioned by Dakota AIM from the US Forest Service and a cultural resource area established for the Lakota Nation, their relatives and their allies. To honour the man whose death was a spark for Indian activism, the 800 acres was named Yellow Thunder Camp and used by the four sacred colours – the white and red man as well as the black and yellow – for all to learn, live and work together with mutual respect for the others right to exist.

As an affiliate of Yellow Thunder Camp, American Indians Against Desecration co-ordinated the legal defence opposing the US Forest Service. Our legal case included testimony from the elders, spiritual leaders, Indian activists, and archaeologists as they stood up for improved cultural management programmes, preservation and Indian religious rights.

Following five years of litigation in which violations to religious freedom were at issue, including the storage and treatment of our ancestors' graves, the United States District Court ruled in favour of Yellow Thunder Camp, declaring the Court's intention to ensure that at least one Indian person in America had the right to religious freedom in his own land. We recognized that the alliance between Indians and archaeologists had significantly contributed to the Court's decision, and we were pleased with the progress made towards human relations and understanding since the days of Gordon Nebraska.

The momentum continued and we joined archaeologists in working towards better preservation for the entire region of the Black Hills, resulting in the budget being doubled twice by the Forest Service and archaeologists employed where before there were none. Slowly, the remains of our ancestors were being returned as greater awareness and understanding developed between archaeologists and Indians. Medicine men from different nations joined the elders and children in returning some 5000 ancestors to their journey in South Dakota alone. As one reburial followed another, the graves of the ancestors surrounded the mass grave of the victims from the Wounded Knee Massacre on the Pine Ridge Reservation.

With renewed enthusiasm and hope, archaeologists and Indians focused on the US Air Force, insisting on additional survey work to identify and avoid significant archaeological sites during the Peacekeeper MX construction project. Finally, in July (1986), with the co-operation of the Pike National Forest in the eastern section of Colorado, we were allowed, for the first time since the arrival of the white man, to return the sacred Sun Dance to the Rocky Mountains, and the dancers dedicated the ceremony to the one half-million ancestors stored in cardboard boxes, paper sacks, and plastic bags. Archaeologist and Indian were learning the advantages of working together, rather than the disadvantages of polarization.

From the bowels of the monster, however, racism and greed were resurrected as the Department of Interior's Consulting Indian Expert dictated a policy on disposition of Indian bodies without one iota of Indian input, review or consideration, placing scientific interest over Indian religious beliefs, practices, and customs.

Objected to by national and international Indian organizations, intertribal and tribal councils, Indian commissions, activist and traditional spiritual leaders, the cavalier dismissal of the Indian concerns would have made a 1920s Indian agent proud.

The arrogance of archaeologists was again illustrated in April when the Executive Committee of the Society for American Archaeology on behalf of all archaeologists in the United States passed a resolution opposing reburial. Reburial might be considered, said the SAA, in cases of 'known individuals from whom specific biological descendants could be traced'. Needless to say, the merits of any reburial request would be determined by archaeologists, based on their opinion and judgement of Indian religious values and interest.

We suggest the Executive Committee of the SAA keep in mind that when the American Indian was developing the richest of cultures in addition to the fundamental principles of democracy, including the right of religious freedom, the Europeans were putting leeches on their ass for medicinal purposes. These are the people that would pass judgement on the level and values of Indian way of life? If one does not know the level and value of his own spirituality – if any – how can he judge another's?

We suggest it was not the American Indian that chose again to polarize relationships between Indians and archaeologists. We suggest that a handful of individuals have conspired for their own purposes and interest to establish unreasonable procedures and policies with the specific intent of excluding Indian input or consideration. We suggest that if anyone is excluded from input into the disposition of our ancestors' bodies, it will be archaeologists. AIAD will strongly advocate and work towards such exclusion as long as that resolution exist.

To that extent, we were very pleased to learn of the conclusions reached by the Black Hills National Forest involving the December 1985 meeting with the Lakota, Cheyenne and Arapaho nations and in which AIAD assisted.

The report says:

> It [is] important that . . . Forest representative come from a 'neutral' discipline, other than archaeology or anthropology. Representatives of those disciplines . . . are viewed with suspicion by the Indian people because their motives in learning about tradition, practices, etc., are interpreted as potentially exploitative. Other resource people are . . . not viewed as a direct threat to Indian culture or spiritual values.

We suggest the insensitivity of leadership among American archaeologists affects anthropologists and archaeologists throughout the world. We suggest that Indian people can be your best friends or your worst enemies, but we will no longer be your collections, specimens or objects of antiquity.

In August 1986 we had the honour and privilege of visiting the elders and spiritual leaders of the O'Odham (Papago) nation in Southern Arizona. 'What message,' we asked, 'would you send to a world organization of archaeologists?'

In the 120-degree heat, the elders spent a considerable amount of time thinking and considering what message they should send to an international gathering of scholars from throughout the world.

Finally, we were instructed: 'You tell them that we do not treat our bones with such disrespect. Those bones are our ancestors,' they said, 'and they are sacred. By disturbing the ancestors' graves and spirits, they have caused many problems and hard times for our people and this makes us very sad. You tell them that the bones of our ancestors must be returned. They are sacred and we do not treat our ancestors with such disrespect.'

With half a million of our ancestors in European laboratories, museums, and universities, we suggest it is now time to have some serious discussions on the meaning of respect.

# 15 Federal Indian burial policy: historical anachronism or contemporary reality?

STEPHEN MOORE

## Introduction

It has been estimated that there are between 300,000 and 600,000 Native American bodies stored in federal institutions, such as the Smithsonian Institution, public and private universities, and museums and private collections in America, and that at least one-half million bodies are held in collections in foreign countries. Indian tribes and national Indian organizations have organized a national drive to get these human remains back into Indian hands for appropriate disposition. Notwithstanding the claims of scientific and educational interests, on moral, religious and legal grounds these remains belong back in the ground or other suitable final resting place.

This impressive collection of Indian remains is not a mere historical anachronism, nor has our society become sufficiently enlightened as to cease being so blatantly racist and disrespectful. Contemporary federal law and policy defines Indian grave sites and human remains as 'archaeolqgical resources' – relics of antiquity – and elevates scientific values over religious and cultural values. As a result, the storage of Indian skeletal materials and associated grave goods continues largely unabated.

This scenario contrasts sharply with the treatment of the human remains of other groups. Non-Indian cemeteries are routinely moved to make way for road and dam construction projects, housing developments, and other improvements in our society. Even 'sensational' archaeological discoveries, as reported in a 3 May 1987 story in the *Denver Post*, ultimately receive different treatment:

### RENAISSANCE REDCOAT

Archaeologists and historians have joined to identify a skeleton found in Philadelphia as that of a British infantryman who apparently died 210 years ago fighting in the American Revolution.

The University of Pennsylvania Museum of Archaeology and Anthropology plans to put casts and holograms of the bones and associated artefacts on exhibit next month under the title 'Last Muster for a British Soldier'. *The remains of the man were reinterred in a formal funeral ceremony attended by British and American veterans.*

Construction workers unearthed the skeleton in 1985 while excavating ground in the city's Mount Airy section. Museum archaeologists used bone fragments to determine the approximate age and health of the man at the time he was killed.

Why have the bodies of the cavalrymen discovered at the site of Custer's Last Stand, Little Big Horn, been reburied when the Sioux warriors killed there have not? How long does an archaeological study of Indian bones take? Do their scientific needs justify curation in perpetuity? Just how much insult to the American Indian is our society willing to tolerate for the sake of a handful of scientists? Do these scientists really produce any information of value to Indians or to the broader society?

This chapter attempts to address these questions by tracing the historical foundation of present-day federal law and policy on this subject, and argues that law and policy must soon change to reflect and protect the fundamental beliefs, attitudes, and rights of tribal descendants to the remains of their dead ancestors.

## The genesis of federal 'ownership' and control of Indian burials

The federal government first undertook cultural resource management near the turn of the century, with the passage of the 1906 Antiquities Act. Spurred by the national archaeological societies of the day, Congress sought to stem the tide of the wholesale destruction of cultural sites in the south-west. A large foreign market in cultural materials had developed, unrestrained by local, state or federal law enforcement. The Antiquities Act, thus, made it a federal crime to 'appropriate, excavate, injure, or destroy any . . . object of antiquity, situated on lands owned or controlled by the Government of the United States' without the permission of the government.

Congress, however, gave no consideration in the 1906 Act to the protection of sites, including burials, for their inherent religious and cultural value. Indeed, the Act served as a means by which the national archaeological community, in the more prominent educational institutions of the day, gained unfettered access to and control over Indian cultural resources located on public and Indian lands. The community of archaeologists saw foreign commercialization as a threat only to their narrow scientific and educational interests, not as a threat to Indian culture and religion *per se*. And the notion that Indian remains located on public lands 'belong to', or are the property of, the federal government – embodied in these first federal laws on the subject – originated not from any established body of common law (as is discussed below) but merely from the effective lobby of a self-serving professional community of interests.

The Act permits the 'examination of ruins, the excavation of archaeological sites, and the gathering of objects of antiquity' only by institutions 'deemed properly qualified to conduct such examination, excavation or gathering'. That the interests of scientific and educational institutions are primarily served by the Act is clear:

> *Provided*, that the examinations, excavations, and gatherings are undertaken for the benefit of reputable museums, universities, colleges. . . . *with a view to increasing the knowledge of such objects, and that the gatherings shall be made for permanent preservation in public museums.*

There is no record of concern for the traditional Indian viewpoint in the proceedings of Congress on the 1906 Act. On the contrary, passages from the hearings before the Senate Subcommittee of the Committee on Public Lands reflect the government's more pervasive ethnocentric stance on traditional Indian culture at the turn of the century. In his testimony before the Subcommittee Office of Indian Affairs' Commissioner, William A. Jones noted, concerning the cliff dwellings on the Southern Ute Reservation in south-western Colorado:

> The Southern Ute Reservation is a treaty reservation, and it will be necessary to negotiate with the Indians to cede or sell that portion of the reservation which contains these prehistoric relics. You authorized us, I think, two years ago to negotiate with the Southern Ute Indians for that purpose. *I have been trying to do so. We have not succeeded so far, but we think that this summer we will succeed. They have an extravagant idea of the value of that portion of the reservation, but I think with a little patience we can get them to cede from the reservation such portions as contain the relics.*

The specific nature of the Utes' objection to ceding that portion of their reservation is unclear from the hearing record; what is apparent is the Commissioner's (and by implication the Office of Indian Affairs') willingness to clear the way for scientific exploration and excavation of the area, irrespective of the nature of the Indian objection. The response to any Indian objection was simply to take the land away from the objecting tribe.

Monsignor O'Connell, Rector of the Catholic University of America, set the tone for the entire congressional proceedings surrounding the 1906 Act: 'these articles of archaeology, etc., are not simply the property of the United States Government, *but in a certain sense the property of the scientific world*'.

The presumption of federal ownership of cultural resources, including Indian burials, continued with the Reservoir Salvage Act of 1960, amending the Historic Sites, Buildings and Antiquities Act of 1935. The federal government's preference for the scientific and educational value of these resources to the exclusion of their inherent cultural and religious value is evident from the Interior Department's endorsement of the Salvage Act.

> This bill has as its object the preservation of historical and archaeological data which might otherwise be lost as a result of flooding caused by the construction of a dam by any agency of the United States or by any private person or corporation holding a license issued by any such agency.

With the increased industrialization and greater federal activity in construction of large-scale multipurpose water control projects, the problem
of salvaging and preserving archaeological and historical antiquities of
national significance in advance of destruction becomes ever more critical.
The bill emphasizes the point that the necessary archaeological and historical salvage should be performed in advance of such construction
activities, and it reflects a growing public awareness of their increasing
loss of this national heritage through such federal and private activities.

As was true of the 1906 Antiquities Act, the effect of the 1960 Reservoir Salvage Act was to legitimate widespread 'looting' and unrestrained expropriation
of sites by the professional archaeological community, and make qualified public
and private museums and other institutions the repository for 'relics and
{human] specimens' removed from sites. It is notable that the 1960 Act marked
the advent of federal financial subsidization of archaeological investigations and
excavations on a broad scale, hastening the 'salvage archaeology' era.
Thousands of Indian 'specimens' were removed, and today remain stored, in
institutions across America as a result of the work of salvage archaeologists.

The National Historic Preservation Act (NHPA) of 1966, amended in part in
1980, also plays a part in Indian cultural resource management. But like the
Antiquities Act and the Salvage Act, it results in little real substantive change in
terms of protecting burial sites and associated sacred materials. Section 106 of
NHPA requires federal agency heads, prior to licensing any federal undertaking, to 'take into account the effect of the undertaking on any [area] . . .
that is included in or eligible for inclusion' in the National Register of Historic
Places. That process entails seeking the comments of the Advisory Council on
Historic Preservation, an advisory office established by the NHPA. But Section
106 is procedural in nature; agency land managers, after securing the Advisory
Council's comments, can choose to ignore the comments and licence or proceed with the federal undertaking. At best the process may result in site avoid-
ance when not too costly from a development standpoint; often the result is
'mitigation', which may mean little more than additional curation and storage
of Indian materials.

## The Archaeological Resources Protection Act of 1979

The presumption of federal 'ownership' and control of Indian burials continues
today in the Archeological Resources Protection Act (ARPA) of 1979. Motivated largely by the inability (if not unwillingness) of federal land management
agencies to enforce the provisions of the 1906 Antiquities Act, ARPA more precisely defines 'archaeological resources' and substantially broadens and stiffens
the range of civil and criminal sanctions which the federal government can
impose on unqualified, unpermitted 'looters'.

ARPA, however, includes Indian graves and human skeletal materials discovered on public and Indian lands as 'archaeological resources', which are the

property of the United States. Moreover, it perpetuates the process of preserving such materials in a 'suitable university, museum, or other scientific or educational institution'.

To Congress' credit Indian tribes or individual Indians must consent to the issuance of ARPA permits for the excavation or removal of archaeological resources on Indian lands owned or controlled by the said tribe or individual. And ARPA requires tribes to be notified before religious or cultural sites can be harmed or destroyed by activities on public lands. But there are no assurances that the 'notice' provision to tribes will effectively alter the land manager's decision, so as to reflect Indian concerns respecting the harm or destruction of a site. In the best of cases managers consult with tribes early on in the land management planning process to avoid culturally and religiously sensitive areas. In the more usual case the manager may take the tribe's views into account, as required by the NHPA discussed above, yet reject them for administrative, economic or political reasons. Notice to, and consultation with, tribal spiritual people must be more than another 'cost of doing business' before these provisions of ARPA will have any significant impact.

Various federal departments and agencies have adopted regulations, policies and guidelines implementing ARPA. One example is a guideline written in 1982 by the National Park Service consulting archaeologist, purportedly for the entire Department of the Interior and its various bureaus (Bureau of Land Management, Bureau of Indian Affairs, Office of Surface Mining, Bureau of Reclamation, etc.). Entitled 'Guidelines for the Disposition of Archeological and Historical Human Remains', the document facially recognizes that the 'proper treatment [of Indian remains] often involves especially sensitive issues in which scientific, cultural and religious values must be considered and reconciled'. To accomplish that end the guidelines – much in the nature of ARPA – encourage early consultation with affected tribes, or, in the case of non-federally recognized tribes, 'ethnic groups'.

But what real difference has ARPA 'notice', or the guidelines' requirement for 'consultation', really meant to Indian people? The answer is simple and unequivocal: very little. For instance, most bureaux and offices of the Interior Department interpret the guidelines as placing the scientific and education value of cultural sites above religious and cultural values. And the common interpretation of ARPA is that it does not allow reburial of Indian remains; that as property of the United States, disturbed remains must be curated and stored in qualified institutions. It seems a cruel joke that the guidelines direct 'any bureau or office of the Department charged with the care of custody of human remains [to] maintain the collection in keeping with the dignity and respect to be accorded all human remains'.

Passed in 1978, the American Indian Religious Freedom Act (AIRFA) would seem to compel a different result. AIRFA expressly protects and preserves American Indians' right of access to sacred sites, *including burial sites*. AIRFA was enacted in recognition of the lack of 'clear, comprehensive and consistent federal policy' premised in a variety of federal laws and the 'inflexible enforcement' of that policy resulting in the abridgment of Indian religious freedom.

From the foregoing discussion it is clear that the spectrum of federal archaeological and cultural resource laws have frustrated Indian religious beliefs and attitudes concerning the burial sites of their ancestors. Yet to date no changes have been made in these laws to reflect AIRFA's articulation of the scope of Indian religious rights under the First Amendment to the United States Constitution.

In sum, contemporary federal law and policy concerning Indian grave sites and skeletal remains is little more than a throwback to the ethnocentric laws and policies of the late 19th and early 20th century. And as long as Indian burial sites, and the human remains and grave 'goods' found therein, are considered to be the property of the United States and treated as other 'relics' or 'objects of antiquity', Indian beliefs and attitudes will be largely ignored and frustrated.

## Defining the nature of Indian rights to, and control of, Indian burials

Few people, other than some physical anthropologists and archaeologists (although by no means a clear majority of their profession), would dispute the notion that Indians and tribes have a superior moral claim to the Indian remains and grave goods, based on traditional religious and cultural beliefs and values. Deeply ingrained religious attitudes toward the dead are found in all cultures worldwide; Native Americans are no exception. Certainly there will be, and are, exceptions, but most contemporary tribal groups have strong objections to the federal government's treatment of their ancestors' remains. Many traditional Indian people believe that the continuing desecration threatens the spiritual balance and harmony of the entire world, not just one tribal community. And many personally feel the spiritual disquiet of their ancestors, whose bodies are stored in plastic bags and airtight boxes in the Smithsonian Institution and other private and public institutions.

Indeed, one would think that on the strength of the moral claim alone Indians would be able to secure the return of their ancestors' bones. And in fact there is legislation pending in the United States Senate which, despite its shortcomings, would begin the systematic process of identifying nationwide the location and tribal affiliation of Indian remains and sacred artefacts, and their eventual return to tribes for appropriate disposition. NARF believes the proposed law – known as the Native American Cultural Preservation Act (S. 187) – is inadequate, because it fails to recognize paramount tribal rights to these materials, thus perpetuating the myth of federal ownership, and because it does not set maximum time limits within which remains and sacred artefacts stolen from graves must be returned to the appropriate tribe.

Laws sometimes have very little real connection to morality or justice, yet are attributed greater weight in our society. Accordingly, tribal advocates feel compelled to construct a legal theory of Indian ownership superior to that of the United States. Without question a legal claim to ownership will have to be established if tribes are forced into court to secure the return of their ancestors' bones.

The question of what legal rights tribes and individual Indians have to the ownership and control of Indian burials on federal lands has not been directly addressed by courts. In the absence of a clear articulation, one must seek analogies in decisions rendered in similar areas of the law. Below is a cursory examination of these decisions.

## The common law analogy

American property law generally vests ownership of objects embedded in the earth in the landowner, under the common law maxim: 'to whomsoever the soil belongs, he owns also the sky and to the depths'. This maxim seemingly vests title to Indian burials in the landowner, whether private or government.

Different, special common law rules apply to gravesites, however. Because no one 'owns' or holds a property interest in a dead body – 'title' to a deceased human being – the common law doctrine of abandonment does not normally apply to burial grounds. When its identity as a burial ground is lost, an obligation continues not to desecrate the graves or dishonour the dead. And descendants are invested with a legal right to prevent and protect a burial site from desecration. Wrongful exhumation is considered an actionable wrong, and reburial, if not done in a decent and dignified manner, renders one liable to tort for damages sustained.

A decision consistent with these common law principles was reached in the context of Indian burials on private lands, in a 1986 case from the Louisiana Court of Appeals. In *Charrier v. Bell*, or the 'Tunica Treasure' case, the court confirmed a superior right in the Tunica-Biloxi Tribe of Louisiana, represented by the Native American Rights Fund, to skeletal remains and associated grave artefacts removed from private property. Between 1968 and 1971, Leonard Charrier, a former prison guard and self-proclaimed 'amateur archaeologist', discovered and systematically removed the materials from approximately 150 burial sites at Trudeau Plantation. Charrier alleged to have the permission of the property owner, in reality only the property manager, to excavate the sites and remove the materials. In 1974 Charrier sued the non-resident owners of Trudeau Plantation to quiet title to the materials after unsuccessfully attempting to sell the collection to the Peabody Museum at Harvard University. The Tunica-Biloxi Tribe of Louisiana intervened in the litigation in 1981, after obtaining federal recognition.

The district court, after a trial on the merits, held that the Tribe is the lawful owner of the remains and artefacts. The Court of Appeals affirmed the district court decision, ruling in effect that the common law doctrine of abandonment did not apply to burial materials:

The intent in interring objects with the deceased is that they will remain there perpetually, and not that they are available for someone to recover and possess as owner.

However, the fact that the descendants or fellow tribesmen of the deceased Tunica Indians resolved, for some customary, religious or spiritual belief, to bury certain items along with the bodies of the deceased, does not result in a conclusion that the goods were abandoned. While the relinquishment of immediate possession may have been proved, an objective viewing of the circumstances and intent of the relinquishment does not result in a finding of abandonment. Objects may be buried with a descendant for any number of reasons. The relinquishment of possession normally serves some spiritual, moral, or religious purpose of the descendant/owner, but is not intended as a means of relinquishing ownership to a stranger. Plaintiff's argument carried to its logical conclusion would render a grave subject to a despoliation either immediately after interment or definitely after removal of the descendants of the deceased from the neighbourhood of the cemetery.

In reaching the decision, the court reasoned that at least some members of the current day Tunica-Biloxi Tribe are descendant from the Indians buried at Trudeau Plantation, and thus have standing to assert legal claim to the materials.

The important, but unanalysed, aspect of this case concerns the superiority of the tribal interest. Fee patent title to Trudeau Plantation was first acquired by grant from the British Crown in 1768, and subsequently conveyed over the years to a number of successive private owners. For the Tunica-Biloxi Tribe in 1987 to still hold a superior interest in the materials, their descendants must have retained – and never abandoned or relinquished – rights to the graves at the time of British occupation and exercise of sovereignty over the area through the 1763 Treaty of Paris. In effect, the British Crown could convey no greater title to a private owner by grant than that which it had. For the Tunicas to have a surviving property interest, that interest must have existed prior to and at the time of grant in 1768. Whether a different result would be reached if burial materials are considered personal property is an open, unresolved matter in the law. And whether the *Charrier* decision can successfully be applied to defeat the United States' claim to ownership of Indian burial site materials is unknown at this point in time.

## Lessons from the United States' extinguishment of Aboriginal Indian title

In the famous 1823 Supreme Court decision in *Johnson v. M'Intosh*, the Court held that upon 'discovery' the European sovereigns held 'ultimate dominion' in land 'subject only to the Indian right of occupancy', also called 'aboriginal Indian title'. Tribes held aboriginal title to lands inhabited since time immemorial. Once the United States was organized and the Constitution adopted, tribal rights to Indian lands became the exclusive province of federal law. This 'use and occupancy' right can only be terminated or conveyed by, or with, the consent of the United States. Until diminished by legitimate congressional act, the Indians' right of occupancy is *as sacred as the fee simple of the whites*'; and '*as sacred and as securely safeguarded as is fee simple absolute title*'.

While there were other purposes, the overriding goal of the United States during treaty making was to obtain Indian lands to foster westward expansion. In exchange for the extinguishment of aboriginal Indian title the United States promised to tribes the exclusive, recognized title to their reservation lands, exclusive use and occupation of those lands, and other rights (e.g. off-reservation rights to hunt and fish), which varied from treaty to treaty, tribe to tribe. After the treaty era ended in 1871 the same federal objectives were achieved by way of legislative agreements and executive orders, either expressly or implicitly ratified by Congress. In this way tribes ceded literally tens of millions of acres of aboriginal territory – and the right of use and occupancy – to the United States.

Did Indian tribes, by way of treaties, agreements, and executive orders, cede and relinquish their rights, however defined, to Indian burials and artefacts to the United States? Did tribes have either the authority or the legal ability to convey to the United States rights to burial sites or collections of remains in burial pits or mounds? The *Charrier* decision makes it clear that a tribe has standing to protect the gravesites of ancestral members from desecration, and to demand and secure the return of remains improvidently removed from burials. *Charrier* and the common law discussed above do not, however, provide complete, satisfactory answers to these questions.

Canons of construction unique to the interpretation of Indian treaties provide helpful insight. These canons require a construction of treaties so as to resolve ambiguities in favour of Indian tribes, and an interpretation of treaties as the Indians would have understood them. And treaties have been interpreted as a grant of rights *from* Indian tribes to the United States; *not* as a grant *to* tribes. Rights not expressly granted are reserved.

In the context of Indian burial sites and grave materials, then, it is hard to conceive of tribes ceding any rights to the United States. In the hour of his death in 1871, Tu-eka-kas, the father of Chief Joseph of the Nez Perces, reminded his son never to sell the bones of his father. Chief Joseph describes the death.

> My father sent for me. I saw he was dying. I took his hand in mine. He said: 'My son, my body is returning to my mother earth, and my spirit is going very soon to see the Great Spirit Chief. When I am gone, think of your country. You are the chief of these people. They look to you to guide them. Always remember that your father never sold his country. You must stop your ears whenever you are asked to sign a treaty selling your home. A few years more, and white men will be all around you. They have their eyes on this land. *My son, never forget my dying words. This*

*country holds your father's body. Never sell the bones of your father and your mothers.'
I pressed my father's hand and told him I would protect his grave with my life. My
father smiled and passed away to the spirit-land.*

*I buried him in that beautiful valley of winding waters. I love that land more
than all the rest of the world. A man who would not love his father's grave is worse
than a wild animal.*

The author is unaware of any discussion of the extinguishment and
relinquishment of property rights in burial sites to the United States in treaty
negotiations; the matter was simply not discussed. In contrast to the 1985
Supreme Court decision in *Oregon Department of Fish and Wildlife* v. *Klamath
Indian Tribe*, silence in the treaties or other agreements as to Indian burial rights
is not, and should not, be viewed as inconsistent with the purposes for the ces-
sion. Then again it is doubtful that Indians in the 19th century were aware of
the avarice the archaeological community would soon engender for Indian burial
remains.

These same questions can be raised in the context of the Indian Claims Commission proceedings. Established in 1946, the ICC was given jurisdiction to
hear five major categories of claims by tribes, bands, or other identifiable
groups of American Indians against the United States. Concerning Indian
treaties, agreements, and executive orders the Commission had authority to
hear:

> claims which would result if the treaties, contracts, and agreements
> between the claimant and the United States were revised on the ground
> of fraud, duress, unconscionable consideration, mutual or unilateral mis-
> take, . . .
>
> *or*
>
> claims arising from the taking by the United States, whether as a result of
> a treaty of cession or otherwise, of lands owned or occupied by the claimant
> without the payment for such lands of compensation agreed to by the
> claimant.

The ICC proceedings contain no evidence of extinguishment of, or compen-
sation for, the extinguishment of rights to Indian burial sites. And the proceedings shed no light on the issue of the authority of tribes to extinguish such
rights.

Arguably, the United States took ceded Indian land subject to an implied or
constructive trust to treat Indian burials in accordance with traditional notions
of respect and decency. A constructive trust is an equitable, remedial device
imposed by courts to prevent fraud, mistake, unjust enrichment or some other
form of unconscionable conduct. Indian people would characterize the federal
government's expropriation of their ancestors bodies for the sake of science as a
mistake, an unconscionable mistake.

# 16 Human bones as symbols of power: aboriginal American belief systems toward bones and 'grave-robbing' archaeologists

LARRY J. ZIMMERMAN

During the past ten years there has been an increasing concern on the part of religious fundamentalist and aboriginal peoples worldwide about the treatment of human skeletons they believe to be from their ancestors. Many have used the bones as an underpinning for political activism, contending that control of the bones by others is simply another form of exploitation. For them the bones have been used in land claims cases and to focus media attention. For others, the concern is strictly a religious one, where the rights of the dead – the ancestors, to many – are at stake. Disturbance or possession of the bones by 'non-believers' is desecration. Whatever the reason, human bones have become symbols of power, both spiritual and political.

Because archaeologists are the individuals who excavate bones, and to some extent are responsible for study and occasional display of them, archaeologists have become a convenient target towards which groups vent their wrath. This has especially been the case in the United States during the past two decades. Native American peoples have actively been seeking to wrest control of Indian skeletons from archaeologists since the mid 1960s. Some attempts have involved violent confrontation, and others have been successfully negotiated compromises involving some restrictions on study, and eventual reburial.

To many traditional Native Americans and activist militants, the image of the archaeologist is that of a grave-robber, and the archaeologist's science little more than another form of exploitation. Yet, more acculturated Indians see the archaeologist as an individual involved in a science that will restore, or perhaps, protect, a vital cultural heritage from certain destruction. This chapter examines the several Indian images of the archaeologist, especially in terms of treatment of human skeletons and belief systems about them. Some assessment of the impact of these images on archaeological objectivity and the Native American view of the past are also made. Examination of Indian statements about archaeologists and the past are very revealing and can be used to elucidate key issues.

### Archaeologists as grave-robbers?

> To us the ashes of our ancestors are sacred and their resting place is hallowed ground. You wander far from the graves of your ancestors and seemingly without regret.

This statement is part of a speech made by Chief Seattle at the signing of the Treaty of Medicine Creek in 1854 (see ch. 13, this volume, for full text), to distinguish between tribal beliefs and what he saw of white people taking legal control of land. The speech has been recalled many times, but most recently is seen as a page of a booklet calling attention to the case of Dino and Gary Butler in Oregon. The two are accused of killing Donald Pier, described as a 'grave-robber'. Though not an archaeologist, he allegedly did loot prehistoric graves (Butler Support Group 1985). That same booklet (p. 14) states in underlined print, 'To disturb a grave is not only an insult to the Spirits of the dead, it is a blatant insult to the creator.' The booklet never directly calls archaeologists grave-robbers, but it certainly suggests that disturbing a grave is not moral when it states, 'To dig up a grave and strip the departed one of . . . treasures that were placed there by relatives would shock and sicken any moral human being' (p. 14). We archaeologists do not like to be labelled 'grave-robber', or 'immoral', but that is how many Native Americans see us.

My crew of archaeologists explained to many Indians on the Crow Creek Sioux Reservation what we were doing excavating the remains of nearly 500 victims of a 14th-century massacre. A range of responses from support to extreme anger resulted, many calling us grave-robbers (Zimmerman & Alex 1981). When we explained that looters had already vandalized the bones, we were asked how we were different. Our response was that we were doing science and that we were protecting the past, always taking care to show respect for the remains we meticulously excavate. This is how we tend to view ourselves and how we tend to differentiate between us and looters, or who we consider to be grave-robbers. But in the view of some Indians, what we do is little different, and they cannot understand why we are interested.

Chick Hale, a Prairie Potawatomi, expressed this concern well at a planning seminar on ancient burials held between Indians and archaeologists in the state of Iowa. He stated,

> What is the difference if you dig burials with a trowel or a bulldozer? Is it any better to go into a bank and steal the money all at once, or is it better to steal it a penny at a time? Burials are not to be disturbed. I have consulted with the elders of others and find the spirituality to be the same. (Anderson *et al.* 1980, p. 12)

A closely related issue for Indians is the need for any kind of study of human skeletons. At a session between Lakota holy men and elders and anthropologists at the 1983 Plains Conference, the audience of anthropologists was asked no less than six times, why they studied skeletons (Hammil & Zimmerman 1983). No answer seemed to satisfy. At the Iowa sessions, the sentiment was the same, and expressed often: 'Why do archaeologists study the past? Are they trying to disprove our religion? We do not have to study our origins. I don't question my teachings. I don't need proof in order to have faith' (Anderson *et al.* 1980, p. 12).

Our archaeological view of the past is apparently disturbing, or at very least, curious, to Indian people. The Indian concerns are at the same time bothersome to us. We remain frustrated by modern Indian groups' disinterest and disbelief in the results of archaeological study (Talmage 1982, p. 44). Perhaps we simply have differing images of the past, and that also causes problems.

## To know the past or to discover it?

Archaeologists and Native Americans view the past differently. We see ourselves as discoverers and protectors of the past. For Native Americans the past is known because it is manifest in the present.

When a group of American Indian Movement (AIM) militants disrupted a dig in the state of Minnesota during the summer of 1971, an archaeology student was heard to say, 'We were trying to preserve their culture, not destroy it.' In recounting this incident, Deloria noted that the archaeologists apparently thought that 'the only real Indians were dead ones' (Deloria 1973, p. 33).

> None of the whites could understand that they were not helping living Indians by digging up the remains of a village . . . The general attitude [of the archaeologists] was that they were the true spiritual descendants of the Indians and that the contemporary AIM Indians were foreigners who had no right to complain about their activities.
>
> (Deloria 1973, p. 31)

To some extent Deloria's observations may be accurate. As a profession we seem to believe that Indians are incapable of preserving their own past or at least are not interested in it.

In a recent article (Floyd 1985) on repatriation of sacred artefacts in museums to tribal groups, the chairperson of the Society for American Archaeology Committee on Native American Relations commented on the recent Indian demands that sacred objects and bones be returned. She is quoted as saying, 'it's good that Native Americans are starting to care about their pasts'. The implication, of course, is that Indians never cared about their pasts before. What we, and Indians, fail to understand, is that archaeologists and many Indians view the past in very different ways. And, if nothing else, this causes major communication difficulties.

Both groups are concerned and continually deal with the past. Notable are the conceptual and pragmatic differences relating the past with the present. For Indians like the Lakota, the past lives in the present. For archaeologists, past and present are related in a linear fashion, with historical retrospection and 'eras' serving as conceptual and linguistic partitions between past and present

(Watson *et al.* 1987). Events begin and end, and other events follow linearly. The Indian 'knows' the past through spiritual sources, ritual, and a rich oral tradition. The archaeologist 'discovers' the past, using predominantly written sources and archaeological exploration and interpretation.

The past is constituted in and informs the present-day Indian. The past is known by and culminates in the present, and the future is largely unknown, but informed and influenced by the past and present. There is no need to investigate the past – it is already known and felt. To the archaeologist, curiosity motivates investigation of the past and prediction into the future. The viewpoint of archaeological science is that investigation into, and examination of, human remains allows us to discover, understand and preserve the past. To the Indian, the excavation and study of burials constitutes desecration of the past, and disruption and exploitation of the present. Turner, the Athabascan Indian author of Chapter 13, summarizes the difference elegantly.

> Human bones are able to talk to the scientists and leave them information. Culture talks to us and gives us messages from the past. Spiritual communication is not a theory, it is a fact. I am not sure what the bones can tell [the archaeologists] of the spiritual beliefs of my people. Even if the bones do communicate, I'm not sure that what they tell you is true (Anderson *et al.* 1983, p. 28).

Turner's view is congruent to that of Esther Stutzman, a Coos Indian (Ross & Stutzman 1984, p. 6): 'The past is obvious to the Indian people, as it does not appear to be obvious to the white man.'

## Natural law and man's law

Another Native American belief system affecting views of archaeology, and also apparently not obvious to archaeologists, is that of the law. Extensive and excellent reviews of laws affecting the treatment of human remains were completed by Rosen (1980), Talmage (1982), and Bahn (1984). Western jurisprudence seems relatively straightforward on the matter, and has been used in court to decide a variety of issues about disturbance and disposition of skeletons. Law has been used both to support and deny Native American views on disturbance of the dead. Yet, law remains a conceptual and practical barrier to communication between archaeologists and Indians (see also Moore, ch. 15, this volume).

In most Western cultures, the legal system provides a means for resolving conflict between opposing groups. But, in conflicts over excavation, study and disposition of Indian remains, this approach has actually intensified the conflict (Watson *et al.* 1987). Archaeologists who oppose restrictions on the excavation of burials and reburial frequently use existing statutes or absence of prohibitive statutes as a defence for their position. We cite laws regarding abandoned cemeteries, private property rights, rights to exhume, ownership rights,

academic and scientific freedom, and historical preservation to justify excavation, study, and perpetual curation of skeletal materials. Armed with court
cases as precedent, and federal regulation and policy, archaeologists feel that
they can rightfully pursue archaeological tasks (see also Ch. 16). What archaeologists cannot understand is that these legal concepts have no antecedent in
many traditional Indian cultures.

Most Native American traditionals believe that burial sites are not fixed
locations, and they cannot be abandoned or disrupted. No individual or group
can 'own' the remains of another person. No need exists to discover and preserve a past which is already known. Clearly, if these concepts do not exist, the
laws of non-Indians that govern the concepts are not valid. They are no defence
for the continued desecration of burial sites. The very concept of statutory law
having jurisdiction over what is a spiritual matter is not acceptable. Native
Americans would, instead, rely on 'natural' law, or that law which is given by
God, to provide guidance as to what they should do. In other words, the source
of statutory law is not recognized and is not a valid defence. The perception of
archaeologists that the law is on their side creates an attitude which is not helpful to conflict resolution. Indeed, the reliance of archaeologists on 'invalid laws'
to defend their position is often interpreted as another form of discrimination
against Indian culture and religion. A 90 year old Lakota elder, Matthew King
(Noble Red Man) summarizes it well:

Let the People sleep in peace. It is a burial ground and also a church for
our Indian people. We cannot change it, because God gave us this country
and he gave us the laws to govern our people. We cannot change it. No
one can change it. We cannot make laws. Sometimes those laws are
made, it's more prejudice. (Hammil & Zimmerman 1983, p. 4)

## Conclusions

If the law and the past are the only two segments of aboriginal American belief
systems to be different from archaeologists, communication problems might be
possible to solve. Sadly, they are not. The conflict is not simply a conflict
between science and religion as some seem to suggest (Overstreet & Sullivan
1985, p. 51), but rather of fundamental differences in worldview. The questions
centre on the past. How does one know the past? Who knows the past? Can the
past be 'owned?' Who should control the past?

Cultural relativism must be applied to the problems. Is the Native American
view of the past less valid than that of archaeology? The frequently uncompro-
mising behaviour of archaeologists seems to suggest that we believe it is. The
fundamental question for our profession should perhaps be whether or not a
recognition of the validity of Indian views will alter our interpretations of the
past. While compromise might limit access to human skeletal materials, our
methods and interpretations will likely not be altered in any dramatic fashion.

On the other hand, failure to recognize the validity of the views and, therefore, not to compromise, is probably the greater threat. Of no minor importance is a question of professional morality and ethics. If we do not consider the views of those we study, we risk violation of some professional ethical codes. Further, such emotionally charged issues seldom work out to the best interests of those cast in the role of exploiter and oppressor. Failure to compromise may limit any future access to prehistoric Native American human skeletal remains as Indians successfully use their symbols of power to raise public sentiment and turn it against archaeology. If this occurs, our ability to interpret the past will be fundamentally altered.

# References

Anderson, D.C., M. Pearson, A. Fisher, & D. Zieglowsky 1980. *Planning seminar on ancient burial grounds*. Iowa City: Office of the State Archaeologist of Iowa.

Anderson, D.C., D. Zieglowsky & S. Shermer 1983. *The study of ancient human skeletal remains in Iowa: a symposium*. Iowa City: Office of the State Archaeologist of Iowa.

Bahn, P.B. 1984. Do not disturb: archaeology and the rights of the dead, *Oxford Journal of Archaeology* **3**, 127–39.

Butler Support Group 1985. *Dino and Gary Butler: a story of struggle to honor life*. Newport, Oregon: Butler Support Group.

Deloria, V. 1973. *God is red.* New York: Delta Books.

Floyd, C. 1985. The repatriation blues. *History News* **40**(4), 6–12.

Hammil, J. & L.J. Zimmerman 1983. *Reburial of human skeletal remains: perspectives from Lakota spiritual men and elders*. Indianapolis: American Indians Against Desecration.

Overstreet, D. & N. Sullivan 1985. *Analysis of human skeletal remains from the Fitzgibbons Site, Gallatin County, Illinois: a draft report*. Wauwatosa, Wisconsin: Great Lakes Archaeological Research Center, Inc.

Rosen, L. 1980. The excavation of American Indian burial sites: a problem in law and professional responsibility. *American Anthropologist* **82**, 5–27.

Ross, R.E. & E. Stutzman 1984. Two views of archaeology. Paper presented at the 49th annual meeting of the Society for American Archaeology, Portland, Oregon.

Talmage, V.A. 1982. The violation of sepulture: is it legal to excavate human burials? *Archaeology* **35**(6), 44–9.

Watson, N., P. Peterson, & L.J. Zimmerman 1987. The present past: an examination of archaeological and Native American views of law and time. Paper presented at the 3rd International Conference on Thinking, Honolulu.

Zimmerman, L.J. & R. Alex 1981. Digging ancient burials: the Crow Creek experience. *Early Man* **3**(3), 3–10.

# 17 *The role of archaeology in nation building*

JO MANGI

## Introduction

The grounds upon which one perceives and bases one's identity with a nation are often personal. No individual can rightfully speak on behalf of the other members. There are nonetheless some common grounds shared by all the members of a nation. Superficial things such as national flags, dress, songs, and emblems; the political ideology upon which the nation is built; and such things as religious beliefs and common history, events when the forefathers of the nation stood together for a common cause, such as the American War of Liberation. Political and patriotic rhetorics often cite examples of the latter two categories as they are by far the most effective tools in mobilising the masses.

Shared experience is the inherent force that holds the many individual nations intact. Papua New Guinea only joined the first category when it gained independence in 1975. Apart from the superficial makings of a nation there is little else.

The use of archaeological discoveries are varied. As the title of my chapter suggests, I would like to look at the role of archaeology in nation building. The use of archaeological findings to boost national pride is nothing new. Writing on the famous Piltdown forgery, Reader (1982, p. 61) ventures to suggest that one of the factors that may have led to the successful perpetration of the hoax may have been nationalist zeal to find the skeleton of the earliest man on British soil.

The primary aim of this chapter is to investigate the possible avenues in which the results of archaeological work done in Papua New Guinea can contribute towards building a nation, in the light of the fact that Papua New Guinea has otherwise little ground in common upon which it can build a strong nation. Presenting a brief history of the country, the first part attempts to justify the claim that Papua New Guineans have very little in common. The second part summarizes the interesting prehistory of the country. Having set the backdrop, the final part returns directly to the main theme of the chapter.

## What is Papua New Guinea?

To appreciate fully the character of Papua New Guinea would require looking back 50,000 years; a task impossible in this context. Here I will only look at what Papua New Guinea is; or what I think it is now.

In the words of Muke (1985, p. 2) Papua New Guinea is a 'nation of a thousand tribes'. Accepting the definition that a nation is a group of people within a geographical location who are economically self-sustaining, politically autonomous, and sharing common norms and values, then every traditional tribe met this criterion. Today, the process of modernization has taken its toll on the traditional tribes. However, many of the underlying social forces are still well and truly alive, despite the fact that they may have taken on a modern dressing.

> In most traditional societies, no matter how altered, the past has imposed a pattern on the present; attitudes towards people within and without the immediate group, attitudes towards marriage, children, pets, land ownership, conflict, loyalty have come from the past.
>
> (Groube 1983, p. 4)

As a vast proportion of the tribes still exist to this day, I would like to take Muke's notion further and say that Papua New Guinea is a nation state of a thousand nations.

## History

The island to the north of Australia became a significant entity to the rest of the world when horse-drawn carts and monarchies were just coming to an end. We entered world history when the European nations of the world were carving up the remaining land masses, each seeking their slice of colonies.

While the land of the 'Black People' (Papua) was known to the European world as early as the late 15th century, it was not until 1874 that the last piece of its coast was mapped. In 1828, the Dutch proclaimed possession of the western half of the island and formally annexed it in 1850. In 1884 Britain established a Protectorate over the southeast and the Germans claimed the northeast, along with the small islands. In 1906 the British handed their Protectorate over to the Australians. At the beginning of World War I, German New Guinea was lost to the Australians. The country was called Papua and New Guinea until self-government in 1973. Political independence was achieved in 1975.

The historical experiences of the people are different. On the coastal frontier the people have been in contact with the outside world for about a century. In parts of the interior of the Highlands it was only about fifty years ago that colonial contact was established. There are no unifying trends in our rather short history; there is no War of Liberation and no military disaster like Gallipoli (Groube 1983).

## Papua New Guinea today

I have maintained the claim that there is little in this country which the inhabitants can grasp in identifying themselves as part of this country. Here I develop the point further by looking at the criteria set out earlier, with the goal of demonstrating the political significance of archaeological research.

### Superficial

The Australian colonial administration made sure that we were well furnished with all the necessary paraphernalia of a modern state before granting political independence. These included the different institutions which are discussed below.

### Ideological

As far as the political ideology of the country is concerned, Papua New Guinea is a modern democracy with a Westminster type of government. The political parties found in the country have very little difference in their political ideology to offer to the people when it comes to voting. Even if there was, to the people in the rural areas of Papua New Guinea, it makes little difference. My personal observations in the past have led me to believe that for the present, it is not what the different candidates stand for, but who and how they are related to the different groups in the respective electorates that counts. The voter is more concerned with the immediate benefits that he will be getting if he gets a relative of his into the Parliament. This is perfectly understandable in the light of the indifference in the attitudes of the bureaucracy towards the local people at all levels; a point I discuss later. The fact that political ideology is of little consequence in determining election winners is clearly demonstrated by the liberty with which these representatives change political affiliations once they are voted in. There is not as much of an outcry from the voters as one would expect if that person was voted in on the merits of the political ideology that he claimed to represent.

While in the long run this picture is bound to change, it is fair to assert that political awareness is still in its youth in Papua New Guinea and to some extent distorted.

### Aesthetic

Credit must be given to the early pioneering churches, especially the more established churches, for their role in the pacification of the country. In many cases they were on the frontier of exploration and many lives were lost. Theoretically, this would provide the ideal uniting factor for the country. But the reality is quite different.

Over the years, in particular the post-independence period, there has been a dramatic increase in the number of Christian denominations found in the country.

Indeed, every Christian sect, from the Mormons – who are here to serve only the 'lighter coloured' population – to Bible-thumping Evangelical and extreme Fundamentalist groups, are found in the country. The fact that the 'type' of Christianity is not specified in the constitution gives any denomination under the Christian banner free entry. Finding no new pastures to convert, these sects go into areas that have members of other Churches and start lobbying; using the same Bible. Tribes, clans, the ethnic groups, and in some cases even family groups, are divided between competing denominations (Groube 1983). There is often total confusion as to what is the real church.

A further discredit to the missionaries is their role in the creation of what I call the 'inferiority complex' problem in the minds of Papua New Guineans. Papua New Guineans are told that they are the 'Black Sheep' that the Bible readily talks about, and that they should be grateful that the missions came to save them from eternal doom. Therefore they have nothing to gain from their traditional society and all to gain by adhering to the Bible. The overall effect on the young generation is to develop a total disrespect for their elders' customs, saying that these are evil ways of the past that are best forgotten. Furthermore, the missionaries are looked upon with such reverence that one begins to wonder if they are the real Gods on earth.

In short, no common grounds can be sought in religion in Papua New Guinea. Interdenominational in-fighting has achieved more in splitting and confusing the people than uniting them all in the harmony of the Kingdom of the Lord.

To this end, one of the inevitable questions is: What has the nation of Papua New Guinea got in common?

Apart from the superficial elements, Papua New Guinea also inherited all the institutions that signify the modern Papua New Guinea state. This includes the education system, the bureaucracy, and the cash economy. Here I look briefly at these institutions and evaluate their contribution – or rather their non-contributions – to the task of nation building.

The education system is geared towards producing people for a modern cash economy that is at the moment underdeveloped. Today, 1 out of every 100 students who enter primary education has a chance of securing paid employment. The rural cash economy is more or less self-sustaining and therefore the bulk of the young people end up in their villages or migrate into towns in search of paid employment.

Once in the village, contact with the outside world is lost. The circulation of the country's newspapers is limited to the town areas. The local radio network is the only medium. Even then, there are often not many radios in any area and generally, over time, interest in radio wanes as other more immediate interests take its place. Life revolves around subsistence farming/fishing, a little bit of cash cropping and the day-to-day activities of the area and other traditional social aspects; including tribal fighting at times. To those that come into towns, life is far worse and often includes at least one trip to the police cell or the nearest prison for some petty crime arising from getting something to eat or to live on.

The bureaucracy has little to offer in this respect. The usual cumbersome problems of bureaucratic red-tape are further enhanced in Papua New Guinea by the fact that bureaucracy is multiplied by a factor of 20, one for the central Government and the rest for the 19 Provincial Governments. While decentralizing the powers, it has also created another 19 mini-nations. Provincial lobbying and the general feeling of competition between the respective Provincial Governments have contributed little to the concept of a united Papua New Guinea.

A further disappointment is the total indifference displayed by the bureaucrats; something that has reached endemic proportion in Papua New Guinea. It stems from the attitude that they know everything and that the fellow countryman that comes into the office is another ignorant villager. The lack of adequate policing of these field officers means that they can get away with such behaviour. The end result is ill feeling between the haves and the have-nots.

The final institution I consider is the economy. There are Papua New Guineans who are millionaires, and there are others who have an annual income of less than K100.00. The economic disparity between the haves and the have-nots is growing. It is interesting to note in passing that there is a positive correlation between the rich and politicians and the poor and non-politicians. The implication is open to suggestive interpretation.

The role of the traditional 'big man' in amassing and redistributing wealth is forever gone. The durability, divisibility, and 'bankability' of modern cash means that all one needs is a paper docket or a plastic card of one sort of another.

## Summary

In Papua New Guinea today, the concept of nationalism has little foundation. Nationalism and unity go together and there are no unifying trends here either. The concept of nationalism is vaguely held even among the educated élite of the country. To the people in the villages and the rural areas – who comprise the bulk of the population – the whole idea is more or less non-existent. If it exists, one can be sure that it is in a distorted version.

It is a *fait accompli* that we suddenly found ourselves 'bundled' together by colonizers, and from then onwards have had to learn to live with each other; we who traditionally had very little in common. Those things that we have in common are the things that we have inherited from the white man. But these, as I have tried to show, have not provided a very good basis on which we could build our common identity. Indeed, they have only helped to split us further.

The difference between the haves and the have-nots, the educated and the non-educated, the antagonism between members of different sects of the same faith, the political immaturity, are real trends and will continue to prevail in our midst unless drastic changes are made; something I do not see happening for some time.

There is also little substance in the idea of unity. Although every effort has been made to bring the people together, our immediate past, which is well within living memory of the older generation or through hearsay from our fathers, prevents this. Today, the bulk of the people in the country readily identify themselves with their ethnic, tribal, or language groups. Even among the working population the affiliation felt for their home areas is more than they feel for their workmates. As the bulk of the people are in the rural area this is no problem. In those societies where a lot of the older generation were alive when the white man first came, which is true of many of the Highland societies of Papua New Guinea, these people see no affiliation or elements of commonality with their neighbours who were bitter enemies traditionally, and not so long ago, let alone with people who were traditionally unheard of from other parts of the country. The rather limited and often grossly distorted accounts that filter back to them only confirms their outlook.

The educated working Papua New Guinean is so caught up in the tidal wave of change that has swept this country from a traditional egalitarian society into the 20th century that he has time for little else; least of all, such sentiment as identity.

## At the crossroads

This is the crossroads. In the words of the Melanesian philosopher, Narakobi (1985, p. 447) the question to ask is: which way now, Papua New Guinea? There seem to be three options.

The easiest option would be to just let things go on and hope that in the end we would come up with something that we can call our own: possibly a mixture of traditional and imported traits. Why bother now? At least we have the superficial elements of unity, and we will slowly develop something more profound.

The second option would be to strive for a homogenized nation whereby diversity in any form is discouraged, minorities suppressed, languages outlawed, aberrant cultures and religions victimized (Groube 1985, p. 295). Many of the traces of our diversity have been or are slowly being obliterated through the activity of missionaries, and the inactivity of the country's younger generation and the decision-making bodies in their lack of initiative to encourage diversity.

However, the task will be impossible at this stage where there is no one ethnic group that dominates the others in size of population or influence. Furthermore, establishing dominance over 700 other groups is quite a challenge.

The final option would be to maintain the diversity while at the same time building a nation based on this diversity. Although appearing contradictory, it is quite self-explanatory.

First, in the face of the world of economically and culturally homogenized nations, the very fact that we are diversified is an element that makes us stand out; it is thus a factor which can be capitalized on. This basically is the concept of unity in diversity.

How do you discover unity at the same time retaining that diversity? The answer, as discovered by so many nations, is history: unity in diversity is found through the past, by paying homage and respect to the memory of the ancestors and by identifying from the past the unity of the diversity (Groube 1985, p. 296). Secondly, there is a positive strength in diversity. It ensures that no one group can become too influential, and start to suppress the others. Papua New Guineans can be reassured that it is impossible in this country for any military coup to succeed. Thirdly, the diversity is a national monument; one to be cherished and maintained. It stands constantly to remind us of what we are and what we were.

While the diversity is unquestionably there in Papua New Guinea, we can still build a nation by seeking out and emphasizing common trends that run through, over and above, the obvious differences. Here I am thinking about the social traits that Narakobi (1985) refers to collectively as the 'Melanesian way'. However, this is in part vague, and the very nature of the social traits makes them prone to change with the changing social environment. He provides a good example of it himself:

> The Wantok System . . . contains significant elements of honour and loyalty that can be developed and applied to modernizing influence. Ancient clan loyalties can be redirected towards loyalty to industry, profession, organization and the nation state. (Narakobi 1985, p. 447).

It is here at last that the results of the work of the archaeologist can come into use.

## Papua New Guinea prehistory

Despite its small land mass, Papua New Guinea contains well over a third of the world's cultures, while its inhabitants speak 700 different languages. The profound diversity has staggered the minds of linguists and anthropologists alike. The formation of the journal of *Archaeology and Physical Anthropology in Oceania* by the University of Sydney was an attempt to solve the mystery of the 'different' races encountered in Oceania, and in particular Melanesia. The change of the title to *Archaeology in Oceania* is a clear indication of the impossibility of the task.

While many theories have been proposed to explain this diversity, these can be broken up into two groups. The first is that the diversity found in Melanesia is the result of multiple migrations from South-East Asia; or what has been expressed by its opponents as the 'rubbish dump theory' (cf Groube 1983, p. 19).

Advocates of this are found in all quarters of the social sciences. Bellwood (1976, 1978) and Wurm (1967, 1972) are representative of the archaeologists and the linguists respectively. Thorne (1971, 1977), following the steps of Birdsell (1949, 1967), continues to advocate multi-pronged migrations into New Guinea and Australia on the basis of anthropometric measurements and the collection of skulls, despite criticism of Birdsell's approach (e.g. Brown 1981).

Equally valid in the light of the current knowledge of this area's prehistory is the theory that the diversity encountered is a direct result of isolation over a long period of time. Supporters of this theory have been thin on the ground, but the number is increasing with more discoveries (see Groube 1971, 1983, Muke 1985). It follows the basic principle of the founder population effect, enhanced by social and geographic barriers. Man has been in 'Greater New Guinea' for the last 50 000 years. Taking a liberal estimate of 25 years per generation, over 50 000 years this yields 2000 generations. This is enough time to diverge. Personally, I favour this theory; I believe that the diversity seen in Papua New Guinea is 'home made'.

## The role of archaeology in nation building

The probable explanation that diversity is a result of internal factors and that Papua New Guineans indeed stem from one ancestral population provides them with much potential common ground. They have a common ancestry from time immemorial, and are what they are because they have had the time to diversify.

I now present a brief chronology of the developments that appear to have taken place since the initial settlement of the island of 'Greater New Guinea' some 50 000 years ago.

Papua New Guinea was most probably settled by a single, original colonizing population, from southern Asia. The initial part of the journey was undertaken in some form of seaworthy craft that took them across the 90 or so kilometres of the Wallace Line. This is the strip of water that separated the Asian and Australia/New Guinea continents with their distinctive flora and fauna. Such craft would represent the earliest form of watercraft anywhere in the world.

Archaeological work in the Huon Peninsula of Papua New Guinea on the raised Pleistocene terraces has produced very clear evidence that humans were living on those terraces as far back as 42 000 years ago (Groube *et al.* 1986). Material from the lower terraces has been dated to the Holocene, at 6000 BP.

While Australia and Papua New Guinea were one land mass, from the time of initial colonialization through to 8000 years ago (as a result of the low sea levels), movement between the two land masses would have been difficult, because much of the area where the Arufura Sea now stands would have been mangrove and swamplands with all the waters from the two lands draining into the future sea (Swadling 1983). This indicates that there would have been little movement between the two areas.

By 26 000 BP man was already in the highlands of Papua New Guinea (cf. White *et al.* 1970), possibly living a hunter-gatherer life.

From the mainland, man went over to the coastal islands as early as 10 000 years ago (Specht 1980), and from there into the Pacific about 3000 years ago. Once man had occupied the island area there was ample time to develop the marine technology to conquer the Pacific. We do not need to hypothesize Asians marching in (see Groube 1971).

During the period between 10 000 and 8000 years BP the sea level rose and thereafter there was increasing diversity from east to west and north to south.

By 9000 years BP there is clear evidence of agriculture in the fertile swamps of the Wahgi Valley (cf Golson 1976, 1977a, b, Golson & Hughes 1977).

Evidence of trade between the coast and the Highlands goes as far back as 9000 years ago (White 1972). Extensive trade networks were developing both in the highlands (Hughes 1977) and on the coastal frontier, where obsidian from Lou Island was traded as far as Moem on the mainland, some 400 kilometres sailing distance from its source.

The diversity encountered by the early pioneers and still witnessed today is easy to understand in light of the fact that people have been long established and have been developing trade relations, allies, and enemies; and all the time changing. Papua New Guineans share a common ancestry and a common past. This is the strength upon which to build a strong nation. The picture presented here is far from complete when one looks at the amount of work that has been done in the area. As more and more work is done we will get a clearer and clearer picture of the amazingly complex past of this country.

## Conclusion

This chapter has examined the potential role of archaeology in nation building in a situation where there is no sense of nationhood and unity. An awareness of unity and nationhood in Papua New Guinea could only be achieved through mass education. The task of creating a sense of awareness amongst the people in Papua New Guinea is not easy in a context where the government believes that the only form of worthwhile investment is to make money, and social issues are very low in government priorities.

### The dissemination of information back to the people

A lot of information is never returned to the people and if it is, not in the appropriate style. A further problem here is that of accessibility. Academic journals can only be obtained from big libraries and through private subscriptions. To the Papua New Guinean these problems multiply, given the fact that English may be a person's third or fourth language.

There are several options whereby this problem can be overcome. The first is to take advantage of the daily and weekly newspapers, and write simple articles that can be circulated, even if it is to a small minority. Other magazines that ultimately get a wider circulation, like in-flight airline magazines, are another possible vehicle. A third avenue is to work through the school curriculum, in particular in the high school. Exposure to Papua New Guinean prehistory should take precedence over learning about other people's pasts.

### Setting up of cultural centres

At the time of Independence, there was only one institution acting as the custodian of the past of the people of Papua New Guinea; that is, the National

Museum. Now there are several other provincial cultural centres. These centres have been set up at the request of the local people, who are beginning to realize that many traditional traits are rapidly disappearing. While working in the Southern Highlands, I came across old men who were concerned at the loss of their cultural materials, and had even got together to raise funds to try and set up a cultural centre. I am trying to help out by writing up some of the information that they gave me, and also trying to negotiate funds to help them start the project. There are similar trends in other Provinces of the country (see Ucko in press).

Archaeology has a lot to contribute to nation building, but there is much to be done. The next decade will decide the direction that the nation will take and forever determine the opinion that the unborn generation will hold of the present generation. If we restore and build up our past, they will be proud. If we do not, they will grow up more lost than ourselves. The onus is upon the *present* nation of Papua New Guinea.

# References

Bellwood, P.S. 1976. Indonesia, the Philippines, and Oceanic prehistory. Paper presented at IXe Congress UISPP, Nice.

Bellwood, P.S. 1978. *Man's conquest of the Pacific*. Auckland: Collins.

Birdsell, J. 1949. The racial origin of the extinct Tasmanians. *Records of the Queen Victoria Museum, Launceston* 2(3), 105–22.

Birdsell, J. 1967. Preliminary data on the trihybrid origin of the Australian Aborigines. *Archaeology and Physical Anthropology in Oceania* 2, 100–55.

Birdsell, J. 1977. Peopling Australia. The recalibration of a paradigm for the first peopling of Greater Australia. In *Sunda and Sahul*, J. Allen, J. Golson & R. Jones (eds). London: Academic Press.

Brown, P. 1981. Artificial cranial deformation: a component on the variation in Pleistocene Australian Aboriginal crania. *Archaeology in Oceania* 16, 156–67.

Golson, J. 1976. Archaeology and agriculture in the New Guinea Highlands. In *Problems in economic and social archaeology*, G. de G. Sieveking, I.H. Longworth & K.E. Wilson (eds), 201–20. London: Duckworth.

Golson, J. 1977a. No room at the top: agricultural intensification in the New Guinea Highlands. In *Sunda and Sahul*, J. Allen, J. Golson & J. Jones (eds). London: Academic Press.

Golson, J. 1977b. The making of the New Guinea Highlands. In *The Melanesian environment*, J.H. Winslow (ed.), 45–56. Canberra: Australian National University Press.

Golson, J. & P. Hughes, 1977. Ditches before time. *Hemisphere* 21(2), 13–21.

Groube, L.M. 1971. Tonga, Lapita pottery, and Polynesian origins. *Journal of Polynesian Society* 80: 278–316.

Groube, L.M. 1983. The ownership of diversity. Paper presented to the Australian Academy of Humanities, Canberra.

Groube, L.M. 1985. Cultural preservation and the national goals. In *From rhetoric to reality*, P. King, W. Lee & V. Warakai, (eds). 294–8. Port Moresby: University of Papua New Guinea Press.

Groube, L.M., J. Chappell, J. Muke & D. Price 1986. A 40,000 year-old human occupation site at Huon Peninsula, Papua New Guinea. *Nature* **324**, 453–5.

Hughes, I. 1977. *New Guinea Stone Age trade.* Terra Australis **3**.

Muke, J. 1985. Access and identity or axes of identity. *Yagl-Ambu* **12**(1&2) 1–8, University of Papua New Guinea.

Narakobi, B. 1985. Which way now, Melanesia? In *From rhetoric to reality*, P. King, W. Lee & B. Warakai (eds), 447–50. Port Moresby: University of Papua New Guinea Press.

Reader, J. 1982. *Missing links. The hunt for earliest man.* London: Collins.

Specht, J. 1980. Preliminary report on archaeological research in West New Britain Province, 1979–80. *Oral History* **8**(8), 1–10.

Swadling, P. 1983. *How long have man been in the Ok Tedi impact region?* Hong Kong: P.N.G. National Museum Record No 8. Everbeast.

Thorne, A.G. 1971. Mungo and Kow Swamp: morphological variation in Pleistocene Australians. *Mankind* **8**(2), 85–9.

Thorne, A.G. 1977. Separation or reconciliation? Biological clues to the development of Australian society. In *Sunda and Sahul*, J. Allen, J. Golson & R. Jones (eds). London: Academic Press.

Ucko, P.J. in press. Irreconcilable issues?: culture houses in Zimbabwe. In *The politics of the past*, P. Gathercole & D. Lowenthal (eds)., ch. 15. London: Unwin Hyman.

White, J.P. 1972. Ol Tumbuna. Archaeological excavations in the Eastern Central Highlands, Papua New Guinea. *Terra Australis* **2**.

White, J.P., K.A.W. Crook & B.P. Ruxton, 1970. Kosipe: a late Pleistocene site in the Papuan Highlands. *Proceedings of the Prehistoric Society* **36**, 152–70.

Wurm, S. 1967. Linguistics and the prehistory of the south western Pacific. *Journal of Pacific History* **2**, 25–35.

Wurm, S. 1972. Linguistics research in Australia, New Guinea, and Oceania. *Linguistics* **87**, 87–107.

# 18  *Dual perceptions of the past: archaeology and Inuit culture*

ELLEN BIELAWSKI

## Introduction

> Native people are different . . . Our thinking is totally different. People
> that are non-Native don't quite understand our way of thinking and
> somehow, if we could close those gaps so they can better understand
> them, I think many good things can happen.
>
> (McMullen, in Berger 1985)

> When archaeologists and other 'experts' challenge the Indians' own idea
> of their history, they implicitly undermine the Indians' sense of absolute
> and eternal belonging to particular places . . . Archaeologists deepen our
> appreciation for and understanding of Indian occupancy of North Amer-
> ica. But archaeological speculations, even when stripped of spurious
> certainties, have implications that many Indians consider to be sharply at
> odds with their own view of themselves and that they fear may even
> undermine their rights.
>
> (Brody 1981, p. 15)

There exist two streams of research into culture and history in the Northwest
Territories of Canada. One is rooted in Western scientific tradition and the
organizing principles of the developed world. Its representatives are members
of the academic community, who tend also to be in the service of the dominant
culture's government either full-time or as consultants. The other stems from
the indigenous cultures, Inuit and Dene, of northern Canada, and is pursued by
native cultural organizations and individuals, singly and through community
heritage projects.

Where is there common ground between these two approaches to docu-
menting and interpreting the unwritten history of the Dene and Inuit peoples?
Is there common ground, and is there truth as it would be defined by either or
both groups of seekers?

This chapter considers differing approaches to 'the past', its interpretation,
and its preservation as espoused by Inuit ('the people', singular Inuk, more
commonly referred to in the anthropological literature as Eskimos), and by
those who research Inuit culture and history. 'Time is not one of the big three

in Inuit Culture' (pers. comm., P. Parker 1982), yet archaeology requires the interpretation of time as it documents the past. The contradiction between these perceptions is fundamental to members' behaviour in Inuit and Eurocanadian cultures. It has hardly been recognized until recently, yet it underlies the more commonly recognized cross-cultural debates in the political, educational, and other realms. It is also fundamental to documentation and interpretation of the Inuit past, and to its present and future survival.

## Inuit perceptions of time

Ethnographic evidence for Inuit perceptions of time yields two conclusions: Inuit both measured time to some extent, and lived always in a timeless present. Franz Boas' classic ethnography *The Central Eskimo* (1888) includes a brief description of when and how Inuit considered the passing of time. Travel was measured by number of days, given by the movement of the sun. Each individual's birth month was indicated at festivals through wearing of the bird skin appropriate to each month (just as Eurocanadian culture indicates birth months with specific flowers and gems). What Boas termed 'a sort of calendar' consisted of dividing the year into 13 months, which varied in name and duration according to the latitude at which each band lived. Each day of each month, however, was exactly determined according to the stage of the moon. The continuity of this calendar through time is best described in Boas' own succinct words:

> The surplus is balanced by leaving out a month every few years, to wit, the month *siringilang* (without sun), which is of indefinite duration, the name covering the whole time of the year when the sun does not rise and there is scarcely any dawn. Thus every few years this month is totally omitted, when the new moon and the winter solstice coincide. (Boas 1974, pp. 644–8, original edition 1888).

Boas' most telling statement for culture historians is: 'Years are not reckoned for a longer space than two, backward and forward' (1974, p. 648). Problems are thus inherent in reconstruction of the past through oral history, in any direct historical approach to the archaeological record, or for some ethnographic analogies such as the duration of seasonal settlement patterns.

It is difficult, using Boas' acerbic account, to know if the brevity with which he considers matters of time in Central Eskimo culture reflects his own interest in other matters, the length of his stay (less than two years), or the lack of Inuit emphasis on matters of time. Other accounts and experience suggest it is the latter, which results in time being rarely mentioned in accounts of Inuit culture, in comparison with material and symbolic aspects.

The timeless present was considered integral to Aivilik Inuit of the ethnographic present (Carpenter 1956); in fact, no chronological chain exists through which events are related to one another. Thus, several elements critical to archaeological interpretation were traditionally absent from the Aivilik Inuit world view. For example, notions of origin and creation are absent; the world is now as it has always been. The 'past' is merely an attribute of the present, as something immanent in all Aivilik being. No word exists for history; both history and the reality described in myth give meaning to all activities and to all existence. Certain songs and secret prayers, as well as material objects, possess the past, but the chronology and history of these are not important as an account of development but as an ingredient of being (Carpenter 1956 but see Anawak 1988).

Language gives further clues to the perception of the Aivilik Inuit past. Events are distinguishable on the basis of having occurred in 'time before known time', which is a different kind of time, rather than an earlier time from now. Carpenter noted the frequent use of a term meaning 'in the time of my grandfather's father', but emphasized:

> which does not refer to an earlier phase of this time, and definitely not to the actual generation of their great-grandfathers. Rather, it is comparable to the phrase *tamnagok*, 'once upon a time', with its double sense of past and future and its true meaning of everlasting now (Carpenter 1956).

The contrast between Inuit perception of time and space is worth noting. Boas described the considerable abilities of Inuit with map-making (1974, pp. 643–4). The knowledge of traditional Inuit, that is, those who have lived on the land, for direction, land marks, and navigation under seemingly impossible conditions is well documented (see Nelson 1969, Hall *et al.* 1976, Binford 1978, and others). It is as if survival depended on concrete knowledge of space, but an abstract perception of time. Knowledge of space and distance on the land, and the ability to communicate this through map-making, was integral to traditional Inuit adaptation. Perhaps a perception of time diminishing emphasis on the sequence of events and lives, and incorporating the past and the future in the present, was equally integral to Inuit survival.

The perception of time by young, contemporary Inuit stands in contrast to the traditional means for reckoning time described by Boas, and the timeless present concept documented ethnographically by Carpenter. Most young Inuit of the Northwest Territories have been educated at least marginally in state schools. Both their study of a southern Canadian curriculum, and the mutual isolation of parents and children which results from years of schooling in English, mean that most young Inuit lack any traditional perception of time or the past. The generation graduated from high school prior to today's graduates was largely educated in mission schools. There, although the emphasis on English literacy produced a generation of excellent English speakers (many of whom are Inuit leaders today), the missionaries also emphasized total denial of Inuit traditional knowledge. Thus we are essentially two generations removed from those Inuit who may understand traditional perceptions of time and the past.

## Inuit and archaeology at present

How then do Inuit perceive archaeology, and how do archaeologists and Inuit interact? What tenets of archaeology, and of an Inuit world-view, are mutually accessible and useful to each other in interpreting the past?

It is necessary to place description of an Inuit view of archaeology in both social and intellectual context. First, from the Inuit point of view, archaeologists are *kabloonah*, white people, outsiders. At best, they are nice enough and fine people as individuals, but they will not stay long, and they will barely begin to understand Inuit and Arctic life. At worst, *kabloonah* are people who come North to take something, usually for profit – be it a service job, or minerals, or artefacts. These judgements are part of the social context of the contemporary Northwest Territories, where the general level of education as an exposure to the outside world is still well below average for a developed country such as Canada. Thus, knowledge of archaeology in particular cannot be expected to surpass a generally low level of understanding about the rest of the world. (Television, of course, provides a window on the outer world, but not knowledge.) Thus some Inuit statements about archaeology must be considered in the generally undeveloped social context, and not be considered specifically and solely directed towards archaeology as a discipline. Such statements have included 'archaeologists dig graves, and old bones, and take artefacts to make money', and 'archaeologists can date objects' but don't know anything else. Furthermore, archaeologists are scientists, or researchers, and most of the things they do out on the land are strange and useless. This perception results because researchers have put little effort into communicating research results to Inuit (Bielawski 1984, 1985). Also, Inuit perceive knowledge, and thus scientific inquiry, differently from members of the Western scientific tradition (Wootten 1983, Bertulli & Strahlendorf 1984, Bielawski 1985).

Archaeology does, however, lie close to the heart of negotiations to preserve Inuit culture. (This negotiation may be termed a struggle, but legions of lawyers, researchers, and co-ordinators confront each other at meetings, not in armed conflict.) Miller's 1980 description of archaeology and traditional Solomon Islands culture is the best description applicable to the gulf between Inuit and archaeologists, and places current research endeavours by Inuit and archaeologists in intellectual context:

> there is nothing in most traditional societies that in any way parallels it [archaeology] . . . its methodology, paradigms and context are all unprecedented . . . in order to become meaningful it must become an integral part of the developing system . . . . and cross the boundary to become identified with many important aspects of traditional life and outlook.
>
> (Miller 1980, p. 710)

Archaeology is coming to be understood as a means to document Inuit culture and heritage. Indigenous organizations such as the Inuit Cultural Institute (in Eskimo Point, Northwest Territories) and the Avataq Cultural Institute of Arctic Quebec are undertaking archaeological programmes through hiring academically trained archaeologists. Singular older Inuit are involved in the use of archaeology to serve the research needs of the Avataq Cultural Institute. Direct practice of archaeology is, however, still the preserve of professional, *kabloonah* archaeologists. Inuit elders are directly involved in archaeological research as informants (Gerlach *et al.* 1985, Bielawski & Kabloona 1985) and in numerous oral history projects. These have been initiated both by university-based researchers and by Inuit organizations. Inuit elders' conferences, which are several days of meetings, tape-recorded and transcribed, consider oral history at length. These have been held in Alaska and Canada, and are also held in conjunction with the Inuit Circumpolar Conference.

It is Inuit youth, however, who are most directly involved in archaeology. Their formal participation ('not as labourers only', Weetaluktuk 1979) was initiated through the Thule Archaeology Conservation Project in 1976 (McCartney 1979). Most, by far, of the education and training for Inuit has been conducted in the Northwest Territories since 1979 by the Northern Heritage Society (see Bertulli & Strahlendorf 1985, and annual reports of the Society since 1979; also Bielawski 1984, 1985). To date, 55 students have participated in a rigorous four-week field school run by the Northern Heritage Society, which includes both practical experience in survey and excavation methods, and an academic curriculum in Inuit prehistory and history, adaptation, material culture, and so on. In the past two field seasons, the Society has added Arctic ecology and earth sciences to its field school; academic lectures are also related to these topics and to a general consideration of science in the Arctic. This programme has been tremendously successful with student participants, one of whom has become an archaeological supervisor for the field school; several of whom have subsequently worked for other archaeological field parties; and at least two of whom are headed for university studies. The education and training programme has been carried out as part of an archaeological research study; the Northern Heritage Society's objectives include a balanced commitment to research and education.

The North Slope Borough of Alaska initiated a similar programme in 1984; and the Government of the Northwest Territories Northern Heritage Centre has also included students in its field crews since 1983.

Young Inuit come to the field school with a blank slate about the past, and about time. Their knowledge, although impossible to summarize succinctly, is almost ahistorical, but not in the traditional Aivilik Inuit sense. It is the knowledge of those living in a culture between two worlds, and these young people communicate with neither world very well. The traditional world of their grandparents, and for some of their parents, is not accessible to them because they lack both the language and the land skills which are the life of Inuit Culture. Many, however, have been exposed to a political view of Inuit claims to traditionally used land. An intellectual, academic view of Inuit culture is not yet accessible to them, because they lack the English literacy required to read the written record from ethnography and archaeology. Their curriculum, prior to attendance at the field school, has not provided them with knowledge of their own history and heritage, nor placed it in a national, global, or temporal context.

Excerpts from journals kept by students participating in the Northern Heritage Society field school illustrate the knowledge possessed by young Inuit before and after participation in research archaeology:

'Cultural heritage can be learned by reading about it, doing it, seeing it . . . it can also be learned by talking to elders or exercising the skill living off the land, also by legends and songs. It can also be learned by archaeology . . .'

'Archaeology preserves the sites and the record of heritage.'

'Today it was a great day for me. It was my first time to see a real old Thule house over in Rocky Point . . . I read some books that Margaret gave us. Some were interesting and I found out more about old Thule houses.'

'It was a very interesting lecture. That's what I call lecture. Talking about how culture is changing and what it means to us.'

'In my point of view there should be more projects like this because it gives students an opportunity to learn more about science, archaeology and biology. I hope to get involved with another project like this . . . It is a very good programme for future students who want to study archaeology.'

One specific example suffices to illustrate the knowledge generally possessed by young and older Inuit about the archaeological record. Almost every Inuit student with whom I have worked has some awareness that something called the Thule (people, or a culture; the concept is rarely clear to them) is ancestral to the Inuit. Few have a clear concept of what ancestral means. Some awareness exists, however, of a people who came before the Inuit. None have any concept of the archaeologist's definition of Thule Culture, nor of the approximately 650-year span ascribed to the Thule occupancy of the North American Arctic, prior to Thule evolution into Historic Inuit bands.

Nevertheless, what is truly stunning is the difference between archaeologists' and Inuit perception of Inuit cultural evolution prior to AD 1000. The entire Paleoeskimo occupation *as archaeologists interpret it*, spanning roughly 3000 years of Arctic prehistory, is unknown to Inuit youth, and, I believe, to their elders. While this occupation is not directly ancestral to Inuit in the linguistic, physical, and material sense that Thule Culture is, Paleoeskimo adaptation was certainly the forerunner of Inuit Culture in both specific and general senses. Inuit do, however, see the evidence for this occupation everywhere on the landscape. Both young and old Inuit are aware of the ubiquitous tent rings, caches, and other stone structures. How is this evidence of extensive human occupation incorporated into Inuit thinking? The Inuit does not usually ask the question asked first by archaeologists about these remains: how old are they? And, secondly, to what culture do they belong? Inuit perception of the visible remains incorporates this evidence of human occupation that archaeologists interpret as pre-Inuit into the timeless present, and thus possesses it. Carpenter writes:

> Wherever they [Inuit] go, their surroundings have meaning for them; every ruin, rock, and cleft is imbued with mythical significance. For example, there lie scattered along the southern shore a number of tiny tent rings which the Aivilik declare to be the work of the Tunik, strangers from the past whose spirits still linger somewhere in the ruins . . . yet the Tunik do not in any sense belong to the past . . . They remain forever in the present, inhabiting the ruins, giving these stones a special quality, bestowing on them an aura of spiritual timelessness (Carpenter 1956).

Arctic archaeologists have perennially debated whether the Tunik legends of the Inuit refer to the Thule Culture people or the earlier Paleoeskimos. To Inuit, it appears that the question is irrelevant. Ethnic identity is a matter of space, of land occupied, rather than of time.

Common ground between Western and Inuit knowledge about the past can be traversed by asking a different question about the Tunik. What is the source of their legendary strength? An archaeologist might pursue this through the concept of adaptation. An Inuk might pursue the question through considering how one learns about new land people occupy and depend upon. This also approaches the question through study of adaptation. Inuit archaeology could direct Arctic archaeology away from limited questions of typology and chronology to broader inquiry into cultural adaptation.

## Synthesis: Inuit cultural knowledge and archaeology

Are approaches that merge traditional knowledge with knowledge of the past derived from archaeology possible? Can archaeologists, native or members of the Western scientific tradition, combine sources of knowledge in a synthesis more powerful than either singular approach? Are there uses for native knowledge beyond ethnographic analogy, which is itself fraught with difficulties? A small number of archaeologists are coming to recognize the wealth of knowledge extant in the global diversity of cultures. Miller (1980), Bielawski (1984), and Denton (1985), discuss treatment of Solomon Islanders', Inuit, and Cree world-views (respectively) as integral to the progress of archaeology in each culture area. Miller suggests that archaeology will only become meaningful to developing cultures through integration with traditional world views. Cultural preservation will follow through documentation and dissemination of knowledge about past ways of life. Certainly this is the case with Inuit as well. Miller also argues for acceptance of dualistic approaches in archaeology. These would recognize the validity of both traditional and contemporary social and economic systems in developing countries. Denton argues that 'the development of native archaeologies requires an ongoing dialogue between traditional scientific archaeology and various native perspectives on the past'.

To believe that archaeology can advance through integration of cross-cultural perspectives is to challenge some fundamental tenets of Western science. To ignore any possible avenue for explaining unexplained phenomena is to deny honesty in scientific inquiry. In a discipline which seeks to explain past human behaviour, ignorance of or lip-service to native perceptions is denial of a potentially fruitful path of inquiry. Archaeology's overwhelming dependence on material culture as the major source of evidence about the past need not limit perception and interpretation of the evidence to material analogies. Dual streams of research, built upon the methods of scientific archaeology and on the world-view of cultures whose evolution is being researched, are to be encouraged. The resulting explanations may merge such concepts as the measured time of archaeology and the timeless present that still provides integrity to Inuit Culture. Efforts to preserve Inuit Culture can only benefit.

# References

Anawak, J. 1988. Inuit perceptions of the past. In *Who needs the past?*, R. Layton (ed.), ch. 3. London: Unwin & Hyman.

Berger, T.R. 1985. *Village Journey*. The report of the Alaska Native Review Commission. New York: Hill and Wang.

Bertulli, M. & Peter W. Strahlendorf, 1984. The Northern Heritage Research Project on Truelove Lowland, Devon Island, High Arctic. Annual Report of the Northern Heritage Society. Yellowknife, Northwest Territories, Canada.

Bielawski, E. 1984. Anthropological observations on science in the North: the role of the scientist in human development in the Northwest Territories. *Arctic* **37**(1), 1–6.

Bielawski, E. 1985. Anthropological models for science in the North: doing and delivering science cross-culturally. Proceedings of the Unesco MAB Northern Science Network Conference, Arctic Science Policy: Local and International Perspectives, in press.

Bielawski, E. & C. Kabloona, 1985. Seasonal and temporal variability on the Barrengrounds: recent finds near Baker Lake. Canadian Archaeological Association, 18th Annual Meeting, Winnipeg.

Binford, L.R. 1978. *Nunamiut Ethnoarchaeology*. New York: Academic Press.

Boas, F. 1888. *The Central Eskimo*. Coles Publishing Company Ltd., reprinted 1974.

Brody, H. 1981. *Maps and Dreams*. Toronto: Douglas and McIntyre.

Carpenter, E.S. 1956. The timeless present in the mythology of the Aivilik Eskimo. *Anthropologica* **3**, 1–4.

Denton, D. 1985. Some comments on archaeology and northern communities. Heritage North '85 Conference, Yellowknife, Northwest Territories.

Gerlach, S.C., M.B. Blackman, E.S. Hall Jr., S. Neakok & R. Ekowana 1985. Custodians of the past: the North Slope Borough Field School. Edwin Hall and Associates, Technical Memorandum 19. Brockport, New York.

Hall, E.S. Jr. (ed.) 1976. Contributions to anthropology: the interior peoples of northern Alaska. National Museum of Man, Mercury Series 49, Ottawa.

McCartney, A.P. 1979. The Thule Archaeology Conservation Project: introduction and Inuit participation. In *Archaeological whale bone: a northern resource*. University of Arkansas Anthropological Papers 1, 99–108.

Miller, D. 1980. Archaeology and development. *Current Anthropology* **21**(6), 709–26.

Nelson, R.K. 1969. *Hunters of the Northern Ice*. Chicago: University of Chicago Press.

Weetaluktuk, D. 1979. Review and recommendations concerning the policy for the conduct of archaeological research in northern Quebec: Inuit perspective. Canadian Archaeological Association 12th Annual Meeting, Vancouver.

Wootten, P. 1983. Science and education: a northern perspective for the northern environment. Manuscript on file, Centre for Northern Studies and Research, McGill University, Montreal.

# Index